Human-Computer Interaction Series

T0214577

Human-Computer Interaction is a multidisciplinary field focused on human aspects of the development of computer technology. As computer-based technology becomes increasingly pervasive - not just in developed countries, but worldwide - the need to take a human-centered approach in the design and development of this technology becomes ever more important. For roughly 30 years now, researchers and practitioners in computational and behavioral sciences have worked to identify theory and practice that influences the direction of these technologies, and this diverse work makes up the field of human–computer interaction. Broadly speaking it includes the study of what technology might be able to do for people and how people might interact with the technology. In this series we present work which advances the science and technology of developing systems which are both effective and satisfying for people in a wide variety of contexts. The human–computer interaction series will focus on theoretical perspectives (such as formal approaches drawn from a variety of behavioral sciences), practical approaches (such as the techniques for effectively integrating user needs in system development), and social issues (such as the determinants of utility, usability and acceptability).

For further volumes:
http://www.springer.com/series/6033

Andrew Crabtree • Mark Rouncefield
Peter Tolmie

Doing Design Ethnography

 Springer

Dr. Andrew Crabtree
University of Nottingham
School of Computer Science
Wollaton Road
Nottingham, NG8 1BB
United Kingdom

Dr. Mark Rouncefield
Lancaster University
School of Computing and Communications
South Drive
Lancaster, LA1 4WA
United Kingdom

Dr. Peter Tolmie
University of Nottingham
School of Computer Science
Wollaton Road
Nottingham, NG8 1BB
United Kingdom

ISSN 1571-5035
ISBN 978-1-4471-6160-8   ISBN 978-1-4471-2726-0 (eBook)
DOI 10.1007/978-1-4471-2726-0
Springer London Heidelberg New York Dordrecht

Printed on acid-free paper

Springer is part of Springer Science+Business Media (www.springer.com)

Contents

Chapter 1
Précis

There is not so much required, any strength of Imagination,
or exactness of Method; or depth of Contemplation as a sincere
Hand, and a faithful Eye, to examine, and to record, the things
themselves as they appear

Robert Hooke

Abstract Ethnographic approaches associated with social and cultural anthropology are common currency in systems design. They are employed widely in academic and industrial reasearch labs, consultancy firms, IT companies and design houses. *Doing Design Ethnography* is about one particularly influential approach: ethnomethodologically informed or inspired ethnography. This chapter provides a brief overview of the ethnomethodological orientation and the 'job of work' using it entails. It outlines the purpose of this book, the authors' experience in doing ethnography for design, and core texts that the reader might also turn to further develop their understanding of the ethnomethodological approach.

Forty years ago ethnography was little more than a blot on the landscape of software engineering and systems development. Twenty years ago it was developing nascent promise. Today it is being taught in computer science departments. Right now it is being employed in academic and industrial research labs worldwide, not to mention a veritable host of consultancy firms and smaller IT companies and design houses. It is being used to understand user requirements, to develop design ideas, and to evaluate computing systems. Ethnography was initially championed in design by Xerox PARC, where the personal computer was developed in the 1970s. Since then other leading technology developers, including IBM, Microsoft and Intel, have also adopted the approach. Despite the transition and broad appeal of ethnography it is curiously hard to define. If one delves into the social sciences, from where it originates, a great many different perspectives on ethnography are to be found and these are increasingly reflected in the fields of Human-Computer Interaction (HCI) and Computer Supported Cooperative Work (CSCW). This book is about one

A. Crabtree et al., *Doing Design Ethnography*, Human-Computer Interaction Series,
DOI 10.1007/978-1-4471-2726-0_1, © Springer-Verlag London 2012

perspective on ethnography in design, derived from a very specific branch of sociology called ethnomethodology. Ethnomethodology was first on the scene, first to be used at Xerox PARC, first to demonstrate the salience of ethnography to systems design, and its studies are still canonical today.

Our purpose here is to explain the ethnomethodological approach to ethnography so that others may learn what is involved in adopting it, using it, and exploiting it in their own work. It requires of the reader that you adopt a distinctive orientation. This orientation is sociological but it is not one that requires that you have a prolonged training in the formal discipline of Sociology. Rather, ethnomethodology takes it that sociology is something that we are all competent in as members of society, that we are all *practical sociologists*. Ethnomethodology's basic premise is that the ordinary activities that make up our everyday lives are sociological achievements that in many and varied ways rely on others for their accomplishment. Whether getting up and out the door in the morning, travelling to work, doing our jobs, or resting and relaxing afterwards, all of these things and more implicate others in their accomplishment even if we live and work alone. Ethnomethodology suggests that we know and recognise this as members of society, know that our ordinary activities involve others, and know that the ways in which we do our activities rely on our mastery of practical sociology: on our mastery of working with others and the things that others do to get the activities we find ourselves engaged in done. Ethnomethodology is an invitation to unpack members mastery of practical sociology as it appears to us in the many and varied settings in which people live and operate and in the lived details of the many and varied activities that people do.

Ethnography is a *tool* that we can use to unpack members' mastery of practical sociology in empirical detail. In doing so it makes visible and available to design reasoning the distinctive activities that populate particular settings, the work involved in doing them, and the work practices that members use to concert their actions with those of other parties implicated in the conduct of a setting's work. Uncovering and recognising the ways in which members concert or coordinate their actions with one another is what practical sociology is particularly concerned with. It is what you and I are concerned with when we walk down the street, buy goods, drive home, etc., even if we don't give it much more than a passing thought, because it enables us to avoid bumping into one another, to determine who is next in line, and to get home without killing anybody. As practical sociologists we know how to concert our actions with other people in order to get the activities we are engaged in done. We know, in other words, how to *organise* our activities and how to do that as a real world, real time sociological accomplishment that other members of the settings we live and operate in know, recognise and can orchestrate their actions with too.

Uncovering and explicating practical sociology, making its workings visible, is a job of work, one that enables system developers to factor the *real world, real time* organisation of human activities into design. Like any other job, it requires skill and competence. This book is an invitation and introduction to that job, one that attempts to convey key aspects of doing it to designers, whether they be undergraduate or postgraduate students or career researchers and design practitioners. We start with an account of the relationship between ethnography and systems design, what it contributes, and why it is still salient today. We then move on to consider foundational principles of ethnomethodology to articulate the distinctive analytic orientation it adopts and applies to ethnographic research. A range of examples that reveal the 'animal in the foliage' – i.e., the organised ways in which members do practical sociology and accomplish ordinary activities – follows this together with some tips for finding it yourself. We then address the core question of method and, surprisingly perhaps, the practical necessity to dispense with it if one is not to lose sight of the animal in the foliage. In turn, given the absence of method, the practicalities of actually doing empirical work, particularly of getting into a setting, assembling a record of the work that occurs there, and getting out are addressed. This is followed by a chapter on the practicalities of analysis and the need to produce 'praxeological' accounts which make the real world, real time character of practical sociology observable. With an analysis of the work of a setting and its real world, real time organisation in hand, we move on to consider a range of practices for relating findings to the design of computing systems, including requirements specification, use cases, scenario-based design and mock ups, along with practical strategies for conducting evaluations. We then consider a range of common misconceptions, misunderstandings and complaints that have accompanied ethnography's migration into systems design before moving on to summarise our journey.

In place of a blow-by-blow account of each of the book's chapters, they each begin with an abstract. The chapters combine in an attempt to support the acquisition of competence in doing design ethnography: in short, learning how to study practical sociology through empirical fieldwork and how to relate findings from this to the construction of computing systems. You might treat the final chapter as something that pulls the various threads of our craft together or as a stand alone piece that provides an overview of the work involved in doing design ethnography. In that respect it might actually be a good place to start if a comprehensive introduction is required.

Ethnography in design is a very different enterprise from ethnography in social science: the accountabilities are different, the needs different, the results and their uses different. Our account of design ethnography is based on our own experience of doing it in both academic and commercial contexts over the last 20 years.

Andy Crabtree is an Associate Professor in the School of Computer Science and Information Technology at the University of Nottingham. Prior to this he worked in the Department of Computing at Lancaster University and Department of Computer Science at Aarhus University; where he contributed to the development of a global customer service system for a major container shipping company. His research focuses on the real world, real time character of social interaction in diverse contexts (including workplaces, mixed reality settings, domestic environments, and the rural economy), and the relationship of studies of interaction to the development of computing systems. His research has made substantive contributions to computer supported cooperative work, human-computer interaction, and ubiquitous computing. He has also made substantive contributions to methodological debates concerning the nature and role of ethnography in systems design and IT research.

Mark Rouncefield is a Senior Research Fellow in the Department of Computing at Lancaster University and Microsoft European Research Fellow. His research is strongly interdisciplinary in nature and has led to extensive and continuing collaborations with colleagues in sociology, computing, informatics and management, both in the UK and abroad. He has particular interest in computer supported cooperative work and the empirical study of work, technology, and organisation. His research includes ethnographic studies of financial services, library services, hotel work, and steel work. Recent research has focused on socio-technical aspects of the design and deployment of technologies in domestic and healthcare settings. He is particularly associated with the development of ethnography as an approach to informing design and systems evaluation and his work has contributed to critical debates concerning the relationship between social and technical aspects of IT research and systems design.

Peter Tolmie is a Senior Research Fellow in the Mixed Reality Laboratory (MRL) at the University of Nottingham. He joined the MRL from Xerox Research Centre Europe, where he previously worked as Area Manager of the Work Practice Technology group. His ethnographic work is extensive and cuts across the workplace (managerial work, consultancy practice, the work of personal assistants, bid management, and remote service assistance); healthcare (decision-making in the treatment of breast cancer); domestic settings (home networks and evolving infrastructures, and living with the energy efficient home); creative industries (pervasive gaming, musical performance and consumption, TV and film production); and leisure industries (tourism and museum visiting practices). His research has made a significant contribution to a diverse range of IT research and system development activities that are concerned to situate computing technology in the everyday lives of people who use them.

All three of the authors completed their PhD theses at the Department of Sociology, Lancaster University, under the supervision of John Hughes, who pioneered the use of ethnography for systems design. Their work has resulted in and contributed to the publication of an extensive range of research reports, scientific papers, journal articles, and a number of books including *Designing Collaborative Systems: A Practical Guide to Ethnography* and *Fieldwork for Design: Theory and Practice*, both of which are published by Springer.

Further Reading

Both of the books cited above will make good companions to the current text. We also recommend a small number of core readings that elaborate the foundations of our ethnographic approach for anyone who might like to delve a little deeper. They include the following:

Button, G. (Ed.). (1991). *Ethnomethodology and the human sciences*. Cambridge: Cambridge University Press.
Button, G. (2000). The ethnographic tradition and design. *Design Studies, 21*, 319–332.

Button, G., & Harper, R. (1996). The relevance of 'work-practice' for design. *Computer Supported Cooperative Work: The Journal of Collaborative Computing, 4*(4), 263–280.

Button, G., & Sharrock, W. (1997). The production of order and the order of production. *Proceedings of the 5th European Conference on Computer Supported Cooperative Work* (pp. 1–16). Lancaster: Kluwer.

Button, G., & Sharrock, W. (2009). *Studies of work and the workplace in HCI: Concepts and techniques.* New Jersey: Morgan & Claypool.

Czyzewski, M. (1994). Reflexivity of actors versus the reflexivity of accounts. *Theory, Culture and Society, 11*, 161–168.

Garfinkel, H. (1967). *Studies in ethnomethodology.* Englewood Cliffs: Prentice-Hall.

Garfinkel, H. (1996). Ethnomethodology's program. *Social Psychology Quarterly, 59*(1), 5–21.

Garfinkel, H., & Wieder, D. L. (1992). Two incommensurable, asymmetrically alternate technologies of social analysis. In G. Watson & S. M. Seiler (Eds.), *Text in context: Contributions to ethnomethodology* (pp. 175–206). New York: Sage.

Garfinkel, H., Lynch, M., & Livingston, E. (1981). The work of a discovering science construed with materials from the optically discovered pulsar. *Philosophy of the Social Sciences, 11*, 131–158.

Hughes, J., Randall, D., & Shapiro, D. (1992). Faltering from ethnography to design. *Proceedings of the Conference on Computer Supported Cooperative Work* (pp. 115–122). Toronto: ACM.

Hughes, J., King, V., Rodden, T., & Andersen, H. (1994). Moving out of the control room: Ethnography in systems design. *Proceedings of the Conference on Computer Supported Cooperative Work* (pp. 429–438). Chapel Hill: ACM.

Hughes, J., O'Brien, J., Rodden, T., Rouncefield, M., & Blythin, S. (1997). Designing with ethnography: A presentation framework. *Proceedings of the Symposium on Designing Interactive Systems* (pp. 147–158). Amsterdam: ACM.

Husserl, E. (1999). *The idea of phenomenology* (L. Hardy, Trans.). Dordrecht: Kluwer Academic Publishers.

Livingston, E. (2008). *Ethnographies of reason.* Aldershot: Ashgate.

Lynch, M. (1993). *Scientific practice and ordinary action: Ethnomethodological and social studies of science.* Cambridge: Cambridge University Press.

Lynch, M. (2000). Against reflexivity as an academic virtue and source of privileged knowledge. *Theory, Culture and Society, 17*(3), 26–54.

Ryle, G. (1968). The thinking of thoughts: What is 'Le Penseur' doing?. *University Lectures No. 18.* Saskatoon: University of Saskatchewan.

Sacks, H. (1984). Notes on methodology. In J. Maxwell & J. Heritage (Eds.), *Structures of social action: Studies in conversation analysis* (pp. 21–27). Cambridge: Cambridge University Press.

Sacks, H. (1992). In G. Jefferson (Ed.), *Lectures on conversation.* Oxford: Blackwell.

Suchman, L. (1987). *Plans and situated actions: The problem of human-machine communication.* Cambridge: Cambridge University Press.

Chapter 2
Ethnography and Systems Design

Software systems do not exist in isolation. They are used in a
social and organisational context. Satisfying these social and
organisational requirements is often critical for the success of
the system. One reason why many software systems are delivered
but never used is that their requirements do not take proper
account of how the social and organisational context affects the
practical operation of the system.

Ian Sommerville

Abstract This chapter elaborates the relationship between ethnography and
systems design. It addresses the turn to the social that occurred in the late 1980s
as the computer moved out of the research lab and into our collective lives, and the
corresponding need that designers had to find ways of factoring the social into
design. It does so from the point of view of people who initially developed the
ethnographic approach for systems designs, notably that cohort of sociologists and
software engineers who came to be known as the Lancaster School. We provide a
brief account of the impetus towards the turn to the social before moving on to
consider how members of the Lancaster School set about addressing this problem of
factoring the social into design through ethnography and what was involved in
doing it. This is not a formal account but rather an informal one based on interviews
with sociologists and software engineers who were there at the off so to speak.
This retrospective brings to the fore the practical concerns that motivated both
parties, the contexts in which they were working at the time, and the foundational
need to develop a constructive relationship between ethnography and systems
design. That is to say, the need to have ethnography help designers figure out
what to build and to help them determine what works and what doesn't. These are
still extremely salient issues today. They underpin ethnography's ongoing relevance to systems design and frame the following chapters in which we explicate the
work involved in doing ethnography and relating it to systems development.

A. Crabtree et al., *Doing Design Ethnography*, Human-Computer Interaction Series,   7
DOI 10.1007/978-1-4471-2726-0_2, © Springer-Verlag London 2012

2.1   The Turn to the Social in Systems Design

If you are at all familiar with ethnography in a design context then one word you are sure to have come across is ethnomethodology. You may hiss and spit when you hear the name or it may pique your curiosity, but however it takes you, you cannot avoid it when considering the relationship between ethnography and systems design. Ethnography is, for some of us at least, nothing more than shorthand for ethnomethodologically-informed ethnography and in that respect you may also have come across the name Harold Garfinkel, ethnomethodology's founding father (cf. Garfinkel 1967), which could well occasion even more hiss and spit, particularly from people who are deeply wedded to theorising as a foundational practice. Garfinkel was a sociologist, a ground-breaking one whose work has had a profound impact on social science around the world. Curiously, however, if you are at all inclined to read Garfinkel's work you won't find anything in it about ethnography and systems design, or at least not anything substantial, nothing more than the odd note really. Ditto Harvey Sacks (1992), the other progenitor of ethnomethodological 'studies of work' (Garfinkel 1986), which lie at the heart of ethnography in systems design, or at least ethnography as we know and practice it. Other versions of ethnography are available but if you want to find out more about ethnography and systems design it's no good reading Garfinkel and Sacks or the multitude of social scientists that offer competing views on social life and its alleged salience to the development of computing systems.

You might turn to the sociologist Lucy Suchman and her PhD dissertation *Plans and Situated Actions: The Problem of Human-Machine Communication*, produced as a result of her pioneering research at Xerox PARC (Suchman 1987). Indeed we would recommend that you do so. It is very accessible and you will learn a lot about ethnomethodology's distinctive analytic orientation along with the shortcomings of cognitive perspectives on human-computer interaction. To complement this, you might also turn to someone who is not an ethnographer or an ethnomethodologist: Jonathan Grudin, whose works, particularly *Interface* (1990) and *The Computer Reaches Out* (1990), played an important role in elaborating the turn to the social from within design. Again, we would recommend it. You will learn how cognitive perspectives remove computers, their designers and users from their real contexts. However, as insightful and relevant as both authors work was and still is, you won't find anything about ethnography in it. Suchman's seminal work provides a sociological critique of models of cognition used in design during the 1980s. Grudin's of the need during the 1990s for interface design, and systems development more generally, to extend out into the social environment. Both authors, along with others, played a formative role in changing designers' perspectives on computing systems and their users, and the need to factor the social into building computers as they reached out from individual users and the research lab into the workplace and beyond. Both heralded the turn to the social, one from within design, the other without, but neither tried to account for how you might use ethnography as a practical means of bringing the social to bear on the actual construction of computing systems.

For an understanding of that particular achievement you need to turn to the UK and Lancaster University in particular, where a small group of sociologists and software engineers set about addressing the problem in the late 1980s. You might turn to the work they produced. The research deliverables where they hammered out what they were doing together, particularly the COMIC deliverables 2.1 (1993), 2.2 (1994) and 2.4 (1995), the conference papers, and the published texts. You could read all of them and you probably should read some of them as what follows is inevitably indexical to them, but, as much for our own interest as yours, we decided that a good (and ultimately more concise) way to introduce 'ethnography and systems design' would be to interview people who were there at the off. We could write a potted history but we thought it might be more interesting to have it from those who did it – from people who started the enterprise, who drove it and shaped it and actually tried to use it to bring an appreciation of the social to bear on the design of computing systems. There were a great many more members and affiliates of the Lancaster School, and others working in a similar vein elsewhere, than we can possibly do justice to in providing this account. Of particular note are Wes Sharrock and Graham Button; both played a strong formative role in shaping the work of the Lancaster School.[1] Other notable characters include the acclaimed author on software engineering, Ian Sommerville (2011); Richard Bentley, vice-president of Progress Software's capital markets; Richard Harper, manager of the Socio-Digital Systems group at Microsoft Research Cambridge; Steve Benford and Tom Rodden, both professors of computing at the University of Nottingham and leading experts in human-computer interaction and collaborative computing; Dave Randall, fieldworker and senior lecturer in sociology (retired); and John Hughes, emeritus professor of sociology at the University of Lancaster. This is what they have to say about ethnography and design, where it came from, what it does, what it gave design, and why it is still relevant today.

2.2 Beginnings

John Hughes. We just wanted to do sociology, our kind of sociology. The three of us – me, Wes Sharrock and Bob Anderson – we were dissatisfied with the way sociology was going: nobody bothered to actually go see what happens, what people do, you know, that kind of thing. So we got a grant to study this multi-site company, basically food supply. Bob did all the fieldwork on that and it resulted in *Working for Profit* (Anderson et al. 1989). Just after that started I met this new assistant lecturer in computing in Bowland Bar. He happened to say that he was working on this automated air traffic control system, which at the time filled me with horror. I talked to Wes and Bob and we thought let's apply for an ESRC grant, which we did and actually got. So we went and talked to the National Air Traffic

---

[1] For a primer in ethnographic studies for design see Button and Sharrock (2009).

Control centre and got permission to send a field worker to West Drayton. Richard Harper did the first fieldwork on air traffic controllers. Then he gave a paper, one of the first papers we did on this, at a conference (Harper et al. 1989). Tom Rodden was there and he was telling Richard that this had computer science value. So when Richard got back he arranged a meeting. That's where it started really, from there.

Richard Harper. I was given a job to work on the first Air Traffic Control (ATC) project. We'd been told to go and see the Royal Signals and Radar Establishment at Malvern in Worcestershire, where they were exploring future forms of air traffic control. They had a demo suite for future air traffic control, which was quite funny 'cause you could actually run false aeroplanes on it and do air traffic control and then if you crashed nothing happened! While we were there, these guys said, "you should go to this new conference that Xerox has invented called CSCW, it's on in Gatwick next year, here's an advert for it." We'd never heard of CSCW. I just thought Xerox was the machine. I scribbled a little sketch of this thing called RD3 that offered enhanced implied collision awareness and then John put it in decent English and we submitted it, not knowing anything about CSCW except what it said on the flyer. The opening premise of the paper was it seemed curious that computer and systems designers should have suddenly discovered an interest in collaborative work because from a sociological perspective it's difficult to find any work that *isn't* collaborative, so what was the work they were modelling before? Anyway, after the conference we got an email from some bloke from computer science. He said, "Do you want to meet in Cartmel bar?" We went downstairs and this bloke called Tom and a bloke called Ian – they had heard about our air traffic control project and wanted to know whether we'd do another one with them? At that time Ian had just got into his textbook about software engineering. He was trying to point out that software engineering is not just a question of the engineering of the software, but of getting a proper sense of the real *human* problem.

Ian Sommerville. Pete Sawyer had a project which was looking at support environments for software engineering and what we decided to do was look at software engineering as a *cooperative process*, rather than to look at what the other environments were doing which was very much to look at *individual activities*. So we looked at various aspects of that and basically what Tom Rodden developed was a very early instance of a sort of mail filtering system where you could actually organise filters so you could organise things into categories, you could organise things around co-workers, and that kind of pointed us towards CSCW as an area. It was at a CSCW conference that we met Richard Harper who was talking about his air traffic control stuff and then that lead us through to meeting with John Hughes. That really was the start of the engagement with them.

Tom Rodden. At the time it happened I'd just completed my PhD and we had a broad interest in CSCW, which was for me principally about the construction of technologies to *support collaboration*, about understanding *distributed interaction* technologically. I noticed that, at the same time, from the other end of campus,

John Hughes and others sought to publish in the very first ECSCW conference, which was enough to suggest that there might be an overlap here. We'd both been doing a range of work in that space and were looking to move onto the next set of things to do, so we thought we should write a joint proposal and do joint work together, which gave birth to the second air traffic control project.

2.3 First Steps

John Hughes. Tom was part of a bunch who was interested in safety critical systems. So we applied, to a different research council this time, for another study of air traffic controllers, this time building in a computing component to it to begin to try to work out how the ethnographies would inform design. Prior to that the main input from the human sciences to computing was HCI – psychology, ergonomics, things like that. So ethnography was quite a new disciplinary input to system design.

Richard Harper. The origins were not on the basis of the methodological propriety of respective parties: one party saying that the other party's methods were fit. It was rather that academically there seemed to be an opportunity for two gangs to do work together.

Dave Randall. I went to Lancaster in 1989 as a research assistant to work on the second ATC project. Its odd how misrepresented that's been. The purpose of this project was to *assess* the value of ethnography in relation to design. People think that the aim was to *demonstrate* that ethnography could contribute to systems design, but it wasn't. It was to try to find whether ethnography *could* contribute to systems design.

Tom Rodden. In the software engineering and requirements engineering community generally at that time, there was a call for a better understanding of the nature of organisations, and the details of it, and that drove a lot of what we did. It was an era of mass embarrassing systems *failures*. Of systems not being workable. Not fitting to organisations. Being unsafe. Unstable. So there was a big call to try and understand what was happening and ethnography became a part of that general turn. It was a big learning curve for everybody. It was about seeking to understand each other's culture. What it is to do the work we do. What the orientation to it was. I adopted a very pragmatic engineering approach which is if you're given a new technique or tool – whatever it is, whether its computational or whatever – what you need to do is understand what it's good for, what it can do and what it can't do and what it costs. So much of our orientation at that point was well, what would you do with this? What's it good for? What would it give you? What wouldn't it give? Where would you use it? Where wouldn't you use it? Very much an inspectional view, a kind of critical eye; not negative just critical in a pragmatic sense.

Ian Sommerville. The first joint project we had was that social analysis of control systems (Bentley et al. 1992). I think it was very successful and I think that was partly because of the people. Richard Bentley was very good and we really had a good system working where there was a debriefing meeting and that was being reflected into the software. The ethnographers were coming up with really interesting reasons why the prototype electronic strip system, had it been produced, wouldn't have been acceptable.

Tom Rodden. That gave birth to my first paper: sociologists can be surprisingly useful (Sommerville et al. 1992). Then a fairly systematic charting of what you get. So the journey from that paper to the control room paper (Hughes et al. 1994) says so far ethnography isn't this big long thing, there are these four different ways in which we've used ethnography, and here's the pluses and minuses, the gains and the benefits, we've got from it.

Dave Randall. After that project we went down to the London Air Traffic Control centre at West Drayton to talk to people about possibly continuing. One of the interesting things that came out of that was that they weren't actually all that interested in the computer science, they were interested in the sociology.

John Hughes. Our motivation was always sociology. The inspiration, insofar as there was one, anthropological: go into some place, hang around, see what people do. A lot of the early papers were working out what the relationship of that to design could be, and us becoming more familiar with the sort of things that computing did.

Dave Randall. I can't remember how far into the second ATC project we were when we went to that first big CSCW conference in Canada. We submitted 7 different things and they all got accepted. There were two papers I think, two workshop proposals, a tutorial proposal, and so on. Every single thing we submitted got accepted and I was very excited. If the truth be told it was very exciting. You felt like you were the centre of attention at that conference. It felt like *this is all new*, but it wasn't of course. Lucy Suchman and Eleanor Wynne had done those studies of office work 2 years before and Christian Heath was doing similar things with London Underground at that time. But I think it hit a nerve. We were making the claim that there *could* be a direct relationship to design here, and we were probably the first people to do that. I don't know that anybody else was actually working with computer scientists and doing ethnographic work at the time, though I do think people got a lot more excited about it than they should have done.

Tom Rodden. It wasn't happening in a neutral landscape though. It was quite interesting. In the U.S. there was more a revolutionary notion of what was happening. For some of the people who had been in this field for a little bit longer there was more of a battleground that I just wasn't aware of which was ethnography, and turning to the social, very much became a fight over HCI: cognitive *versus* social. I didn't care. Didn't get engaged. It wasn't part of what we were thinking or doing or anything like that.

2.4 Faltering Towards Design

John Hughes. I think it a good idea that you have design teams using somebody who's got a kind of *sociological sensitivity*. Ian was often talking about trying to formalise it but I don't think he got very far. I don't see how you can. But I think it's probably right that computer design – I mean design of systems which are to support human activities, I'm not talking about designing chips, the really technical things – I think it's probably right you have some sociological sensitivity in there of the kind that ethnography can bring to it. You don't want social theorists or post-modernists in there, that's a luxury you can well do without, but a service discipline, you know, to inform, to sensitise to the *human context* in which designs will have their voice, if they are to have a voice at all.

Richard Bentley. From a computer systems design point of view I need to start understanding what the use case is, what the process is, what the requirements are *for the system*.

Tom Rodden. Requirements are a funny bugger, and requirements engineering. Requirements teams are generally quite small and requirements teams write documents which are then enacted by larger numbers of people. So the whole process has a pyramid feel to it, from requirements to design out to implementation. Ethnography scales up through that process.

Ian Sommerville. You've got to remember the point of a lot of new systems is to change things. One of the misconceptions that is commonly made in requirements engineering is that the process involves collecting the requirements then building a system to these requirements, whereas quite often the process is, "We're not interested in how you do things, this is how you're going to do things in future." It's doomed in most cases. But nevertheless software engineers often don't want to know *what people do*. They don't want to be told, "these things are important you can't change them" because they want to change them, and then they change them. It's a disaster.

Tom Rodden. I'm a big believer that large-scale IT systems failures do one major thing: they surface the failures of your organisation. They surface its properties and failures and therefore understanding its properties and failures is really important. Given that, and given that you as IT developers will find yourself in the frontline carrying the can for this, knowing the nature of those organisations, knowing the nature of those people, becomes a critical part of doing that job if only so you know what not to build. We talked a lot about this. We deliberately said what we are trying to do is give you *sensitising* information. We're not giving you results. We're sensitising you to the nature of work and its organisation.

Richard Bentley. That was the thing for me. There was definitely value added. There was definitely interesting insights. The big take-away for me was sensitisation.

Ian Sommerville. You get information about the *social interactions* in the setting, which other design and analysis methods simply don't capture. For me a lot of the value – and this is coming at it from quite a conventional engineering background – was to sensitise me to all these *social* and *organisational* issues about systems. I think that's a real value. I think that it has helped the requirements engineering community, that sensitisation. There is definitely some sensitisation.

Steve Benford. Sensitising is the key word. Sensitising designers to the limitations of the things they are currently thinking.

Dave Randall. I think the most important thing in ethnography is simply getting designers sensitive to the issues that the people who use systems confront. I think it's an ongoing problem. It's the "techy knows best problem" – we can do all sorts of gee-whiz things, we're great with html and xml and so on and so forth; we can do all sorts of wild and wacky and wonderful things. The user is just this vague symbolic presence in all this and I do very seriously think that what ethnographers should be able to do is get designers used to the idea that users are *real people* with *real practical issues*. Ethnography ought to be about a reality principle.

Ian Sommerville. Ethnography doesn't rule out any design options but it tries to tell you something of the consequences of the choices that you make. I think it highlights things which are of significance and says if you muck around with that you may have problems.

Tom Rodden. So a nascent set of concepts started to appear actually having more legs and more depth to them than what other people were doing at that time. Those *sensitising concepts* then became useful for people who did not have access to people with a long training in the social sciences: aide memoirs, lists of 'be carefuls', pay attention to, be aware of, think about, etc. We played around a lot about how to convey them so that they didn't get reduced to a formulaic doing of things. So that we conveyed the intention of making people sensitive or aware of these things without being overly prescriptive.

2.5 Informing Design

John Hughes. First accept for a general premise that if you're going to design something you need to know something about the *qualities* you're designing for.

Tom Rodden. Humans are here to stay. Technologies come and go and fashions come and go. People remain people and there's much about technology that's *about people:* about what they decide, what they know, what they do, how they go about doing it. Ethnography has a salience because we keep forgetting that. We get lost in everything else.

John Hughes. From the point of view of doing the kind of sociology we were doing, ethnography delivered very well. Of course a lot of Garfinkelian entered into the kind of analysis you do. The turn to ethnomethodology wasn't just an accident though. It was the result of dissatisfaction with mainstream sociology and attraction to the symbolic interactionist tradition. That moves into ethnomethodology and those kinds of studies. You know, studies of work, which could be used as a critique on existing methods, but it was *more than critique*.

Dave Randall. The promise of ethnography was not that it would provide answers that other methodologies cannot provide but that it could *respecify problems*. It could make you think differently about problems, draw your attention to things you might not have thought of.

Richard Bentley. The best way I could articulate it is when I've been looking at ideas for new developments or new solutions, or I'm looking at projects, the question I ask is, what's the use case? I know that has all kinds of connotations, it can be cast in many ways, but ethnography certainly sensitised me to understanding what people *do*, to *how* they do their job today, what the *critical aspects* of that are, and actually understanding that and articulating it through some kind of use case description which then feeds in to some kind of solution.

Tom Rodden. Its contribution is mundane. It isn't dramatic or revolutionary. It's about the everyday nature of work, the mundane everyday nature of the world. Its contribution is to ground things in that rather than to allow them to be overly abstracted. Where's the science? Where's the big theory? There isn't one. Its contribution is very much one of working through what the doing of an activity, an endeavour, is in sufficient detail so that you can understand enough about what a technology will need to do to survive, by which I mean it's going to get put in a place and it will need to function within that place and so understanding the detail of it becomes important, understanding the nitty-gritty of the work and what the issues that might emerge from that are. So its contribution is very much about the detail of work, about conveying work as it is understood *by the people who do it*.

Richard Bentley. The fundamental argument that we need to understand how people do their jobs today to design systems to help them do them better tomorrow is ultimately how I think of ethnography: a deep understanding of how work gets done in order to better support that. But, if I'm building a computer system – a new system, a new piece of technology to support people – I might actually want to *change how* they do their job. There are some facets of what people do today that are bound up with the legacy systems they're using or the constraints of the environment they're working in that are not actually beneficial, not actually fundamental to their jobs, which you don't need to preserve and take account of. They're actually things you need to get rid of because they're functions of the systems that they're using right now. In building a new computer system to support this or that activity, I'd actually want to have them not have to do these things. So I get the deeply immersive description of what's going on but tell me, from what's going, what things are critical, what would I *need* to build into the design of a computer system, and what things are non-critical and the consequences of the environment they are in at the moment?

Richard Harper. I think that most people who do ethnography in the academic world have a spectacular inability to use that sensibility to explore artefactual changes of the world made possible by design interventions. Regularly, weekly, I meet anthropologists and I'm gobsmacked at how sort of frigid and autistic they are when it comes to imagining design possibilities or how the world might change. I think if you're doing ethnography it seems intrinsic to observation and grasping and feeling inside the worlds of those that you're studying that you get a sense of how those worlds are *assembled* and thus you therefore also have a sense of how it can be *reassembled*. If that's not possible I feel like saying what are anthropologists doing then? How can you possibly not see this all the time whenever you go out into the world? For me, I cannot see how ethnography isn't about how the world's *made* and therefore how the world might be *made differently*. Of course, anthropologists and sociologists do talk about how the world is made but what they talk about is pretty much what Huw Benyon talked about in *Working for Ford* (1973), which is not the work – *not* the thing that you would actually observe if you were doing ethnography – but the stories people tell about the political arrangements at work.

Tom Rodden. One way I used to talk about this is, what you're going to see here is what the day-to-day being an X is, where X is an air traffic controller, policeman, bank teller, etc. That's what you're going to get from us. And I used to say, surprisingly it looks like no one's bothered going and looking before! That's part of what was at play: the surprising thing is that no one's gone and looked at the work *before* they build things for it. A big part of that then became whether they had or they hadn't and what you can gain from it? This became quite a critical question because often what would happen is we would present the stuff and people would say that's obvious and we would say if it's so obvious why haven't you taken it into account, why was the system *built in a different way?*

Steve Benford. As a designer, you clearly have a set of assumptions about what problem the system is addressing, or what innovations it's bringing. Ethnography often challenges those assumptions, revealing the 'rude' realities or actuality of making the thing happen and work. In that sense it may be critical of grand visions but it's not necessarily pejorative. It's not to say that to have a grand vision is wrong or irrelevant. Rather, ethnography is a very good way of finding out some interesting things that might be worthy of further exploration or of changing your view. The most powerful thing in broad terms is that it's about agenda setting. It actually raises quite *big* issues and *refocuses* you as a designer.

Dave Randall. I've always had that "tool in the toolbox" attitude, that ethnography is one of the things you look to do good design rather than bad design. It doesn't answer all your questions – it can't answer all your questions – but it is the sort of thing you should look to try and get people to move away from a technical conception of human life and work. It's not the only way of thinking about that sort of thing, but it is well suited to it.

Tom Rodden. I don't think ethnography's foothold is just particularly in requirements engineering. You see it quite a lot now, through a shift that started in the 1990s when it started to have a stronger evaluative purchase than it did at the beginning. Part of writing the control room paper was to orientate people to the fact that you could use it evaluatively as well as use ethnography generatively. Up until that point our orientation had been much more generative: study an environment, build a new technology as a result of what you study, rather than look at technology and how it is used *in situ*, in a place.

Steve Benford. Computer science proceeds through proof by existence, by building things and trying them out. So something that gives you some purchase on how people *experience* the things you build and the issues that arise is great. If you are trying to build and deploy systems then you need, at each stage, to learn about how people experience them and feed that back into design. Ethnography is, I think, a highly appropriate and relatively quick way of doing that.

Tom Rodden. Computers are really hard work. It's not easy to build this stuff and the minute you start building it, it becomes myopic. Therefore, before you commit to building a thing, pause, think, *look*. Don't get yourself in a situation where you're canning an investment because it won't work. Go and look at the setting and the target space. Get to know the practical scopes, limits, and bounds of what you're building for. Before you spend a large amount of your time, a large amount of your organisation's resources, and commit to a programme of work, I would always strongly advise *go and have a look* before you make those commitments. Don't make them until you've had a look at what it is you're doing and at the context in which you're doing it. Ethnography is one of the tools that delivers an understanding of the context you're acting in. Ethnography is one of the best techniques for doing that. That's its foundational value for me.

2.6   Key Issues Framing the Relationship

There are no doubt innumerable ways in which you could read the interview extracts presented above. To complement that we would add several key observations of our own.

The Need for Practical Sociology Within Design
It may seem strange to speak of practical sociology. Stranger still to suggest that system design has need of it. Yet this is exactly what occasioned ethnography's relationship with and involvement in the development of computing systems. The turn to the social was predicated on the recognisable paucity of existing models of work and organisation that underpinned widespread and 'embarrassing' failures of systems design. The need to understand the social emerged from *within* systems design then, driven by the lack of fit systems had with the real world character of work and its organisation and spurred on by a collective call to attend to collaborative work and the development of distributed interactive systems.

The Need to Incorporate a Sociological Sensitivity into Design
The need to understand the real world character of work and organisation – i.e., the *social* character of work and organisation – demands that systems design develop its own sociological sensitivity. This involves uncovering practical sociology: using an ethnographic approach to go and look at work and organisation and to analyse it in terms understood by parties to the work and in the details of work's social or collaborative assembly.

The Need to Bring This Sociological Sensitivity to Bear on Systems Design
Even if you have developed a sociological sensitivity, and done so in the empirical details of a setting's work and its organisation, this is still not enough. It is also necessary to *apply* that sensitivity and the empirical insights developed through its application to what then gets designed. It is necessary for ethnography to move beyond critique and shape the actual construction of computing systems through requirements engineering and systems evaluation.

The concerns that software developers had with practical sociology – with understanding how people work with others and using that understanding to shape design – are as salient today as they were 20 odd years ago. Whether they are used in the workplace, on the streets, or in the home, computing systems are social through and through. The social character of computing systems *is* the real world character of computing systems. Accordingly, our aim in the following chapters is to elaborate practical sociology, how to develop sensitivity to the phenomenon, and how to make use of that sensitivity so that designers may capitalise on the foundational value to be had in going and looking at what people do.

References

Anderson, R., Hughes, J., & Sharrock, W. (1989). *Working for profit: The social organisation of calculation in an entrepreneurial firm*. Aldershot: Ashgate.
Bentley, R., Hughes, J., Randall, D., Rodden, T., Sawyer, P., Shapiro, D., & Sommerville, I. (1992). Ethnographically-informed systems design for air traffic control. *Proceedings of the Conference on Computer Supported Cooperative Work* (pp. 123–129). Toronto: ACM.
Benyon, H. (1973). *Working for Ford*. London: Penguin.
Button, G., & Sharrock, W. (2009). *Studies of work and the workplace in HCI: Concepts and techniques*. New Jersey: Morgan & Claypool.
COMIC Deliverable 2.1. (1993). *Informing CSCW system requirements*. http:// www.comp.lancs. ac.uk/computing/research/cseg/comic/deliverables/D2.1.ps
COMIC Deliverable 2.2. (1994). *Field studies and CSCW*. http:// www.comp.lancs.ac.uk/ computing/research/cseg/comic/deliverables/D2.2.ps
COMIC Deliverable 2.4. (1995). *CSCW requirements development*. http:// www.comp.lancs.ac. uk/computing/research/cseg/comic/deliverables/D2.4.ps
Garfinkel, H. (1967). *Studies in ethnomethodology*. Englewood Cliffs: Prentice-Hall.
Garfinkel, H. (1986). *Ethnomethodological studies of work*. London: Routledge.
Grudin, J. (1990). Interface. *Proceedings of the Conference on Computer Supported Cooperative Work* (pp. 269–278). Los Angeles: ACM.

Grudin, J. (1990). The computer reaches out: The historical continuity of interface design. *Proceedings of the CHI Conference on Human Factors in Computing Systems* (pp. 261–268). Seattle: ACM.

Harper, R., Hughes, J., & Shapiro, D. (1989). Working in harmony: An examination of computer technology in air traffic control. *Proceedings of the 1st European Conference on Computer Supported Cooperative Work* (pp. 73–86). Gatwick: Computer Sciences Company.

Hughes, J., King, V., Rodden, T., & Andersen, H. (1994). Moving out of the control room: Ethnography in systems design. *Proceedings of the Conference on Computer Supported Cooperative Work* (pp. 429–438). Chapel Hill: ACM.

Sacks, H. (1992). In G. Jefferson (Ed.), *Lectures on conversation*. Oxford: Blackwell.

Sommerville, I. (2011). Requirements engineering. In *Software engineering 9* (pp. 82–117). New York: Pearson.

Sommerville, I., Rodden, T., Sawyer, P., & Bentley, R. (1992). Sociologists can be surprisingly useful in interactive systems design. *Proceedings of the 7th Conference of the British Computer Society HCI Specialist Group* (pp. 341–353). University of York, UK. Cambridge: Cambridge University Press.

Suchman, L. (1987). *Plans and situated actions: The problem of human-machine communication*. Cambridge: Cambridge University Press.

Chapter 3
Our Kind of Sociology

> *If we figure or guess or decide that whatever humans do, they are just another animal after all, maybe more complicated than others but perhaps not noticeably so, then whatever humans do can be examined to discover some way they do it.*
>
> Harvey Sacks

Abstract The previous chapter considered the emergence of systems designers' concern with practical sociology, specifically the lack of fit their systems had with the real world character of work and its organisation and the need to develop a sociological sensitivity in order to address the problem. This chapter explicates the sociological foundations of the ethnographic approach adopted by the Lancaster School. It first and briefly considers the emergence of ethnography as a social science approach, then, in more detail, our use of it to study practical sociology. We articulate the first principles of an ethnomethodological approach to ethnography, including the key notions of work, natural accountability, and reflexivity. We present and elaborate a set of sensitising concepts supporting the study of work, including practical action and practical reasoning, interactional work, work practice, and the machinery of interaction before turning to consider the ethnographer's task, including the practical consequences of the ethnographer as an adjunct to social life and the commensurate need to develop 'vulgar competence' in a setting's work. In conclusion, we review the key issues discussed in this chapter and present a series of practical guidelines that may be derived from them for the conduct of ethnographic studies.

3.1 Ethnography

The impetus towards practical sociological involvement in systems design revolved, as John Hughes put it in the previous chapter, around "doing the kind of things that anthropologists do" – i.e., going into some place, hanging around, and seeing what people do there. In anthropological terms practical sociological

A. Crabtree et al., *Doing Design Ethnography*, Human-Computer Interaction Series,   21
DOI 10.1007/978-1-4471-2726-0_3, © Springer-Verlag London 2012

involvement in design relies on 'ethnography', an approach to the study of social life developed by Bronislaw Malinowski *circa* 1922 to characterise the work he conducted while marooned in the Western Pacific during the First World War. Malinowski's predicament was brought about by the threat of internment in Australia, where he had gone as a fresh-faced graduate to conduct fieldwork. Although of Polish origin, Malinowski's Austrian citizenship marked him out as a potential enemy alien. Atlee Hunt, permanent head of the Home and Territories Department, intervened at the request of Walter Baldwin Spencer, pioneer of anthropological studies of aboriginal life. Hunt allayed the fears of his colleagues in government and also managed to secure a tidy sum of funding – £250, some $20,000 in today's money – to sponsor fieldwork in New Guinea. One might think the situation an anthropologists' dream come true. Malinowski describes it as follows:

> Imagine yourself suddenly set down surrounded by all your gear, alone on a tropical beach close to a native village, while the launch or dinghy which has bought you sails away out of sight . . . Imagine further that you are a beginner, without previous experience, with nothing to guide you and no one to help you . . . This exactly describes my first initiation to field work on the south coast of New Guinea. I well remember the long visits I paid to the villages during the first few weeks; the feeling of hopelessness and despair after many obstinate but futile attempts had failed to bring me into real touch with the natives.

Hardly an auspicious start to the ethnographic enterprise, though the situation clearly improved. So much so that, when reported in 1922, Malinowski's novel approach came to mark a step change in the way that anthropology conducted its business (Malinowski 1922). Prior to his enforced immersion in Melanesian life, anthropology was largely done through fieldwork in its most basic sense. That is, it involved going out into the field, looking at people and what they do, and gathering a 'corpus of exhibits' to elaborate the lives of others: not only accounts of folklore, custom, and habit but also local artefacts, photographs, measurements of people, etc. Fieldwork was itself a significant development in anthropology, transforming it from an armchair pursuit busied with the cataloguing of travellers' tales into a discipline occupied by direct *empirical* inquiry.[1] Nonetheless, fieldwork was and is an activity essentially conducted at one remove from 'native' life, marked by forays out of the field camp and the conduct of interviews with 'informants' rather than actual immersion in whatever it is that the natives do. Malinowski's misfortune changed all that and he subsequently urged his peers to "get down off the verandah" and "grasp the native's point of view" before standing back to provide a more detached assessment or 'analysis'.

Today, an almost biblical confusion of tongues compete to tell us what ethnography is, though much of what is called ethnography in the computer science literature is merely fieldwork as outlined above. Ethnography cannot be reduced

---

[1] See, by way of notable examples, Franz Boas' 1883 study of Eskimos on Baffin Island in Canada, Walter Baldwin Spencer and Francis Gillen's 1894 study of aboriginal life in central Australia, and Alfred Cort Haddon's 1898 'Cambridge Expedition' to the Torres Straits.

to just going and looking and gathering a corpus of exhibits, however (Bittner 1973). It is not a mere method of observation and data collection. Ethnography is more than just fieldwork. It first requires immersion in the everyday activities of a setting or place, situating oneself in the 'phenomenal field' as it were and seeing what is done there from a native's or a members' point of view. Then it requires that we analyse what we have seen so that we might provide a professionally defensible and, in a design context at least, a demonstrably useful account of the lives of others (Button 2000). There are two key components to ethnography then: fieldwork *and* analysis, and it is with regard to the latter that the clatter of tongues is most pronounced, even in computer science.

Ethnographers offer innumerable ways of analysing everyday activities. Malinowski employed a 'functionalist' analytic to the things that he saw in the field: to the Kula Ring, for example, which consists in the exchange of necklaces and armbands and which Malinowski saw as an exercise in social cohesion. Thus, analytically, the Kula Ring 'functions' in its performance to bind island society together. Functionalism is just one of a huge array of analytic perspectives developed by social analysts. It is viewed as something of an aberration these days. Marxism, Freudianism, Feminism and a host of other perspectives on society and culture have been superseded by post-modernity too, with Deconstructionism (Derrida 1967) and Critical Theory (Adorno and Horkheimer 1972) now providing influential viewpoints on everyday life. No matter. The issue here is that the multiplicity of analytic perspectives available means that in practice there is nothing that can be definitively called ethnography. Rather, a cacophony of different ethnographies emit discordant if not contradictory messages about what ethnography is, what it does, and what it should be.

3.2 First Principles of an Ethnomethodological Approach

Our own approach to ethnography is ethnomethodological in character (Garfinkel 1967). Ethnomethodology doesn't do experiments or conduct its business through surveys or focus groups or interviews or any other methodological contrivance. Instead, through fieldwork, through going and looking at what people do, it focuses on naturally occurring activities: on human action as it spontaneously arises and as it is done by whoever is party to it. Below we articulate first principles of the approach before moving on to consider what is involved in addressing them through fieldwork.

3.2.1 Work

Ethnomethodology focuses very specifically on the 'work' that a setting's members engage in to accomplish the naturally occurring activities they are involved in. The notion of 'work' employed in ethnomethodological studies derives from

Harvey Sacks' reflections *On Doing 'Being Ordinary'* (1992c) where he introduces us to the idea that no matter how mundane and familiar our activities might be, it takes practical effort on our behalf, and on that of the others involved too, to make them happen:

> Whatever we may think about what it is to be an ordinary person in the world, an initial shift is not to think of an 'ordinary person' as some person, but as somebody having as their job ... doing 'being ordinary'. It's not that somebody *is* ordinary ... it takes work, as any other business does.

It is extremely important to appreciate that when Sacks speaks about 'work' in this way he is not necessarily speaking about paid labour. Rather, he is talking about the practicalities that people must necessarily address to get ordinary activities of all sorts done – ordinary practicalities that we are so used to as members of society and the social settings we inhabit that the effort involved in doing them is often overlooked and passes us by without pause for thought, which is not to say that we are 'unconscious' of them. Even the mundane conversations that we engage in require that we do *something* to make them occur: try it now and see. Similarly, it takes 'work' to walk down a street and it takes 'work' to decide what to do this evening just as much as it takes 'work' to do more complicated things, like process a customer order, fix a photocopier, or forge a piece of steel. The idea of 'work' refers then in a very ordinary sense to all the things that people have to do to accomplish the activities they engage in and all the things that people have to do to get their activities done may be part of an organised system of paid labour or they may not. So for us, the idea of 'work' refers to anything and everything that people *do* wherever and for whatever purpose they do it for. 'Work' is the primary focus of our brand of ethnographic studies; so much so that, bearing the above caveats in mind, we will drop the quotation marks and simply speak of work from here on in.

Sacks' distinctive concern with the work involved in the accomplishment of naturally occurring activities orients us to a world of 'achieved ordinariness' – i.e., to a world in which people actively *make* the activities they are engaged in into the ordinary activities that they are for themselves and the other members around them. That's not say that we spend our time continually fretting about whether or not our behaviour might seem out-of-the-ordinary in any way. Rather, as Sacks (ibid.) observed, it's hard to proceed in anything other than an ordinary fashion:

> ... it's perfectly available to anybody to spend an afternoon looking at a wall. You could choose to do that. If you take drugs you're permitted to do that. But unless you take drugs you would not find yourself allowed to do it, though nobody's around. That is to say, in being an 'ordinary person', that's not a thing you could allow yourself to spend the day doing. And there is an infinite collection of possibilities, of things that you couldn't bring yourself to do; not out of boredom, though that's one way you could formulate it, but in the midst of the most utterly boring afternoon you nonetheless would rather live through the boredom in the usual way – whatever that way is – than see whether it would be less or more boring to examine the wall or to look in some detail at the tree outside the window.

Essentially, foundationally, we want to know what doing 'being ordinary' consists of for the members of the settings we investigate and how they *make* or *assemble* or *put their activities together* in the doing such that they turn out to be the most ordinary things in the world.

Another way of putting it is that our studies are rooted in a distinctive disciplinary orientation to the performance of human action, not in a theatrical or 'dramaturgical' sense (Goffman 1959), but rather in the mundane sense of how people do the things that they ordinarily do. By invoking the ordinary and mundane we are not merely saying that we wish to understand how people cross the road or buy bread or watch TV, etc., though such things are not excluded from our studies. Rather we mean to say that the object of our studies is whatever is ordinary and mundane to the people we study. That might include pilots, air traffic controllers, bankers, scientists, mathematicians, and a host of other domains of human action where the activities that constitute them are utterly mundane *for those who do them*. Flying, after all, is no less an ordinary activity to an airline pilot than calculating *Pi* is to a mathematician or washing dishes to a potboy.

3.2.2 Natural Accountability

It is foundational to our studies too that a setting's work is 'naturally accountable' (Garfinkel 1967). This means that the members of a setting can see the work that is going on around them and know what it is that they and the other parties to the work are doing. Furthermore, and unproblematically, members can offer an account of what they can see and what they are doing that others will recognise too: a natural account of action seen and done in the doing of the ordinary work of a setting: of queuing to buy coffee, of walking, running, riding; of driving, waiting at traffic lights, picking the kids up; of working, having a meeting, shopping, and all of the rest of the mundane things that make up the work of the particular settings you might encounter in everyday life and which, in turn, make up the society at large. Any competent member of the ordinary society presumes that their own actions, and those of the other people around them, are naturally accountable. Society's members hold each other to that maxim. If, in the course of action, members cannot see and someone cannot provide a natural account for their actions then they are in trouble. If you doubt it, try it and see. Try, for example, walking into the house without greeting the other members of your family and then ignore them when they ask you to account for your conduct and see just how quickly things turn nasty. See how saying that you were only doing an exercise in a textbook doesn't help you because doing that, for members, is quite demonstrably and emphatically *not* a naturally accountable feature of entering the family home.

The naturally accountable character of everyday activities is an achieved outcome of their conduct, which is to say that in making their activities happen – in the work of assembling and accomplishing them – members attend as a matter of course to making them naturally accountable. This enables members to make whatever it is they are doing into the ordinary things that they are for themselves and the other people around them. We want to know how they do that, because that's where practical sociology is located and to be found – because in doing their work members display for others what it is they are doing and by making visible what they are doing others can see and recognise what is being done and can therefore concert their actions accordingly: e.g., they can walk down the street, cross the road and drive in each other's company and do so in ways that ordinarily avoid collision. Practical sociology resides in the ways in which work is made naturally accountable, with those ways being known in common and used by members to organise their activities in real time. Unpacking the naturally accountable work of a setting is the primary concern of our kind of ethnography and the effort to elaborate practical sociology.

3.2.3 Reflexivity

Our studies not only reveal what it is that the members of a setting do and the naturally accountable work they engage in but also how, in doing that work, members *reflexively* organise it as a practical sociological enterprise. The notion of reflexivity is common currency in the social sciences. It has radically different meanings. For most social scientists it is an instruction to carefully consider the impact of the researcher on representations of other people. It is used to remind us that ethnography is not only about going and looking at what people do but that it is also and in significant respects about 'writing culture' too. The production of textual representations is said to be enormously problematic and full of risks that we need to be particularly mindful of, not least of which is the projection of ourselves and our own interests onto the lives of those we study (Hammersley and Atkinson 1983). Consequently, we are urged to be cautious, to exercise reflexivity in our studies. It might be thought that this means we need to reflect on our own conduct when doing fieldwork and writing accounts of what we have seen. This is good advice but there's a lot more to it than that. We won't digress other than to say that contemporary concerns with reflexivity derive from something called the 'crisis of representation' in the social sciences, which seemed to undermine ethnography's objectivity and legitimacy as a rigorous if not a scientific endeavour (Marcus and Fischer 1986). Michael Lynch (2000), a sociologist at the forefront of debates on science and technology, provides us with a concise summation of the problem with reflexivity as it is commonly understood in the social sciences today:

> In a world without gods or absolutes, attempting to *be* reflexive takes one no closer to a central source of illumination than attempting to *be* objective … Studies of 'our own' investigative practices may, in some cases, be interesting, insightful and cleverly written, or they may come across as tedious, pretentious and unrevealing. Close textual studies of scientific or administrative reports may reveal significant contingencies covered over by unequivocal claims, or they may turn up nothing of great interest to anybody. *Ordinary* and *occasional* virtues and difficulties can be ascribed to thinking about what one is doing or reflecting on the moral consequences of one's actions, but reflexivity *in general* offers no guarantee of insight or revelation.

So where does that leave us? Apparently it's impossible for us to study practical sociology in an objective fashion, which means that whatever we do we are condemned to an infinite regression of subjective interpretations of the things we see in the field and to continuously struggle to be reflexive about our representation of them with no guarantee that it will make a blind bit of difference! There is an alternative. It's not one that's going to enamour you with a great many social scientists. Nonetheless, it works for us. First off, how about we dispense with the 'objective-subjective' dichotomy? You really don't need to get embroiled in it to study the naturally accountable character of a setting's work (Sharrock and Anderson 1991). If you take even a cursory look around you the chances are that you will see, and see at-a-glance in a great many cases, what it is that those around you are doing. You probably don't think that a very remarkable achievement. Indeed, you probably think the naturally accountable character of the activities around you is unworthy of remark. Why, after all, would you remark on what is plain for any member of the setting you are in to see? It would be absurd to say to those around you, 'I see you are having a meeting', 'ordering a coffee', 'eating lunch', 'walking', etc., as a mere matter of observation, wouldn't it? For the ethnographer, however, that you can see what those around you are doing is very remarkable indeed.

Think about it: in your ordinary capacity as a member of the various settings you inhabit in the course of your everyday life you can see much of what those around you are doing at-a-glance, just as they can see the same of you. This is not a matter of objectivity or subjectivity. It is not an ability you have courtesy of some scientific training, nor is it your subjective interpretation, something that you and you alone see and know. It is an intersubjective matter of fact for you and the other members of the setting you are in – *you and your fellow members* can see what is going on, just as what occurs in other settings is intersubjectively recognisable by their members too (Berger and Luckmann 1966). It is a condition of your own and others' membership that you see the activities going on around you in naturally accountable ways: as having a meeting, ordering a coffee, eating lunch, walking, etc. Naturally accountable activities are, for members, intersubjectively recognisable. Look around again. If you are in a place you often inhabit or frequent what you see will be utterly familiar, something seen but usually unnoticed or taken for granted and treated as the most unremarkable of things that anyone around here knows and has no need to speak of as such.

Now ask yourself a question: if what any member of a setting knows of 'what goes on around here' is usually not worthy of remark, how do members make their activities naturally accountable in the course of doing them such that any other member can see what it is that they are doing here and now? Ask yourself, in other words, how members provide for the intersubjective recognisability of their activities such that you can look around you and see what it is that they are doing at-a-glance, and they can see the same of you? Look again. Whatever is going on around you, the work you observe is bound to be *incarnate* or embodied and animate and it is by virtue of this that you can see what it is that is going on. If you look a little closer you will see that work incarnate is replete with natural accountability: the movement and arrangement of bodies speaks volumes to you as a member, as do the various pieces of equipment, materials, artefacts, resources and tools you see people exploiting, and then you may hear what people are saying and this too elaborates what is going on.

Importantly, you will not hear people saying what is going on in so many words, unless you or someone else interrupts them or in other ways calls their actions to explicit account. What you will see and hear is people *doing* their work, *doing* queuing for food, *doing* having a meeting, *doing* eating lunch together, etc., in specific details of bodily movements, arrangements of people, uses of equipment, materials, artefacts, tools, resources and turns at talk. In specific details of the embodied work of a setting members make their activities into the naturally accountable and intersubjectively recognisable things that they are for 'anyone around here'. There is, then, an *incarnate reflexivity* built into naturally occurring activities. This kind of reflexivity is not an intellectual reflexivity, not something you have to think about as a researcher or analyst, but an essential feature of the work involved in assembling and accomplishing an activity, any activity. It means that in doing work members make it accountable and in doing so reflexively organise whatever it is that they are doing: having a meeting, queuing for coffee, eating lunch, etc., one not the other, and not something else but just this thing here and now that 'anyone around here knows'.

So put yourself in the ethnographer's shoes – *the professional stranger's shoes*. Our job, more often than not, is to go into settings in which we do not know what 'anyone around here' knows. So how do we find out? It is no good following current advice in the social sciences and doing reflexive ethnographies – i.e., reflecting on our own conduct and its impact on our representation of others. Being reflexive might make you into a very nice person or equally someone who never quite knows what to say let alone what happened right in front of your very own eyes. In any case, and the case could of course be catastrophic if the latter applies, it will lead to an infinite regression of subjective interpretations having little, if any, connection to what people actually do. Instead we need to uncover reflexivity as an incarnate feature of naturally occurring, naturally accountable activities (Czyzewski 1994). That means we need to turn to the work of a setting, not to ourselves, and develop a distinctive *analytic orientation* that enables the empirical discovery of the work involved in assembling and accomplishing naturally occurring activities and the ways in which they are reflexively made into the naturally accountable, intersubjectively recognisable, socially organised activities that 'anyone around here knows'.

3.3 Studying Work

Our approach to ethnography turns reflexivity into a members' problem, a problem of assembling naturally occurring activities and, in the course of doing so, making them accountable to others so that they can concert their actions accordingly.

We want to know how members do that. Before we go and look, before we do fieldwork, it is necessary that we adopt an appropriate analytic orientation so that the work of assembly comes into view. That orientation is articulated by a set of *sensitising concepts* (Blumer 1969), which are elaborated below.

3.3.1 Practical Action and Practical Reasoning

When we speak of naturally accountable activities, what is it that we are speaking of? The social sciences offer a plethora of definitions of 'activity' and its correlates 'action' and 'agency'. We are not interested in any of them insofar as they are artefacts of reflexive reasoning in the social sciences. Instead we are interested in activity, action, and agency (etc.) as ordinarily understood by the members of society from within the settings in which they operate. From this perspective, the notion of naturally accountable activities might be seen to refer to that enormous variety and heterogeneity of things that members *do* – to that vast 'plenum' of distinctive and different naturally occurring activities that members produce and accomplish through their own agency and action. The question is this: what can we say about naturally occurring, naturally accountable activities in the face of seemingly infinite and endless variety?

When we look, and you might do that again right now wherever you are, we see that members are essentially engaged in some form of *practical action and practical reasoning* (Garfinkel and Sacks 1970). Those around you might be standing in line queuing for coffee, they might be talking to one another to work out what kind of coffee each of them wants, they might be reading, praying, preaching, painting a picture, discussing the weather, gossiping, calculating the cost of goods, splitting atoms, singing, dancing, begging, directing traffic, doing handstands or pirouettes. Whatever it is that they are doing, it will be accountable to members in terms of practical action and practical reasoning. For members, there is *no time out* from practical action and practical reasoning, even our sleep is accountable to it in the language of nightmares and dreams, bad backs and indigestion, etc., and death is no exception either. Practical action and practical reasoning is the very stuff of ordinary, everyday life, no matter how esoteric or mundane it may appear to be. Whether one is a coroner, artist, astronaut, opera singer, schoolteacher, nurse, policemen, factory worker or full time mother, everyday life is replete with practical action and practical reasoning. The mother's just as much as the coroner's; the opera singer's just as much as the nurse's. Any one of them will tell you as much if you ask.

Well, what of it? If practical action and practical reasoning is the stuff of everyday life *for members*, then it should be the stuff of everyday life for the ethnographer too. It is the ethnographer's primary task to investigate the practical action and practical reasoning that inhabits a setting. By doing so you will be able to identify the naturally accountable activities that populate it and, in turn, come to elaborate the work of a setting and its reflexive organisation. Practical action and practical reasoning beg basic questions. What do you do? How do you do it? When and where do you do it? With what? With who? Then there are questions and issues that emerge in response. Attending to practical action and practical reasoning provides us with a segue into a setting: provides or furnishes us with a concrete *starting point* and focus to our enquiries – a starting point and *ongoing focus* that is salient to members and thus salient to our understanding of the naturally accountable activities they routinely engage in and in which computing systems may be or are already embedded and used. No matter the setting, no matter how familiar or strange, investigating practical action and practical reasoning will quickly uncover the day-to-day business of a setting and orient our studies to salient topics for the members whose business it is and for designers who wish to build computing systems that resonate with, support and enhance it.

Take, for example, the practical action and practical reasoning implicated or involved in the use of Online Public Access Catalogues (OPACs) in libraries. It might be that designers are interested in learning from the use of these how they may develop new digital libraries (Crabtree et al. 1997). Your initial investigations might find a range of different members implicated in their use, including members of the public and library staff. You might also find, given what members of the setting tell you, that different categories of 'user' embed OPAC in different kinds of practical action and practical reasoning: that members of the public embed OPAC use in searching the library catalogue; whilst library staff may embed it in filtering work, for example. 'Searching' and 'filtering work' thus present themselves as salient topics for further investigation. Like the characterisations offered of practical action and practical reasoning in all kinds of settings, these are *members' glosses* on naturally accountable activities. To 'anyone around here who knows' they speak volumes, but to the uninitiated they only index or point to an unknown assemblage of naturally accountable activities. They do not describe them. As such, they gloss over and leave untouched the practical action and practical reasoning implicated in their actual accomplishment. Treated as members' glosses on naturally accountable activities, such characterisations present themselves as salient topics for further investigation, topics which may be unpacked by attending to and describing the *interactional work* implicated in their accomplishment.

3.3.2   Interactional Work

This idea orients us to the 'haecceities' of practical action and practical reasoning or, in more prosaic terms, to just how the practical action and practical reasoning involved in an activity is embodied and brought about in real time, in the real world. 'Interactional work' refers us to the concrete courses of practical action and practical reasoning constitutive of any activity's production, performance, and achievement 'here and now', as it is really and actually done by the particular members of a particular setting (Garfinkel 1986). Interactional work is 'equipmentally-affiliated' – i.e., it involves the use of tools, artefacts, and materials. It is the embodied 'stuff' that goes on in front of our very eyes when the members of a setting *do* practical action and practical reasoning and it draws our attention to the plainly observable fact that practical action and practical reasoning is done through *interaction*, either with people or with a setting's equipment or, as is more often the case, with both. Wherever we look we find people engaged in interactional work. Whether it is the interactional work of walking down a street, or driving, or crossing the road, or the interactional work involved in doing the myriad human activities and jobs of work that are going on around us. No matter how trivial, mundane, ordinary and familiar the activities around us may appear to be, their accomplishment wholly consists of interactional work. It is our task as ethnographers to attend to that work and unpack it, to describe it carefully, in the ways in which it is actually done, and to make it available to analytic account and design reasoning.

By way of example, consider practical action and practical reasoning in the library again, and 'filtering work' in particular. Library staff might tell us if we ask that it is "all about helping people find what they want" and "about getting details out of people so that we can find what they are looking for". When we look to see how they *do* this we might see something very much like the following:

Fieldwork Extract
Sarah: Could you tell us where market – what was it – market intelligence?
Lisa: Yeah.
Sarah: Market intelligence . . .
Staff: Marketing is C floor. (Points to OPAC located at service desk) Do you know how to use the screens?
Lisa: Yeah but . . .
Staff: You need to find the classmark for the book. (Staff leaves the help desk, leads Sarah and Lisa to a free OPAC terminal nearby and initiates a 'title' search.)
Lisa: It's not a book.
Sarah: It's like information, information about these particular products and services. It's called market intelligence and leisure intelligence et cetera et cetera.
Staff: And is that the name of . . .
Sarah: That's the name – market intelligence and leisure intelligence. It's not a book as such. It's usually in the reference library.
Staff: Is, is it a serial?
Lisa: Yeah.
Staff: It's a serial. (Staff initiates a 'serial' search on OPAC.)
Lisa: It's a journal.
Sarah: It's not so much a journal but it does come out every few months.
Staff: (Browsing the 'serial' search retrieval list) Is it marketing intelligence and planning? Is that the one? (Staff points to an item on the retrieval list) T6 – it's a journal.
Sarah: No. It's not a journal.
Staff: Do you want to check at that and find the journal itself? (Staff points to the item's classmark on the OPAC screen)
Sarah: Been there.
Staff: But have you actually looked at the classmark?
Lisa: Yes.
Sarah: Yes.
Staff: You've looked at that and it's not what you're looking for?

Sarah:	It's not what I'm looking for.
Staff:	Right. But that's the title of the book you're looking for – marketing intelligence?
Sarah:	Market intelligence, and its got a list of all the products and services – it's basically a reference book – and it tells you about particular market products and services and what to look for.
Staff:	You've checked in the reference area?
Lisa:	Well, no.
Staff:	Right.
	(Staff takes Sarah and Lisa to the reference area, returning alone to the help desk some three or four minutes later)
Another member of staff:	What was it she wanted? What did she ask for?
Staff:	Marketing intelligence.
Other member of staff:	Marketing intelligence?
Staff:	Which is a joke [inaudible]. She didn't want that. I eventually got out of her that it was breweries, which we've got in the reference area.

This is the interactional work of 'filtering work'. This is how 'filtering work' gets done in a library. This is what is plain to see when we look at this kind of 'filtering work' being done and what anyone can go and see for themselves, at least while physical libraries exist. Naturally the details of its accomplishment will vary from case to case. Not everyone will want the same article. Maybe only one person will ask library staff for help, maybe three or four need assistance together. Maybe it will take more or less work to resolve the search. Naturally, a host of unpredictable contingencies may impact 'filtering work'. What is predictable, however, is that despite contingencies 'filtering work', like any practical accomplishment, will be done through interactional work. It is also the case that careful description of interactional work will reveal distinctive assemblages or 'families' of *work practices*, which provide for the routine accomplishment of naturally accountable activities even in the face of contingency.

3.3.3   Work Practice

The idea of 'work practice' indicates that there is something essentially stable about the interactional work involved in the accomplishment of practical action and practical reasoning. It doesn't mean that interactional work isn't amenable to change through social or technical engineering, that there is something immutable about the interactional work of a setting that inhibits this, only that the interactional work of a setting gets done in much the same ways on one occasion as it does on another until significant changes are implemented; then it gets done stably in new ways and so on *ad infinitum*. Interactional work is, then, *reproduced* and *reproducible*. What provides for this reproducibility is work practice, which is to say that the doing of interactional work consists in the doing of distinct practices that provide for its accomplishment on occasion after occasion in the face of all manner of familiar and unfamiliar contingencies. Work practice elaborates practical sociology and provides for the recurrent accomplishment of naturally accountable activities (Button and Harper 1996). Think about it, or better still go out and see for yourself, how people cross a busy road if you want to get an immediate handle on it. Look at how pedestrians make their intention to cross the road accountable to drivers: look at how they look not only left and right but also at how they seek out the attention of the drivers of nearby vehicles with their look; look at how the drivers of those vehicles accountably register the pedestrian's look by looking back at them; look at how the exchange of looks then provides for crossing a busy road and how the refusal to exchange looks inhibits crossing. What you will see in watching members do this is the *methodical* use of looking to accountably accomplish crossing a busy road and you will see it in use time and time again.[2]

The methodical character of interactional work – the procedural ways in which it is done – underpins and provides for the notion of work practice. Work practice draws our attention to the methodical or procedural ways in which interactional work is accomplished. Thus, if we return to our example in the library, we find that 'filtering work' is accomplished in methodical ways. We see, and can see in case after case, that searches are initially made accountable through the provision of a *specifically vague* description, such as "market intelligence". This is a vague description insofar as it covers many things and so just what is wanted is not at all clear but, at the same time and without contradiction, it is also specific and directed as the information required is, in some yet to be articulated way, non-etheless understood by members to be connected to some specific matter, in this case "marketing". Specifically vague descriptions provide a starting point and warrant for further inquiries. The connection between them and the information actually required consists of a course of interactional work that revolves around the methodical use of OPAC to elicit descriptions that are intelligible in terms of the library catalogue's organisation. Library staff and users thus orient to and employ OPAC search categories to work up library-relevant descriptions of the information which is required: e.g., that the information required is not "a book" but "a serial", which provides a rather more specific sense of just what is being searched for – not just something in the area of marketing but a "marketing serial". These basic or preliminary information requirement categories may not be suffi-cient to identify just what is being sought after, however. Rather, they work or are used by members to narrow down the search and warrant continued collaboration. Simply put, being able to establish a preliminary information requirement category means that the search *can* proceed further. It does so through the elicitation of the users' prior search activities, which are drawn upon to formulate more specific library-relevant information requirement categories. There is then a whole method-ical *machinery of interaction* that has been played through here to the point where it can be established that the required item is not in a "journal" but a "reference book".

---

[2] You will also see that some people routinely violate the method: children and old people frequently dash across unannounced or shuffle out into the highway with head fixed on the road beneath their feet. From the members' perspective, these are not competent ways in which to cross a busy road: one need not necessarily sit inside a car on such occasions to see and hear what drivers make of it.

With this information in hand, staff can then act appropriately, in this case taking the users to the marketing section of the reference area in the library and to a finite collection of relevant materials.

3.3.4 The Machinery of Interaction

The identification of work practice, of the methodical or procedural ways in which members assemble and conduct naturally accountable activities, brings a distinctive 'machinery of interaction' into view; an intersubjective or social machinery used by members to produce, perform, and accomplish naturally accountable activities (Sacks 1984). The machinery reveals how members reflexively order and thus *organise* the naturally accountable activities they engage in. We can see, for example, that members order the accomplishment of 'filtering work' through the provision of specifically vague descriptions to initiate intermediated searches, through the collaborative use of OPAC to work up preliminary information requirement categories, and through appealing to users' search histories to formulate more specific information requirement categories. Thus, vague descriptions offered by a host of different library users in search of a myriad different items can time and time again be parsed, through the methodical use of OPAC and appeal to the users' search histories, into descriptions that make sense in terms of the library catalogue's organisation and permit the finding of sought after items and relevant information. If you doubt it, go and look at what happens at any library help desk, because the machinery is at work there and plain to see.

The machinery of interaction and, with it, the incarnate organisation of work might be characterised as 'the animal in the foliage' – i.e., something that is right in front of our eyes, seen *but unnoticed*. As members we usually concern ourselves with what we are doing, not with how we are doing it, and so pay little attention to the methodical ways in which we conduct our work. Like the watch on our wrist or clock on the wall, we don't look at the mechanism but use it to tell the time. Uncovering or discovering the machinery of interaction is, however, ethnomethodologically-informed ethnography's prize. Finding it is what doing ethnography as we know and understand it is all about. It isn't especially difficult to do but it does require that we pay careful attention to that which we would ordinarily, as members, let pass us by and in other circumstances intellectualise.

Take 'filtering work' again, by way of example. The term is a professional one. It belongs to the language of librarianship and it has been studied by practitioners and academics alike. Seminal among these are the studies of Robert Taylor (1968), who noted that librarians have developed "rather sophisticated methods of interrogating users". Furthermore,

> These methods are difficult to describe, indeed some believe they are indescribable ... [Because] we are dealing here, of course, with a very subtle problem – how one person tries to find out what another person wants to know, when the latter cannot describe the need precisely ... The negotiation of reference questions is one of the most complex acts of human communication. In this act, one person tries to describe for another person not something he knows, but rather something he doesn't know.

Taylor was the first to describe the handling of reference questions as 'filtering work', and the term soon dropped into common parlance among librarians to describe a distinctive feature of their daily business. Taylor suggested that 'filtering work' is organised by parsing descriptions of the information requirement through five filters. The filters work to articulate (1) the general character of the search, (2) the user's interest and (3) motivation, (4) the relationship of the inquiry to the catalogue's organisation, and (5) what might constitute an acceptable answer to the query. Clearly, there are resemblances between Taylor's account and our own: specifically vague descriptions may well be characterised as descriptions that articulate the general character of the search, for example, and the methodical use of OPAC evidently serves to establish the relationship of the search to the library catalogue. However, at no point in the description of these filters will you find an account of the interactional work implicated in the practical accomplishment of 'filtering work'. It is absent from the account, as are the work practices that provide for its real world, real time organisation. In place of an incarnate social machinery, Taylor, like many other professional social analysts, offers us an abstract account of 'filtering work. An *analytic gloss* on 'filtering work' which loses the phenomenon as it is seen, done, and understood by members.

The local, situated, and occasioned accomplishment of naturally accountable activities is too often ignored by professional studies, seen as fleeting, mundane, trivial and idiosyncratic, of relevance at best to only these people 'here and now' and hardly the stuff of rigorous inquiry. Do not be so quick to dismiss what is happening in front of your eyes 'here and now' when doing fieldwork, however. That whatever is happening *is happening at all* is worthy of the ethnographer's attention, because if it is happening then it's happening in some way: through the use of some incarnate social machinery which elaborates the setting's work and its naturally accountable organisation. You ought, then, to attend very carefully to what is happening in front of your eyes and listen very carefully to what you hear. In turn, you will be able to account for the real world, real time organisation of a setting's work and thereby identify concrete (rather than imagined) 'human activity systems' that are relevant to systems design (Checkland 1999).

3.4 The Ethnographer's Task

Although you will need to examine at least one instance of each of the various activities that make up a setting's work and are deemed relevant to design, you don't need to observe a great many occurrences of an activity-being-done to uncover its incarnate organisation. A certain number of samples of an activity-being-done is not required. We are not in the business of quantification and statistical analysis. Generalisation doesn't have to turn upon mathematical procedure. One instance will do, if you attend to it carefully, in detail, because its description will reveal the social machinery that *any* competent member uses to accomplish a setting's work (e.g., 'filtering work'). To be clear about what we are saying here: methods are not tied to individuals. Individuals use them but they are intersubjectively distributed, which is to say that *all* competent members use the machinery. Consider the following statement, by way of example, and what Harvey Sacks (1992b) has to say of it:

> When I hear 'The baby cried. The mommy picked it up,' one of the things I hear is that the mommy who picks the baby up is the mommy of the baby. Now it's not only the case that I hear it that way – and of course there's no genitive there to say 'its mommy picked it up,' 'his mommy,' 'her mommy' – when I hear it that way a kind of interesting thing is that I also feel pretty confident that all of you, at least the natives among you, hear that also. Is it some kind of magic?

It isn't, of course. As competent speakers of natural language we hear that the baby's mommy picked it up even though the two sentences don't say so because we all know, understand, and use the *same* machinery of talk. In this case, *membership categorisation devices* (ibid.) – collections of natural language categories such as 'father', 'mother', 'baby', 'uncle', 'grandmother', etc., which we use to characterise relationships between people – and *tying rules*, which provide for our hearing that the categories 'baby' and 'mommy' are first and second parts *of a pair*, that they belong together, and that the mommy is therefore the mommy of the baby even though nobody actually said so (Sacks 1992a). Remarkable isn't it? Even something as simple as a couple of sentences exhibits a distinctive social machinery at work which is used by any competent member but cannot be reduced to the individual reader. The same is true of our other activities. You don't need 10, or 100, or 1,000 instances of people doing intermediated searches in libraries to uncover the social machinery that provides for that accomplishment then. Each and every instance will *display the machinery at work*. Another way of putting it is, "tap into whomsoever, wheresoever, and you get much the same things" (Sacks 1984). Go back to the coffee shop, out onto the streets, venture into the library, and you will see that time after time, on occasion after occasion, this is indeed the case because the machinery is there for any competent member to see, and most of us are competent enough to buy a cup of coffee, cross the road, and even search for a little information in a library. Recognising the social machinery implicated in the accomplishment of more unfamiliar activities may take a little more work.

Whether studying familiar or unfamiliar activities, or activities in which you are or are not a competent member, the ethnographer's task is the same: to describe the achieved ordinariness of a setting's naturally accountable activities in details of the haecceities that observably and reportably animate them. In other words, you need to attend carefully to what people do and describe the discrete courses of practical action and practical reasoning that make up the interactional work of a setting and the work practices that members use methodically to organise that work and make it accountable. In turn, this will enable you to identify the machinery of interaction that provides for the work's intersubjective recognisability and its reproducibility by members on other occasions. The consequences of this are profound: adherence to these maxims means that the ethnographer is, essentially, an *adjunct* to naturally accountable activities. Someone who trades upon and makes visible for others a setting's members manifest competence in the particular things they do and the particular methods they use to do it.

The ethnographer as adjunct to the work of a setting is in many ways at the heart of the enterprise. One conducts fieldwork not to become another competent member of a setting as such, but to *explicate* and *make visible* the work practices and social machinery that animate a setting's work in real time. It is not about 'going native' then, but rather about grasping the actual work of the setting and the methods at play and then being able to stand to one side, as an adjunct to that work, and point out its accountable features, all of the cogs and wheels of the social machine so to speak, and demonstrate to others just what it is that they do. So, at no point in doing a study is your personal perspective an issue. That would miss the point of being such an attentive student of and apprentice in a setting's work. Instead, your attention ought to be wholly arrested by just what it is that the competent members around you do and the methodical ways in which they do it. The art of the competent adjunct is to be able to make that visible in a way that anyone else looking at the machinery at work might also be able to see that it does indeed work in just the ways you say it does. Your opinion regarding the efficacy of the machinery, and what place you might think it has in grand schemes of society, are irrelevant to this exercise. Indeed, they would serve to make the work *less visible*, substituting what members do and how *they* do it for what *you* think about what they do and how you perceive it to have sociological significance. It need not be the case then that the ethnographer is doomed to be ensnared in an infinite regression of interpretations, no matter current advice and received wisdom, for if you do a study properly it will reveal the ways in which *members* themselves 'interpret' or make sense of and understand their actions – fundamentally, how they themselves make their actions *accountable*.

What we are driving at here, and insisting upon as something that ought to be sacrosanct, is the primacy of the members' perspective. Ethnography can be about turning the ordinary things that people do into examples, cases, versions even, of 'bigger' phenomenon at work in the society at large. You could do such things with your observations, but were you to do it you would lose sight of the everyday work of a setting and its 'endogenous' or local organisation. In doing so you would be making ordinary action into something else, something outside of the setting and its member's ken, transforming their ordinary business into some other kind of phenomenon. So what? It's a perfectly legitimate practice if you are an anthropologist or sociologist. Indeed, transforming the members' perspective is required of the anthropological or sociological analyst. It is their stock-in-trade, for without the transformation there is no anthropology or sociology (etc.) and we are not saying that it is without use. It is not our job, however, to speak to anthropology or sociology but to systems design, and that requires a rather different order of account from ethnographic approaches in the social sciences at least. One which suspends analytic reflexivity and instead reveals incarnate reflexivity and the real world, real time organisation of human action so that computing systems meet the needs of their users as manifest in the actual accomplishment of their work.

We must insist on primacy of the members' perspective then. It roots design in real contexts of use, real settings, populated by real users, doing real activities with real bits of equipment and tools. A necessary corollary to this, one that applies just as much to adjuncts as to fully paid-up practitioners, is that the production of empirical ethnographies (in distinction to analytically reflexive ethnographies) relies on the development of 'vulgar competence' in members' work (Garfinkel and Wieder 1992). Vulgar is not a pejorative term, it does not mean common or rude. Rather, etymologically, it means ordinary. It is a requirement then for you to develop an appreciation of the ordinary competences that the members you are studying themselves *possess and employ* methodically to get their activities done, to make them accountable, and use to recognise what those around them are doing too. The requirement to develop vulgar competence is a requirement for you to get to know the work of a setting such that you can see what 'anyone around here' can see in the ways that they see it. It is a requirement for you to develop a members' familiarity with the work of a setting so that you can see the work from the perspective of its members. It is not, however, a requirement for you to go native and provide a personal account or 'auto-ethnography' of a setting's work (Hayano 1979). To reiterate, your personal views are not relevant.

The ethnographer's job of being an adjunct to a setting's work is to look and see how the work is done and organised on the 'shop floor' as it were. If you are doing fieldwork in an unfamiliar setting this will be a relatively straightforward task in the sense that everything will be new and strange to you and you will have much to learn. If, however, you are studying familiar activities, like those that go on in the home, you also need to treat what you see as 'anthropologically strange' – i.e., you need to pay *extraordinary attention* to familiar activities and hold them up to careful scrutiny so the animal in the foliage that you usually ignore comes into view and you can both see and notice the incarnate machineries of interaction organising the setting's work. A useful technique to employ for getting a handle on the work of a setting and its organisation is 'bracketing'. We did it with 'filtering work'. It's a simple device for making a members' gloss on practical action and practical reasoning into an object of sustained enquiry. The brackets say 'look at this'. They say 'ask questions' about how this kind of practical action and practical reasoning gets done. They say 'carefully describe' the interactional work that provides for that accomplishment.

With the interactional work of the setting in hand you will then be able to see for yourself how the work is done and provide a 'defeasible account' of the machinery that members use to organise it – i.e., you will be able to provide an account that members will be able to *verify*. What you find will not be news to the members whose activities you have been studying because you will not (or should not) be transforming the ways in which they conduct their activities into versions of something else. Your findings will be news to those parties who are at some remove from the setting's work, however, including systems designers. Through them, members of the design team will come to see what activities go on in a setting, how they are done, who is involved in doing them, what resources they draw upon, what skills are involved in using them, and so on, and thereby start to develop an understanding of the possibilities for systems design.

3.5 Practical Guidelines

Before moving on, let's take a breather and sum up what we have been saying about ethnography, particularly about what is involved in *doing it*. There is already quite a lot to digest.

Immerse Yourself in a Setting
In a design context ethnography requires that you immerse yourself in real world settings of relevance to your design task. You can't do it from your office chair, or by phone, or by post, or by administering a questionnaire, or by doing an experiment in a lab. You have to do fieldwork. You have to *go and look* at what people actually do in the places they actually do it. If you are involved in building library search systems, for example, go and look at how people do searching in libraries. If you are building inventory systems, go and look at how people keep inventories. If you are building knowledge-based systems, go and look at how people assemble and construct the kinds of knowledge that your system has to support. Whatever the design task or problem, the first step in doing ethnography is to identify an appropriate setting and to immerse yourself in its work.

Focus on What Is Happening in Front of Your Eyes
This may seem like an obvious point but it is important not to get too carried away by your research brief or design agenda and ignore what is actually happening on the ground. It is all too easy to focus on issues that you think important at the expense of understanding what the setting's members actually do and the ways in which they actually organise work in real time. Pay close and careful attention to what is happening in front of your eyes then and *let what you see guide you*. This is not to say that you need take every single thing that people do into account. It would be pointless looking at what the cleaners do if you were developing a system to support customer service work in an office, for example. You need to be in the right place, with the right people, and that may take some working out. Once in the company of those people, however, do not ignore or readily discount what you see. It may seem like people are doing silly or trivial things, but then a great many human activities can look that way if you don't pay sufficient attention.

Develop Your Competence in the Setting's Work
Paying close and careful attention to whatever is happening when people do their work will enable you to *see what's happening from the perspective of members* and thus help you develop an appreciation of the competences involved in doing it. You might attend to the following features of work to help you do so:

(a) *Attend to practical action and practical reasoning*
Attend to the distinct courses of practical action and practical reasoning that members engage in as a feature of actually doing their work, and the descriptions or 'glosses' they use to characterise these when you ask them what it is that they are doing. Bracket members' glosses on practical action and practical reasoning in order to make them into objects for further scrutiny.

(b) *Scrutinise interactional work*

Scrutinise members' glosses on practical action and practical reasoning by attending to and describing the interactional work they actually engage in to accomplish the work their characterisations refer to and gloss. Look at the things they actually say, the people they actually talk to, and the equipment they actually use, and provide a detailed account of what is actually said, by whom, using whatever materials, tools, resources, etc.

(c) *Identify work practice*

Analyse your descriptions of interactional work to identify the work practices that members use to accomplish it. Your analysis should reveal the methodical character interactional work has for the parties to it, and in turn, display the social machinery that members use to make their work accountable and to reflexively organise that work.

Verify Your Findings with Those Who Do the Work

It is a good idea, good practice even, to present your findings to the members whose work you have studied. Your account of the interactional work and social machinery that members engage in and use to organise their work should be intersubjectively recognisable. That means that if the setting's members don't recognise their work and its naturally accountable organisation in your account of it, *you have issues*. If they do recognise it but raise questions, concerns, caveats, and otherwise tell you about significant aspects of their work that you have missed, then you have more fieldwork to do. Fortunately, in raising such issues, they will have already told you what to go and look at.

We appreciate that these guidelines don't actually tell you how to do ethnography. What they hopefully do *do* is give you a rather more concrete sense of what doing ethnography is all about and what is involved in carrying it out. We also appreciate that these guidelines raise as many questions as they answer, especially with regard to the methodical or procedural character of a setting's work, which is obviously core to the enterprise. What we want to do next is figure out how you can go about seeing the animal in the foliage and thus find the methods that provide members with a social machinery for making their activities into the naturally accountable, intersubjectively recognisable activities that they demonstrably are for them.

References

Adorno, T., & Horkheimer, M. (1972). *Dialectic of enlightenment* (J. Cumming, Trans.). New York: Herder & Herder.

Berger, P., & Luckmann, T. (1966). *The social construction of reality: A treatise in the sociology of knowledge*. New York: Anchor Books.

Bittner, E. (1973). Objectivity and realism in sociology. In G. Psathas (Ed.), *Phenomenological sociology: Issues and applications* (pp. 109–125). New York: Wiley Interscience.

Blumer, H. (1969). Science without concepts. In *Symbolic interactionism: Perspective and method* (pp. 153–170). Berkeley: University of California Press.

Button, G. (2000). The ethnographic tradition and design. *Design Studies, 21*, 319–332.

Button, G., & Harper, R. (1996). The relevance of 'work-practice' for design. *Computer Supported Cooperative Work: The Journal of Collaborative Computing, 4*(4), 263–280.

Checkland, P. (1999). *Systems thinking, systems practice*. Chichester: Wiley.

Crabtree, A., Twidale, M. B., O'Brien, J., & Nichols, D. M. (1997). Talking in the library: Implications for the design of digital libraries. *Proceedings of the International Conference on Digital Libraries* (pp. 221–228). Philadelphia: ACM.

Czyzewski, M. (1994). Reflexivity of actors versus the reflexivity of accounts. *Theory, Culture and Society, 11*, 161–168.

Derrida, J. (1967). *Of grammatology* (G. C. Spivak, Trans.). Baltimore: Johns Hopkins University Press.

Garfinkel, H. (1967). What is ethnomethodology? *Studies in ethnomethodology* (pp. 1–34). Englewood Cliffs: Prentice-Hall.

Garfinkel, H. (Ed.). (1986). Introduction. In *Ethnomethodological studies of work* (pp. vii–viii). London: Routledge.

Garfinkel, H., & Sacks, H. (1970). On formal structures of practical action. In J. C. McKinney & E. Tiryakian (Eds.), *Theoretical sociology: Perspectives and developments* (pp. 160–193). London: Apple-Century-Crofts.

Garfinkel, H., & Wieder, D. L. (1992). Two incommensurable, asymmetrically alternate technologies of social analysis. In G. Watson & S. M. Seiler (Eds.), *Text in context: Contributions to ethnomethodology* (pp. 175–206). New York: Sage.

Goffman, E. (1959). *The presentation of self in everyday life*. Garden City: Doubleday Books.

Hammersley, M., & Atkinson, P. (1983). *Ethnography: Principles in practice*. London: Tavistock.

Hayano, D. (1979). Auto-ethnography: Paradigms, problems and prospects. *Human Organisation, 38*(1), 99–103.

Lynch, M. (2000). Against reflexivity as an academic virtue and source of privileged knowledge. *Theory, Culture and Society, 17*(3), 26–54.

Malinowski, B. (1922). *Argonauts of the western pacific: An account of native enterprise and adventure in the archipelagoes of melanesian New Guinea*. London: Routledge.

Marcus, G., & Fischer, M. (1986). *Anthropology as cultural critique: An experimental moment in the human sciences*. Chicago: University of Chicago Press.

Sacks, H. (1984). Notes on methodology. In J. Maxwell & J. Heritage (Eds.), *Structures of social action: Studies in conversation analysis* (pp. 21–27). Cambridge: Cambridge University Press.

Sacks, H. (1992a). Tying rules. In G. Jefferson (Ed.), *Lectures on conversation* (pp. 150–156). Vol. 1, Pt. 2, Fall 1965, Lecture 4. Oxford: Blackwell.

Sacks, H. (1992b). The baby cried. The mommy picked it up. In G. Jefferson (Ed.), *Lectures on conversation* (pp. 236–242). Vol. 1, Pt. 3, Spring 1966, Lecture 1. Oxford: Blackwell.

Sacks, H. (1992c). Doing 'being ordinary'. In G. Jefferson (Ed.), *Lectures on conversation* (pp. 215–221). Vol. 2, Pt. 4, Spring 1970, Lecture 1. Oxford: Blackwell.

Sharrock, W., & Anderson, R. (1991). Epistemology: Professional scepticism. In G. Button (Ed.), *Ethnomethodology and the human sciences* (pp. 51–76). Cambridge: Cambridge University Press.

Taylor, R. (1968). Question-negotiation and information seeking in libraries. *College and Research Libraries, 29*(3), 178–194.

Chapter 4
Finding the Animal in the Foliage

The 'foliage' is the local historicity of embodied shop practices.
The 'animal' is that local historicity done, recognised, and
understood as a competent methodic procedure

Harold Garfinkel

Abstract In the previous chapter we suggested that practical sociology may be studied empirically through the use of ethnography, which entails fieldwork or going and looking at the naturally occurring work of a setting, and the application of an analytic perspective to uncover the organisation of a setting's work. We suggested, too, that there are a great many analytic perspectives available but that we focus exclusively on ethnomethodology and the naturally accountable character of work and its organisation. Uniquely, this perspective concentrates on the *methodical* ways in which a setting's members assemble, build up or put their work together, and make it accountable to others in doing so. Work practice is another term for the methodical assembly of work and finding it is ethnography's task as it makes visible a social machinery of interaction that a setting's members use to do and organise their work. This machinery is usually 'seen but unnoticed', which is to say that members know and make use of it but pay little heed to it; instead they get on with whatever it is they are doing through its use. Like the animal hiding in the foliage, we need to attend carefully to the machinery of interaction to make it out and make it available to design reasoning. The issue we want to elaborate here is how we can find the machinery of interaction. To put it another way, how *do* we uncover work practice and make members' methods visible? By way of an answer we want to explore a range of examples which articulate different orders or modal expressions of the phenomenon at work. The examples should not be read as definitions, only as concrete cases that display the methodical character of work.

A. Crabtree et al., *Doing Design Ethnography*, Human-Computer Interaction Series, DOI 10.1007/978-1-4471-2726-0_4, © Springer-Verlag London 2012

4.1   The Methodical Character of Talk

Talk is the most obvious and pervasive way in which members conduct their work and make whatever it is that they are doing into an intersubjectively recognisable and naturally accountable activity. It is often the case in our capacity as ordinary members of the settings we inhabit that we only have to hear a snippet of talk to figure out what is going on between the parties to conversation and recognise what it is that they are doing. Take the following extract (Sacks 1992d); as mundane a piece of conversation as you are ever likely to hear:

Lana: Hello.
Gene: Is Maggie there.
Lana: Hh, uh, who is calling.
Gene: Uh this's Gene – Novaki.

You can probably recognise, at-a-glance, what is going on here: a phone call, and more precisely the beginning of a call or a phone call opening. You might also recognise, were you to treat this as an 'anthropologically strange' or unfamiliar event, rather than something that is utterly commonplace, some distinctive inter-subjective or social features of phone call openings: that the person who answers the phone always speaks first, for example, or that the person who answers is not necessarily the person called, and that in such cases people who answer phones but haven't themselves been called have ways of establishing the callers' right to call, by asking them who they are. You can see these things at work in the snippet of talk above. What you might not notice straight off, however, even though you are intimately acquainted with it, even a master in the use of it insofar as you are a competent speaker of natural language, is that these features of a phone call opening exhibit how members go about assembling *all* talk.

Take a closer look. No doubt you can see that the talk consists of utterances that follow on from one another; that these utterances are produced interactionally by alternate speakers; and that they come in adjacent pairs: e.g., Lana's question "Hh, uh, who is calling" is paired with Gene's answer "Uh this's Gene – Novaki". It might seem trivial at first glance but these adjacent pairings of utterances are used by members to make the work they are engaged in accountable. This particular *pairing* of question and answer is used to make it accountable in the unfolding flow of answering the phone that the person who has answered the phone wants the caller to establish his right to call, to furnish grounds for calling as it were and to furnish grounds for continuing the call. The question and answer pairing is used to establish that. Seeing and recognising this is what a member's competence turns upon and Gene responds accordingly, identifying himself as someone the intended recipient of the call (Maggie) knows. This is not a cold call then, but a call from an acquaintance. As members who are competent in answering phones, we know this, we see and recognise what Lana and Gene are doing even though what they are doing is not said in so many words. Rather, they use the simple pairing of question and answer to conduct the work. More than that, they use the pairing of question and answer in a methodical way to establish the caller's right to call. In saying this we do not mean that questions and answers are methods but that in the course of our interactions we *use them methodically*. Interactionally, we know that asking someone "who is calling?" is not simply a request for them to furnish their name, it's a request that they furnish their credentials. A name may suffice, as it does on this occasion, but were the call from a sales person, for example, or some other stranger more would be required. The asking and answering of questions is used by members as an interactional method. We know and use them in methodical ways ourselves to handle calls from unknown parties.

Adjacent pairings of actions are not limited the asking and answering of questions. They are infinitely variable. They are also the "building blocks" of interaction (Sacks 1992c). We use them to assemble our conversations and we use them to assemble other activities as well. As we shall see, the use of technology of all kinds, be it telephones, paper mail, photographs, mobile and virtual technologies, etc., is inextricably tied to them. You cannot separate out the use of technology from the adjacent pairing of actions in which its use is interactionally embedded. You may well be able to ignore the phenomenon – a great many methods in the social sciences and the more specialised field of human computer interaction guarantee that you will do so – but for members the use of technology is not separable from the adjacent pairing of the particular actions in which it is interactionally embedded.

The telephone is a perspicuous example of that: anyone can see that 'using the telephone' is intersubjectively accomplished and accountably organised through the adjacent pairing of utterances that make up 'the call'. What makes that accomplishment accountable – what makes what Lana and Gene are doing recognisable to us as fellow members, for example – is not the pairing of particular actions but the methodical ways in which the pairs are *used*. It is not adjacent pairings of utterances or actions more generally that are of interest to us then, but *what attending to their use reveals:* members' methods for using technology and embedding it in everyday life. As Sacks (1992d) puts it with reference to the telephone,

> Here's an object introduced into a world around 75 years ago. And it's a technical thing which has a variety of aspects to it ... Now what happens is, like any other natural object, a culture secretes itself onto it in its well-shaped ways. It turns this technical apparatus which allows for conversation, into something in which the ways that conversation works are more or less brought to bear ... ... This technical apparatus is, then, being made at home with the rest of our world. And that's a thing that's routinely being done, and it's the source for the failures of technocratic dreams that if only we introduced some fantastic new communication machine the world will be transformed. Where what happens is that the object is made at home in the world that has whatever organisation it already has.

There is a strong implication for systems design in this observation: if we want to understand use settings, computer users and technology use, we need to develop a keen appreciation of "the organisation that the world already has" because technology is "made at home" within it. That organisation comes into view when we attend to a "drastically simple" and "utterly pervasive" phenomenon (Sacks 1992c): the building blocks of interaction or the adjacent pairings of actions in and through which interaction is built up and assembled.

The assembly of interaction is not restricted to talk and the telephone. It extends far beyond conversation and is foundationally implicated in the incarnate organisation of human activities and technology use in all their rich variety, which is to say that adjacent pairings of utterances *and* other forms of action are the building blocks of interaction everywhere. Conversation analysts, who see themselves as the successors to Harvey Sacks work, are likely to take issue with the suggestion and our account of adjacency pairs. We are not doing conversation analysis, however, or trying to elaborate everything Sacks had to say about them. We are trying to put you onto a fundamental feature of interaction *everywhere*. One that you can orient to *whatever* the work you are studying in order to *search for* and *locate* members' methods and the machinery of interaction they use to conduct and organise their activities. The building blocks of interaction are not restricted to talk but are used by members to assemble activities of all kinds. If you pay careful attention to them – if you look to see how any course of interactional work is observably and reportably assembled through the pairing of adjacent actions – the methods that members use to make their activities accountable will come into view. The following examples seek to elaborate the proposition and provide some demonstrations of the phenomenon at work.

4.2   The Methodical Character of Asynchronous Action

Action may be synchronous in nature, as above where one action immediately follows another, or asynchronous. Asynchronous action is temporally distributed. It is naturally accountable nevertheless, and frequently made so by members in methodical ways through adjacent pairings of material artefacts and objects. The handling of mail in the home provides a lucid example (Crabtree 2003). Handling mail is a mundane matter that occurs on a daily basis across a great many homes. Through it we receive invitations, appointments, bills, important household documents, and more. Despite the enormous variety of homes and heterogeneity in their layout and furnishing, a distinctive social machinery for handling mail can be found to operate across many of them (Fig. 4.1).

In the first instance mail arrives somewhere, not anywhere, but at some specific place: the mailbox, apartment pigeonhole, front door, etc. Mail is delivered to a specific *collection point* then, which any competent member of the home knows. It is also known that any member of the home may collect the mail, though this may be constrained on occasion by age, the height of the mailbox, doors, etc. That anyone in the home may collect the mail does not mean that anyone can open it, however. Consequently, mail items are often moved from the collection point to a *sorting point* where it can be established what the mail is and who is entitled to open it. Kitchen tables, desks, trolleys in the hallway all provide commonplace examples of sorting points.

Fig. 4.1 New mail has arrived and needs sorting

It may be that the person who collects the mail is the same person who sorts it, and it may not. The collector may simply drop the mail at the sorting point and leave it for someone else to sort sometime later. Either way, the placement of mail is a highly nuanced affair, with specific placements providing specific accounts as to what needs to be done with the mail and what its placement means. Placing the mail at the front of the kitchen table, for example, may provide an account that says, without a word being spoken and at-a-glance, that 'new mail has arrived and needs sorting'. Alternatively, someone might do the sorting and place mail in locations that are relevant to recipients; let's call it a *relevant recipient point*. This placement may be at a similar location to that where mail is sorted, e.g., somewhere else on the kitchen table, or it may be in a different location entirely – on a chair where the recipient usually sits or on a nearby nest of tables, even outside a bedroom door (Fig. 4.2).

It may also be the case that the mail is opened or unopened. Items such as postcards, thank you cards, round robins and others that provide news that extend beyond the named recipient are frequently placed at relevant recipient points to display at-a-glance, and again without words, that 'something of interest and relevance to you' has arrived, whereas more personal items may be left unopened in the same location to the same effect.

A great many items we receive through the mail require further action of us. This too is handled through the placement of mail and in ways that reflect, at-a-glance, the priority household members attach to it. It may be that immediate action is required, that a bill has to be paid, for example. In such cases we find that household

Fig. 4.2 Mail has arrived that is relevant to you

Fig. 4.3 Mail items requiring immediate action

members place items in locations to display that such action is required and where they are likely to remember to undertake it – *immediate action points* as it were, such as in the porch near the car keys, in front of the computer, near the mobile phone charger, etc. (Fig. 4.3).

Fig. 4.4 Mail items pending future action

Items that require or may require that action be taken sometime in the future, that is items where action is pending, are placed in different locations or *pending action points*, such as in a pile at the back of the kitchen table, on top of the stereo or a bookshelf, in a letter holder, etc. (Fig. 4.4).

Mail pending future action is often differentiated: bank statements, records of mortgage payments, insurance certificates, and other important household documents are often placed in a pending pile awaiting future sorting and filing. Such things as invitations, appointments, shopping vouchers, promotional offers, concert tickets, and other *event*-based items find themselves placed in alternate locations, however, alongside relevant artefacts such as calendars, shopping lists, and takeaway menus. Noticeboards, kitchen walls and cupboard doors, are common examples of *pending event points* (Fig. 4.5). Pending event points keep items relevant to up and coming events ready to hand and on display and thus work to maintain household members' awareness of them.

Other kinds of mail displays are also to be found in the home too. Notably locations where such things as birthday cards, thank you cards, and the like, are routinely placed. Let's call these *social display points*. They may merge with pending event points – postcards are often found on noticeboards, for example – or the locations may be discrete: mantelpieces, windowsills, and shelves are commonly employed to display items from friends and family (Fig. 4.6).

There is, then, a distinctive methodical organisation to mail handling. Its specific manifestation will vary from home to home according to its layout and furnishings, and aspects of it such as placement for relevant recipients will be

Fig. 4.5 Mail items relevant to up and coming events

Fig. 4.6 Social displays of mail

constrained by household population. Nonetheless, where and when household members have need to organise the handling of mail, and a great many of us do have such need, then it is done through the *methodical placement* of mail items, proceeding from collection points, to sorting points, to relevant recipient points, and to a range of relevant handling points thereafter. The methodical placement of mail is elaborated by a distinctive set of adjacent pairings. These are not simple pairings of the order 'question-answer', but are responsive to a range of possible actions occasioned by the arrival of mail. Thus, sorting occasions a range of recipient placements and once the mail is read one of a range of actions is provided for through subsequent placement: immediate action, pending action, pending event, social display. This set of adjacent pairings reveals a machinery of interaction for handling mail and making accountable to household members what needs to be done with it. Thus, at-a-glance, without a word being said, household members can see that 'new mail has arrived', 'mail has arrived that is relevant for you or for me', 'this mail item requires immediate action', 'that will wait' or is 'up and coming', and so on.[1]

4.3   The Methodical Character of Synchronous Action

Of course a great many embodied actions are done synchronously, in situations where our own actions are interleaved 'here and now' with those of the other people we are co-located with, and also involve the methodical use of objects, artefacts, materials, etc. A relatively simple example of this commonplace kind of synchronous action is provided in the mundane activity of looking at photographs with family or friends, something that most of us have had occasion to do in the past. The following example elaborates the methodical ways in which the viewing of physical rather than digital photos is assembled and intersubjectively organised by a small group of family members. The participants in our study, Andy and his wife, Suzie, are paying a family visit to his brother, Billy, his wife, Louise (or Lou), and their children, Sam and Lydia. Lou has recently been sorting through some family photographs preparatory to archiving them, and this turns from a passing topic of conversation into an occasion to view the photographs themselves. Like mail handling, these instances of photo viewing reveal a distinctive machinery of interaction that extends beyond the particular case where we observed it at work. Next time you find yourself looking at a collection of physical photos in the company of others, the machinery will be available for you to see at work too.

Louise retrieves a folder of photographs from a cupboard in the living room and sits down on the floor so that the children can gather round her. Suzie joins them on the floor too, and Billy and Andy sit on adjacent settees. Louise takes the photos out of their folder and starts leafing through them, telling the assembled

---

[1] All well and good but one might ask, what has this got to do with systems design? See Harper and Shatwell (2003) by way of an answer.

company who is on them, and placing photos that have been looked at in front of her on the floor:

Fieldwork Extract
Andy: Is that your Grandad?

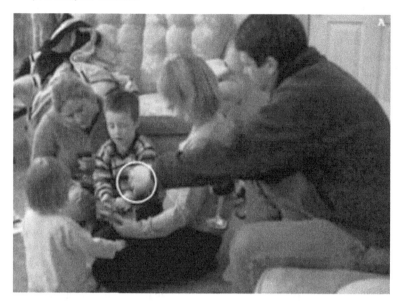

Lou: *Points to the photo on top of those in her hand. She's looking at Sam as she does so, who has picked a photo up off the floor.*

Lou: That's my Grandad. He was a real character. You remember Great Grandad don't
       you Sam? *Lou tilts the photo in her hand towards Sam as she continues to point at it.*
Sam: Yup. *Sam puts the photo he has picked up off the floor down and takes the photo off
       Lou instead.*
Andy: Let's have a look.
Sam: *Turns the photo to Suzie, who he is sat next to.*
Suzie: *Leans in towards Sam to look at the photo he is holding.*

Andy: Let's have a look.
Sam: See, we're at my house.
Suzie: Yeah.
Sam: *Puts the photo on the floor.*
Lou: *Picks the photo up.*

Lou: That's Grandad there. *She passes the photo to Andy.*

Lou: *Turns to the next photo in hand, which Sam is already trying to take off her.* And that's
    Granddad there – she slides the photo off the deck – and there.
Sam: *Takes the photos off Lou and holds them up in front of Suzie.*

Lou: Grandad lived just long enough to know that Lydia was born; he died about three
       days after.
Suzie: Ahhh.

Andy: *Holds the photo out towards Lou.*
Andy: How old was he there then?
Lou: *Turns towards Andy and takes hold of the photo as well.*

Lou: 90, 91.
Andy: Were he!
Lou: Yeah.
Andy: Fit bloke.
Lou: Yeah.
Andy: *Lets go of the photo.*

Lou: He lived a good life.
Andy: Yeah.
Lou: He really did.
Sam: *Moves around to Andy, holding up the photos he has been showing Suzie, which are also of his Great-Grandad.*

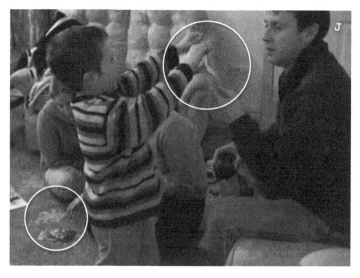

Lou: *Puts the photo she and Andy have just been talking about on the floor, and then turns to the next in hand.*

This short sequence of interaction displays a distinctive machinery of interaction that the participants exploit as they work through the photographs. In the first instance it can be seen that looking at photographs is organised by participants through the distribution of turns that provide for sharing them. This is done in conversational ways through the pairing of adjacent utterances, and it is also done in material ways through the placement of photographs relative to those utterances.

If we look we can see then that Andy's initial question "Is that your Grandad?" is paired not only with an answer from Louise but an answer that is prefaced by her pointing a finger to the photograph in question. This pairing of adjacent utterances *with* material actions establishes a *mutual orientation* to a specific photo. This continues as the action unfolds and elaborates members' methods for doing 'sharing photographs'. Thus, we can see that Lou's question to Sam – "You remember Great Grandad don't you?" – is paired as the pointing continues with tilting the photo towards him, which invites Sam to look and even take hold of it. We can see that Sam's subsequent taking and turning of the photograph towards Suzie is paired with an account of the photograph – "See, we're at my house". We can see that Suzie acknowledges that Sam's account was directed specifically to her by pairing the verbal account "Yeah" with leaning in bodily towards the photo to display her orientation to it. Suzie's acknowledgement provides Sam with an opportunity to continue talking, but instead he brings this turn to a close by placing the photo on the floor.

We can see too that Andy's request to view the photo is delayed until Sam and Suzie's turn is completed and that compliance with his request to "have a look" is done by Lou pairing an account of the photo – "That's Grandad there" with her picking it up off the floor and handing the photo over to him. This shows how the second part of an adjacent pairing of actions can be complied with in other ways than immediate adjacency, where there is a clear orientation to provision of the second part even if it is delayed. We can see that working through the stack of photos continues as Lou pairs her bodily orientation to the next ones in hand with an account of them – "And that's Granddad there, and there." The next turn is prefaced as before by Sam taking the photos in hand from Lou and again orienting them to Suzie. The orientation of the photos is paired concurrently with an account from Lou – "Grandad lived just long enough to know that Lydia was born; he died about 3 days after." Suzie acknowledges the orientation of the photo to her by Sam and Lou's account as complementary actions and, again, the acknowledgement is done by pairing her bodily orientation to the photographs with a verbal account – "Ahhh."

We can also see that Lou's account of the photograph is heard by Andy to be of broader topical relevance, relating not only to the photos that Sam is holding and Suzie is looking at but also to the one that he is holding, and that further topically relevant questions may be begged of it – "How old was he there then?" Andy's question is paired with the action of holding the photo he is has in hand out towards Lou to display who the question is directed at. This enables Lou to recognise that a question is being asked specifically of her and she responds to the question being asked by taking hold of the photo in question and pairing it with a relevant account – "90, 91." It can also be seen that having joint ownership of the photograph, literally taking hold of the photograph together in this case, occasions further discussion. Andy shows that he has finished doing so by letting go of the photo, which is ultimately acknowledged by Lou by putting the photo on the floor to show that the turn is coming to completion. At the same time as this particular exchange is being brought to a close, Sam brings the photos of his Grandad that he has in hand and has been showing to Suzie and holds them up for Andy to see as well. Andy takes hold of one of them and the sequence continues to unfold through the use of the methods that have elaborated the sequence thus far.

Those methods elaborate a distinctive machinery of interaction for sharing photographs. They are made visible through the assembly of adjacent pairings of utterances and material actions. The pairings *reveal* members' methods for doing 'sharing photographs'. Those methods provide for the use of photographs through the combination of a range of material actions – including bodily movements, orientations and gestures – with verbal utterances. Methodically, the pointing finger enables members to identify just which photograph a question is being asked of. Methodically, tilting or turning or holding a photo out towards a particular person enables them to recognise that they are being addressed. Methodically, the tilting and turning of photos by one party to a recipient, and concurrent descriptions of them by another, are heard to be tied together and to complement one another. Methodically, recognition is done not only through words but also by physically orienting oneself to the tilted and turned object or even taking joint hold of it. Methodically, other turns at viewing a particular photo are put on hold until the current turn is done. Methodically, letting go of a jointly held photo or putting it down (e.g., on the floor) or passing it on, makes it visible that this turn is complete. Methodically, the speaker's bodily orientation to the photos in hand says that a next photo is being discussed as much as the words that accompany it do.

This much and more can be seen in the sequence above. The sequence is not exhaustive; members' methods for sharing photographs are even finer-grained than this (Crabtree et al. 2004). Nonetheless, the methods at work here provide a social machinery that enables members to see 'which photograph is the current topic of conversation', 'which photograph questions are being asked of', 'which photograph you are talking to me about', 'which photograph someone else wants to look at', 'which photograph another is asking questions of', 'which photograph answers are being given to', 'which photograph someone has finished talking about', and 'which photograph is next'. If you doubt it, go and get your old photos out and look at them with your family or friends. You will see the machinery at work as together you go about *making* them into accountable objects and thus get the work of sharing done.

4.4 The Methodical Character of Distributed Action

A great many naturally accountable activities happen online these days. Digital technology increasingly enables *distributed action*, where members' in one location interact with parties in another location at some geographical remove. Distributed action is an ever more common mode of action. It can occur asynchronously or synchronously and can combine physical and digital action, or embodied action taking place in the real world and interaction taking place online in virtual worlds as well. The following example addresses the methodical character of distributed action in real and virtual environments (Crabtree and Rodden 2009). It is an example drawn from a novel form of gaming which has become popular over recent years: Alternate Reality Gaming. Specifically, it is drawn from a game called *Uncle Roy All Around You.*

The game situates some players on the streets of a city, Manchester in the UK in this case, and some players online anywhere in the world. The street players are equipped with GPRS-enabled PDAs, which display a map of the gameplay area in the city. Street players report their positions by tapping 'I am here' on it. They receive clues from the game server and its operators, aka 'Uncle Roy', directing them around the gameplay area and text messages from online players. Online players are immersed in a virtual representation of the gameplay area. They have avatars that they use to roam around it and when street players declare their position for the first time, they become visible as avatars (highlighted by a red ray of light) in the virtual world as well (Fig. 4.7).

A description and photograph of each street player is also available to online players and street players can respond to their text messages by recording short audio messages. The aim of the game is for street players to find a postcard somewhere in the physical gameplay area, which in turn triggers a response from Uncle Roy leading to instructions being released to online players.

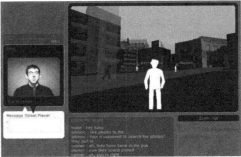

Fig. 4.7 Street player with PDA and online player in the virtual game play world

These are used by online players to guide street players to Uncle Roy's office and an intimate encounter.[2] We join a street player, Patrick, a few minutes into the game:

Fieldwork Extract

Patrick: *Reports his location on Portland Street on the PDA and receives a clue from Uncle Roy in response* – 'Wai Yin. Translate: men cannot enter. Make appropriate move. 23 minutes remaining.' – Wicked, right, China Town.

Patrick: *Starts walking along the street, reading a message on the PDA; he laughs.* Someone's telling me I've got a nice jacket on. *Selects record audio.* Thanks Nicole, it's very comfortable and it's keeping me very warm tonight, so thanks for that.

Patrick: It's bizarre in it. *Carries on walking, turns towards a man and woman coming towards him.* Excuse me? Do you know where China Town is?

Man: That way. *Points to a street across the road.*

Patrick: Right, down there. Wicked. Cheers mate. *Man and woman walk on.*

Patrick: It's where there's the big gate.

Patrick: *Crosses the road and looks at the PDA.* Right, Dave's just sent me a message: go into the graffitied phone box by the railings. So I'm going to send him a little message now. *Selects record audio.* Dave, can you direct me to it? I'm outside the red phone box outside er – *looks around for a street sign* – oh bollocks, outside Reyner Street. So yeah, if you want to direct me there that would be wicked. Cheers mate.

Patrick: Right, I'm on my way to China Town. *He crosses Reyner Street, still walking down Portland Street; looking around as he walks; sees another red phone box down Charlotte Street and heads towards it.*

Patrick: *Approaches phone box; looking at PDA.* Is he (Dave) trying to goose me here? He's telling me that I've got to have a look on top of the phone box. And Nicole, who likes my jacket, is saying that her postcard's here as well. So. *Patrick opens the phone box and looks inside and exits shortly afterwards.* There's nothing in there.

Patrick: *Looks around and notices a postcard on the floor outside the phone box, which he picks up.* All right. It says tell me about someone from your past who never leaves you. Right, OK. *Selects record audio record.* Nicole, Nicole, tell me about someone from your past who never leaves you – that's what it says on your postcard and it's on – *looks around for a street sign* – Charlotte Street.

Patrick: *Looking at PDA.* Right, and apparently there's another one. There's a phone box – Dave's telling me there's a phone box over by Portland Tower.

Patrick: *Turns around and heads back down Charlotte Street, towards Portland Street.*

Patrick: *Walking down Charlotte Street, sees another phone box.* Ah right. *Selects record audio.* Dave, is it the one over the road from Portland Tower?

Patrick: *Walks over to the phone box.* There's two of them actually. *Looks inside and then walks off towards Portland Tower.*

Patrick: *Looks at PDA as he approaches the road. Selects record audio.* No Nicole. Nicole, it's not a riddle, it's the clue that's on the postcard on Charlotte Street phone box. Do you want to text me the name of someone from the past who never leaves you.

Patrick: *Crosses the road in front of Portland tower and checks his PDA again.* Right, Uncle Roy's getting a bit annoyed because I'm not telling him where I am. *Reports his location and then reads a message:* All right, that's Nicole (who has supplied a name of someone who never leaves her, thus triggering the release of instructions by Uncle Roy).

---

[2] For a more detailed account, see www.blasttheory.co.uk/bt/work_uncleroy.html

There is a strong assumption built into the design of this game, and other experiences that combine real and virtual action, which is that the online players' view of the world *correlates* with the street players' view of the world. The assumption has it that online players inhabit a virtual environment which is a facsimile of the real environment, and that online players therefore share the same perspective as street players. The fieldwork extract strongly suggests otherwise. While both sets of players may see specific structures, street layouts and street furniture, they do not see them in anything like the same way. This is not simply to say that virtual representations are necessarily abstract and lack the vivacity of real life. It is to say that while players may see the same structural arrangement of buildings and streets, etc., they do not *share* same point of view on those arrangements. They do not do so because they are not actually in the same place, looking at the world *from* the same point of view. One is 'here' on the streets, the other 'there' online. Ordinary troubles one encounters on the streets, such as 'which way do I go from here?', or 'which way is this or that place?', cannot be resolved in ordinary ways then: by asking someone to point out the way for you, for example. Obviously you can't do that if you aren't actually in the same place as the person you are asking directions of. You have to find other ways to achieve a *mutually intelligible orientation* to the world, and that is what is going on here.

Merging real and virtual action relies upon participants being able to establish mutually intelligible orientations to the world. It is not something that stands at the periphery of this distinctive kind of distributed action but is something that runs throughout it, moment-by-moment as it were. This is easily done when we are co-present, as with sharing photographs where moment-by-moment we create and sustain mutually intelligible orientations by pairing our accounts with material actions, but material action is not available as a shared resource here in the same methodical ways because the two parties can't actually see one another's actions. Alternate methods are required for the job then. When we look to see what these consist of, when we inspect the interactional work of the setting, we see that achieving a mutually intelligible orientation is a built in feature of way-finding or navigating the city streets. Thus, we can see that Dave's message to "go into the graffitied phone box by the railings" is heard by Patrick as an instruction to find a specific place somewhere in the city. We can see that instructions to find locations are paired with requests for directions to those places: "Dave, can you direct me to it." These second part pairings are accompanied by 'personal coordinates', e.g., "I'm outside the red phone box outside er – *looks around for a street sign* – oh bollocks, outside Reyner Street. So yeah, if you want to direct me there that would be wicked. Cheers mate." These coordinates orient the online player to the street player's current location and enable online players to plot directions to the location they seek.

The street player does not wait for specific directions to be delivered but proceeds on his way, following the clues provided by Uncle Roy. He does not go blindly about this however, but visually searches the streets to see if he can identify the place or places that online players have asked him to find. In other words, instructions to find specific places are also paired with actions that amount to 'scanning' the streets to find candidate locations or places that might well be those that are sought after. The result is that another red phone box is seen by

Patrick as a good candidate, especially given new messages from the online players saying that a "postcard is here", "at this phone box", and that he should "look on top" of it to find it. Thus 'scanning' the streets for candidate locations is paired with 'directional accounts' or accounts from online players, which direct the street player's looking. These may, or may not, be accurate. To say that the post card is "here", for example, is actually extremely vague in this situation, as it is not based on an up-to-date location report. Patrick has not reported his location on the PDA since Portland Street. He has only furnished a verbal report, and that was outside a red phone box on Reyner Street. Finding Nicole's postcard in a phone box on Charlotte Street is purely serendipitous then: nothing in what Nicole has said has furnished Patrick with actual directions to *this* red phone box. That her card was found is the happy coincidence of Patrick trying to find Dave's postcard.

Of course, directional accounts may be more precise as, for example, when Dave instructs Patrick that his post card is in "another phone box over by Portland Tower". That is a rather more serviceable formulation than "the graffitied phone box by the railings". It is still ambiguous, however, as can be seen in Patrick's request for a more detailed specification of location: "is it the one over the road from Portland Tower?" The directional account is not only paired with 'scanning' for candidates then, but with requests for more detailed accounts of location which may be used to confirm or reject candidates. In this case, a more detailed account is not required from the online player, as Patrick quickly establishes, by looking in the phone box and seeing that there is no postcard there, that this is not a candidate location after all.

The interactional work of the setting reveals that way-finding is organised in real time through the ongoing *construction* of a mutually intelligible orientation to the streets between geographically dispersed parties to interaction. Methodically, that orientation is done moment-by-moment at geographical remove through the delivery of instructions to find specific locations. These instructions are paired with requests for directions and the provision of personal coordinates. These in turn furnish online players with a start point from the street player's current location to accompany the end point or destination that has already been specified. Methodically, instructions to find locations are paired with 'scanning' the streets to find candidate locations. Methodically, the personal coordinates provided by street players are paired with directional accounts of varying degrees of accuracy. Methodically, directional accounts are paired with requests for more detailed accounts of location to confirm or reject candidate locations. Methodically, where way-finding is not interrupted by the game server (as it is in this case), the iterative pairing of instructions, scanning the streets for candidate locations, providing directional accounts, and formulating more detailed specifications of location to confirm or reject candidates, works to *narrow down the gap* from a constantly moving 'here' to some very specific destination 'there'. Thus, the assembly of a mutually intelligible orientation to the streets reveals the methodical character of way-finding's work and elaborates a distinctive set of work practices for coordinating distributed action across real and virtual environments. In turn, those work practices display an incarnate machinery of interaction for handling the asymmetry that is inherent to action distributed across real and virtual settings.

4.5   Identifying Members' Methods

The point of providing examples of "members' methods" is not to use them to formulate some definition of the phenomenon; it is not to say that *this* is what they are and what they consist of. Rather, our aim is to sensitise the reader to the phenomenon by giving concrete examples of it at work. These examples are not to be treated prescriptively. They should not be read as instructions to go and find the same modalities of action and methods at work in other settings. Rather, they should be read as examples that try to articulate the diversity of the phenomenon: that it spans verbal action, asynchronous and synchronous material action, and real and virtual distributed action as well. What the examples show is that one can tap into the methods that members use to organise their activities at any point, whatever the modality or modalities of action. Don't restrict your studies to our examples then, they are only elaborative of Sacks' (1984) maxim that "there is order at all points".

Our examples will not tell you what to look for in each and every case. So, rather than treat our examples as some kind of template, read them instead to develop your own awareness of and sensitivity to the different modalities of action that you see, and can see, going on around you. Read them to see that whatever it is that those around you are doing, the modality in which it is expressed, can be inspected to see how it is being assembled or put together. *Whatever* the modality of action, it is being observably assembled in front of your very eyes through the adjacent pairing of actions. Those pairings reveal members' methods for assembling work and making what they are doing accountable. Your task as an ethnographer is to uncover the methodical character of naturally accountable activities. To do that you need to go out into the field, go to where the action is, immerse yourself in the work of a setting and attend carefully to the observable and reportable ways in which members assemble and make whatever it is that they are doing *mutually intelligible*.

Our examples don't provide you with a recipe for doing that. What they *do* do though is elaborate a grossly observable feature of interaction that you can orient yourself to on any occasion of inquiry to identify the methods members use to construct and coordinate mutually intelligible courses of action. This general feature of interaction is derived from Harvey Sacks' notion of adjacency pairs. We say 'derived' because it is not Sacks' account of adjacency pairs that concerns us so much as the underlying logic of his analysis and thus the distinctive way in which he *reasoned* about interaction and *made it analysable*. We take analytic inspiration from Sacks then, nothing more. Looking at our examples it is plain to see that the methodical character of the naturally accountable activities they report is made visible by members *through* the pairing of adjacent actions – i.e., through the observable and reportable ways in which members see their own and others' actions as being accountably related in the very course of interaction itself. In short, attending to the adjacent pairing of actions orients us to how it is that members see their actions as belonging together, such that the placement of a mail item by someone's seat, for example, tells both the giver and receiver that 'this is for you', just as the tilt of the photograph says to both parties involved that 'we are talking about this particular photo'.

The logic of Sacks' analysis is one, essentially, that orients us to interaction such that it is seen by those who are involved in doing it to be built up through the putting together of particular actions in a symmetrical fashion (Sacks 1992a). The symmetry is accountably produced through the pairing of adjacent actions which clearly complement and complete one another, whether continuously 'here and now' or discontinuously sometime later: by turning your head to look at the photo thus offered, for example, or by picking up the mail left just here for you where you always sit. By looking at how naturally occurring activities are accountably constructed through the pairing of adjacent actions we may come to see the methodical character of action. In turn, we are able to offer analytic accounts of the intersubjective or social organisation of human activities that avoid the standard substitution of the members' perspective for the analysts'. Instead, our studies illuminate distinctive work practices and machineries of interaction that 'anyone around here' knows how to use and that members together employ to order the activities they engage in.

We have chosen several mundane examples to demonstrate the point. There is nothing esoteric about answering a phone, handling the mail or sharing photographs. Most of us will have had occasion to do these things or at least will have seen them done and so, on the basis of the ordinary competence we have developed through personal experience, most of us will *recognise* the methodical character of the work involved in their accomplishment (Sacks 1992b). Your studies will need to enable that too and thus make visible the methods that members use to conduct their activities and make them accountable *to one another*.[3] Work practice, to use another term for members' methods, changes from activity to activity but that does not mean that there is nothing for you to grab onto. Time after time, in setting after setting, you can attend to the *building blocks* of interaction to tap into the phenomena. Without presupposition as to just which methods could be at work you can nevertheless orient yourself to and explicate adjacent pairings of actions to reveal the animal in the foliage. It takes more than just seeing alternate blocks of light and shade and colour to see it: it takes seeing how the parts go together.

4.6 Practical Guidelines

Once again our reflections on doing ethnography have doubtless left the reader with a great deal to absorb. In that case, it is perhaps worth drawing out the key features of what we have been saying here.

---

[3] For further examples see Hughes et al. (1992), Button and Sharrock (1997), Garfinkel (2002), and Livingston (2008).

Find the Animal in the Foliage – The Machinery of Interaction
The point and purpose of ethnography for us is to *uncover the machinery of interaction* that members employ to conduct and organise their work. The machinery consists of members' methods or work practices. They are known in common, seen and used by members but usually go unnoticed: members instead attend to the business in hand rather than to the methodical ways in which they go about doing it. If we are to draw them out of the foliage, if we are to notice them, we need first to attend to the modality of action.

Focus on the Modality of Interactional Work
Specifically, we need to focus on the modality of interactional work, on the particular manner in which interactional work is visibly articulated and expressed by the parties to it as it unfolds. If the work of a setting is done through talk then we need to focus on talk; if it is done through material action then we need to attend to material action; if it is done in embodied ways then we need to attend to embodiment; if it is done virtually then we need to attend to the virtual, and so on; and we need to attend to the spatial and temporal (synchronous, asynchronous, distributed) character of verbal, material, embodied and/or virtual action because the *method is in the mode of action's doing.*

Attend to Actual Sequences of Interactional Work
If we are to find members' methods we need to attend to actual sequences of interactional work. Talking to people – interviewing them – is not sufficient because that is not where the animal resides. Talk can shed light on features and characteristics of the animal but we actually need to see the work being done to have any possibility of it coming into view. So you need to observe people *doing the work* and attend carefully to the *actual sequences of interaction* in and through which it is done.

Examine How Actual Sequences of Interactional Work Are Assembled
Look to see if you can find how parties to the work build it up or put it together over the course of interaction. Use the logic of adjacency pairings to see how the assembly is done. Pay careful attention, then, to the particular actions that members do to construct the work and pay particular attention to how those actions complement and complete one another. The aim in doing this is to see how particular actions form the parts of adjacent pairings of action that are oriented to as belonging together by the parties to the work.

Explicate the Accountable Character of Members' Methods
The identification of adjacent pairings of action reveals the methods that members use to assemble their work and make it accountable. It is essential that you explicate the accountable character of members' methods – i.e., that you describe what turns upon the use of the methods made visible by adjacent pairings of actions for members doing the work: that you are being asked for your credentials in order to determine your right to call when being asked who you are, for example, or that mail placed next to your seat is for you, or that in turning the photograph towards you it is being made accountable that it is available for you to look at it, etc. Make it

clear what the method *does* then, what it is used for and how it is used by members to make their actions mutually intelligible and to concert or coordinate those actions in the doing of them.

The question of method is a central one in systems design, as it is more generally. Indeed, it is a constant preoccupation of the sciences. What we want to do next is consider the question in more detail, to move beyond our examples and elaborate what is involved in actually 'going about' finding the animal in the foliage.

References

Button, G., & Sharrock, W. (1997). The production of order and the order of production. *Proceedings of the 5th European Conference on Computer Supported Cooperative Work* (pp. 1–16). Lancaster: Kluwer.

Crabtree, A. (2003). *The social organisation of communication in the home*. Proceedings of the 8th Conference of the International Institute of Ethnomethodology and Conversation Analysis, August 6–9, Manchester.

Crabtree, A., & Rodden, T. (2009). Understanding interaction in hybrid ubiquitous computing environments. *Proceedings of the 8th International Conference on Mobile and Ubiquitous Media*, Article No.1. Cambridge: ACM.

Crabtree, A., Rodden, T., & Mariani, J. (2004). Collaborating around collections: Informing the continued development of photoware. *Proceedings of the Conference on Computer Supported Cooperative Work* (pp. 396–405). Chicago: ACM.

Garfinkel, H. (2002). An ethnomethodological study of the work of Galileo's inclined plane demonstration of the real motion of free falling bodies. In *Ethnomethodology's program: working out durkheim's aphorism* (pp. 263–285). Lanham: Rowman & Littlefield.

Harper, R., & Shatwell, B. (2003). Paper mail in the home of the 21st century. In *Inside the smart home* (pp. 101–114). London: Springer.

Hughes, J., Randall, D., & Shapiro, D. (1992). Faltering from ethnography to design. *Proceedings of the Conference on Computer Supported Cooperative Work* (pp. 115–122). Toronto: ACM.

Livingston, E. (2008). *Ethnographies of reason*. Aldershot: Ashgate.

Sacks, H. (1984). Notes on methodology. In J. Maxwell & J. Heritage (Eds.), *Structures of social action: Studies in conversation analysis* (pp. 21–27). Cambridge: Cambridge University Press.

Sacks, H. (1992a). Accountable actions. In G. Jefferson (Ed.), *Lectures on conversation* (pp. 72–80). Vol. 1. Pt. 1, Fall 1964 – Spring 1965, Lecture 10. Oxford: Blackwell.

Sacks, H. (1992b). On sampling and subjectivity. In G. Jefferson (Ed.), *Lectures on conversation* (pp. 483–488). Vol. 1. Pt. 3, Spring 1966, Lecture 33. Oxford: Blackwell.

Sacks, H. (1992c). Adjacency pairs: Scope of operation. In G. Jefferson (Ed.), *Lectures on conversation* (pp. 521–532). Vol. 2. Pt. 8, Spring 1972, Lecture 1. Oxford: Blackwell.

Sacks, H. (1992d). A single instance of a phone-call opening: Caller-called, etc. In G. Jefferson (Ed.), *Lectures on conversation* (pp. 542–553). Vol. 2. Pt. 8, Spring 1972, Lecture 3. Oxford: Blackwell.

Chapter 5
Dispensing with Method

> *An alternative would be to assign exclusive priority to the study of the methods of concerted actions and methods of common understanding. Not a method of understanding, but immensely various methods of understanding are the hitherto unstudied and critical phenomena.*

Harold Garfinkel

Abstract Methods are the *sine qua non* of scientific endeavour. They are commonly held to provide for rigor and reproducibility of both approach and results, yet we have none to offer. Indeed, we steadfastly refuse to impose methods on the study of practical sociology. Why? Because *a priori* methods, or methods devised outside the actual circumstances and situations being studied by people who are not party to the work under investigation, lose the phenomenon: lose *members' mastery* of practical sociology. You don't need methods to develop competence in a setting's work or to uncover the naturally accountable ways in which members do it and reflexively organise it. So how is ethnography to proceed then? The absence of method – of formula, of prescription, of step-by-step approach – does not mean that advice cannot be offered, or that common tools and resources cannot be used. Our aim in this chapter is two-fold then. Firstly to elaborate the practical necessity to dispense with method. Secondly to elaborate how to approach fieldwork, including configurations of fieldwork for design, and common tools and resources you might employ to elaborate a setting's work and its real world, real time organisation.

5.1 The Practical Necessity for Dispensation

The social sciences are replete with special methods for conducting research. That they are possessed of such methods enables us to reason about them as scientific activities. Ethnography in the broad sense of the word – i.e., in anthropology, sociology and other disciplines – is no different. It is not our purpose to provide

A. Crabtree et al., *Doing Design Ethnography*, Human-Computer Interaction Series,
DOI 10.1007/978-1-4471-2726-0_5, © Springer-Verlag London 2012

an exhaustive review of the methods that are available to the fieldworker, a great many textbooks already do that job. We note however that they cut across five general categories:

- *Textual methods*, which rely on the participants in a study self-reporting, usually through the use of diaries or similar devices.
- *Observational methods*, which rely on the fieldworker seeing the work of a setting first-hand.
- *Audio-visual methods*, which exploit audio recorders, video recorders, and photography to capture aspects of the setting's work.
- *Verbal methods*, or interviews of which there are a great many types ranging from the structured to the unstructured.
- *Digital methods*, which are largely derived from HCI and exploit such things as keystroke logging and gaze tracking to capture human-computer interaction.

If you were to read the literature you would find that a great many methodological distinctions exist within each of these categories. Take the literature on observation, where you will find distinctions between participant observation (where one becomes involved in the work of a setting), direct observation (where one is not involved in the work but present), and covert observation (where one may be present but those being observed are not aware of it). Or again, take the literature on interviews where you will find an enormous variety of methods on offer: open-ended, fixed response, topical, historical, biographical, contextual, focus groups, etc.

A great many methods are offered by ethnographers and qualitative researchers more generally – i.e., those researchers who do not work in a quantitative or numbers-oriented tradition. Fundamentally, all social science research methods fall into one of two camps: qualitative or quantitative. The essential difference between the two is not that one does research by numbers and the other does it by some other kind of measurement; fieldworkers of various analytic persuasions may well run numerical operations on their findings. The difference is that qualitative research is not fundamentally about numbers and numerical methods of measurement. Rather, numbers – statistics – are used to support fieldwork insights, not as primary findings or phenomena in their own right. Of course, there are those who seek to combine qualitative and quantitative methods, so-called 'mixed method' approaches where the objective is to quantify qualitative findings and thus establish 'scientifically' defensible measurements as opposed to what have occasionally been characterised by hardline methodologists as subjective almost 'journalistic' approaches that rely upon the interpretations of the fieldworker. While qualitative purists may well take issue with such approaches and characterisations, we are not persuaded by arguments on either side of the debate. The reason for our lack of interest, let alone conviction, in the arguments for this or that methodological approach is that we have no work for research methods to do – any research method, be it qualitative or quantitative in nature. Rather, our interest lies in *treating methodological matters as members' concerns* and in identifying the methods members use to address them.

One does not need an armoury of research methods to do that despite the thought that surely some research method must be needed to uncover the incarnate ways in which members methodically organise their affairs. By way of example and of dispelling that insistent thought let us first consider the application of a social science research method to a mundane activity: driving across a four-way stop or intersection where two streets cross.[1] In countries all over the world the flow of traffic through this kind of intersection, and others too, is regulated by rules and regulations. Signs are often placed at them which reflect and index these, such as 'stop' or 'give-way'. Where stop signs are placed the driver is supposed to come to a full and complete stop. Where more than one driver arrives at different parts of the intersection, then the one who arrived first has right of way. Where two drivers arrive at the same time then, depending on which side of the road vehicles travel on in the country in question, traffic on the left or right takes precedence. A reasonable social science inquiry might set out to explore the social character of driver behaviour at four-ways stops in order to understand the social factors that are implicated in road traffic accidents at such locations. The enquiry might reasonably be conducted by devising a method for identifying car drivers and the ordinary activities that they engage in. The method might consist of identifying and applying categories of perceived social and situational relevance: e.g., age, gender, race, type of car, age of car, stop behavior, type of infraction. The method might be applied by embedding the relevant categories in a chart or table and then standing at the roadside and observing what goes on at four-way stops in order to fill in the chart.

There is nothing unusual in this kind of method. We see it at work in diverse situations from high-street questionnaires to traffic monitoring and roadside checks. Livingston characterises it as 'street corner Durkheim', after the founding father of sociology. While Durkheim's work is often eschewed by social scientists today, the method persists and works by rendering or transforming ordinary action into a collection of count-able indicators, tokens or signs, which reveal distinct demographic patterns. In the case of the four-way stop, for example, statistical analysis of the results might reveal that older drivers observe the instruction to stop or give-way more than younger drivers, that women do so more often than men, or that young white males in fast cars have the highest rate of infraction. In turn, this might inform policy-making, leading to public awareness campaigns or even an increased level of pre-license training for young drivers.

All well and good. However, at no point is the interactional work of crossing the four-way stop uncovered by the research method. Absent also are the methodical ways in which drivers themselves organise interaction at four-way stops, thus navigating through them safely or not. The method does not make visible, for example, that most drivers 'roll' up to and through the intersection and do not stop, that they often 'sneak out' in front of oncoming traffic causing oncoming vehicles to slow down, that they 'piggy-back' cars that are crossing in front of

---

[1] The example is not our own. It is taken from Eric Livingston's unpublished primer for students, *The Ordinary Society*, and rendered in our own words.

them and occasionally cut other drivers up in the process, that they take turns by 'flashing' one another across with headlights, that they balk and stall on occasion, that they get angry with one another, gesticulate, make rude gestures, and honk their horns whether to convey their displeasure or to 'chivvy' a hesitant driver along. Even something as mundane as crossing a four-way intersection is replete with it's endogenous or internal organisation. It is an incarnate organisation produced in the methodical ways of crossing the road. Not in blind obedience to rules and regulations but in rolling along, sneaking out in front of others, piggy-backing, flashing one another across, chivvying others along, and so on in all its accountable detail. The research method misses the methods that members use to organise the flow of traffic at intersections, methods drivers are keenly aware of and acquainted with and which they recognise and use in the company of others to navigate their way across intersections. The point is this then: no matter the merits of social science research methods or any others, *they lose the very phenomena we seek.*

5.2 Professional Indifference

Our reservations about the need for research methods lies in the demonstrable fact that whatever they do, they do not uncover the endogenous organisation of naturally accountable activities. Consequently, our reservations extend beyond anything that might be described as scepticism, healthy or otherwise, to active professional *indifference* (Lynch 1993). What do we mean by this? We do not mean we have no interest in research methods or their achievements. Clearly they are critical to a great many forms of inquiry and their use may be studied as a job of work in its own right. We mean that in doing fieldwork we can have no interest in research methods or their achievements as they lose the phenomena we seek: namely, members' methods for conducting and concerting their activities, and with them members' mastery of practical sociology. Our indifference is not "naughty advice" (Garfinkel 2002b). It is not about disrespecting social science research or any other kind of research. It is about not buying into research methods, not making them foundational to *our* studies, because if we do, we lose our phenomena and the ability to uncover practical sociology in empirical detail. Our indifference is not an attitude. It is a professional action which requires of us that we set research methods aside and learn for ourselves what methods could be at play in the current situation of enquiry – i.e., in the work of the field setting.

The professional notion of indifference derives from studies of scientific practice, and from Edmund Husserl's phenomenology in particular. Husserl, a philosopher, was interested in the epistemological foundations of science. In short, he wanted to know how science knows its objects (Husserl 1999). The obvious answer is through the Scientific Method. Not many social scientists are likely to accept that today, if for no other reason than that it would appear there is no Scientific Method but rather a heterogeneous array of scientific methods having no essential commonality. The relative character of scientific method wasn't what troubled Husserl, however. His problem was that, when he looked at scientific activity, scientific methods appeared to come *after* discovery and thus have a *post hoc* relationship to knowledge.

An example might help to clarify the point and its significance: on the evening of January 16th 1969 at the Steward Observatory in Arizona astronomers John Cocke, Michael Disney and their colleagues discovered a degenerate neutron star or 'pulsar' (Cocke et al. 1969). Cocke and Disney recorded part of their night's work on audiotape, particularly a series of 'Runs' or observational episodes during which the discovery of Pulsar NP 0532 was made. Pulsar NP 0532 is a 'transcendent astronomical object', an 'independent Galilean object', which in more prosaic terms means that it is available to astronomy as a mathematically describable feature of the universe and one that exists independently of particular observers: Cocke and Disney, for example. Pulsar NP 0532 is, in other words, 'out there' – an objective feature of the universe for astronomers and others to see. Three social scientists, Harold Garfinkel, Michael Lynch and Eric Livingston, set out to explore how the discovery was made and examined the tape to address the issue (Garfinkel et al. 1981). What interested them in passing through the tape was how Cocke and Disney's observations clearly evolved from identifying *a vague object of sorts* to identifying an independent Galilean object that transcended their local experience. The question is, how?

The following edited excerpts are taken from Runs 18–22 and show something of the work of the discovery. Run 17 detected no pulse.

Run #18
McCallister: There's a nice dip on that side of the sky. I'm going to turn this thing down.
Disney: We've got a bleeding pulse here.
Cocke: Hey! Wow! You don't suppose that's really it, do you? Can't be.
Disney: It's right bang in the middle of the period. Look, I mean right bang in the middle of the scale. It really looks like something from here at the moment to me.
Cocke: Hmm.
Disney: And it's growing too. I won't believe it until we get a second one.
Cocke: I won't believe it until we get the second one and until the thing has shifted somewhere else.

In this sequence of talk, and through the use of the astronomical equipment to hand, "a nice dip on that side of the sky" reveals a "pulse", but it is not a given pulse, not an objective pulse. While the pulse's factual status is suspected by the astronomers, it is nevertheless doubted at this point in time. At this point in time the pulse is a vague object of sorts, one lacking definition. Consequently, in their conversation together, Cocke and Disney formulate conditions to verify the factual status of the object to hand. These include (#1) reproducing the Run such that a second pulse is detected, and (#2) looking for a shift in the object's onscreen representation. This latter condition is predicated on their working knowledge of the equipment and the commensurate suspicion that the visibility of the object "right bang in the middle of the scale" may be a technical bogey: a subsequent correct reading should place the object elsewhere on the screen.

Run #19

Disney:	Beginning.
Disney:	My God, it's still there. It's as good as it was, or better than it was last time.
Cocke:	It disturbs me, that's right in the middle of the screen.
Disney:	It isn't John, look.
Cocke:	It's moved a little bit.
McCallister:	If you get the right frequency then it'll be more or less the same place, wouldn't it?
Disney:	It should be more or less; you won't be exactly the same place.
Disney:	That's a bloody pulse isn't it!
Cocke:	Let's move off that position and do somewhere else and see if we get the same thing. I hope to God this isn't some sort of artefact of the instrumentation.

In this sequence of talk, the astronomers try to reproduce the prior observation subject to the verification conditions they have specified. Condition #1 is readily satisfied in this Run, indeed it's "better than it was last time". The satisfaction of Condition #2 is still in dispute, however. Although the on-screen representation of the pulse has shifted a little, it is not enough to determine whether or not the pulse is "some sort of artefact of the instrumentation". Judgements as to the factual status of the object are suspended and a further verification condition is formulated. Condition #3 specifies moving the telescope 0.25 of a millimetre northwards. This positional check confirms that the equipment is working properly and results in Run 20 in the reproduction of the pulse and a shift in its on-screen position corresponding to the movement of the telescope: a pulsar has indeed been detected.

Having established the 'immanent facticity' of the object to hand – i.e., its situationally factual status, its factual status 'here and now' – Cocke and Disney set about formulating ways in which the independent Galilean status of the object may be established. This will enable the existence of the pulsar to be publicly verified by other members of the astronomical community. In order to achieve this, they examine their data for its measurable properties, such as photons per second (Run 22). With these exact scientific measures, other astronomers may reproduce the observation and see Pulsar NP 0532 for themselves.

Run #22

Disney:	We should be able to work out how many photons coming in per second to this pulse, right?
Cocke:	Well, we should be, yeah.
Disney:	Can we get the actual number; can we read off digitally the number of photons in each channel subsequent to this?
Cocke:	Oh yeah.
Disney:	Now the fun begins, we've got to write out some sort of programme to reduce this tape and have the whole lot go in so
Cocke:	I don't think we need to reduce the damn tape.
Disney:	No.
Cocke:	We have – we'd have to reduce the tape only if we saw nothing or just a bare little hint of something.

This brief account of the discovery of Pulsar NP 0532 illustrates the discovery as the product of the astronomers' intersubjective efforts to make the pulsar into a professionally accountable object. It makes it visible that their night's work is busied with the assembly of accounts: accounts which identify "a nice dip on that side of the sky", which is "better this time" and eventually "a bloody pulse" possessed of exact coordinates and measurable properties. We can see that those accounts are assembled methodically, not only by organising the night's work in terms of an unfolding series of 'Runs', but *within* those 'Runs', through the methodical application of working knowledge of the equipment and the skies to conversationally formulate a series of increasingly precise verification conditions and methods of satisfying them. While it is possible to see the discovery of the pulsar in terms of a numerical collection of methodical observations and measurements, this overlooks the naturally accountable ways in which the pulsar was actually discovered. The numerical collection of observations is a methodical *outcome* of the naturally accountable work of discovery, as are the situationally independent measurements that provide for Pulsar NP0532's independent Galilean status – i.e., its status as a scientific object which is demonstrably out there in a real and mathematically describable universe for astronomers.

The example illustrates the reason why Husserl advised indifference as an essential procedure in studies of science and why we advocate the policy generally and would have you apply it to the study of work in any setting: scientific methods are the outcome of discovering work and thus *already know their objects*.[2] Furthermore, there is a 'praxeological gap' between scientific method and knowledge. The gap consists of this: the next time a group of astronomers wants to see Pulsar NP0532, they will find themselves engaging in the intersubjective work of verification. However, the methodical ways in which Cocke, Disney and their colleagues did this work was not reported in the scientific report of the discovery. Instead those methods were treated, as science universally treats them, as situational contingencies of no worth: they are not transcendental, they are not mathematically measurable, and they are not situationally independent of those who do the work. They are members' methods, not scientific methods. Nonetheless, they are essential and indispensable insofar as scientific methods are always accompanied by members' methods on actual occasions of their use and rely upon them for their accomplishment. The two are 'chiasmically chained' (Merleau-Ponty 1968), which is to say that they are genetically tied, not in a literal sense but in the sense that they are *intertwined* (Husserl 1970), like a DNA helix.

It is in this sense that Husserl spoke about the 'genetic origins' of knowledge and the 'vital practices' (as in living, embodied, incarnate) that knowledge production relies upon. Scientific methods everywhere, be it in social science research, astronomy, biology, mathematics, medicine, etc., are intertwined with and rely upon members' methods for their accomplishment, yet the latter are rarely attended to even when a setting's members make enquiries into the organisation of their work and its conduct. The function of professional indifference is to bring members'

---

[2] Thus the social science researcher charting demographic patterns at the four-way stop already knows what the phenomena looks like, for example: that orderliness at the intersection is a property of age, gender, race, etc., rather than of rolling, sneaking out, piggy-backing, flashing, chivvying, etc.

methods to the fore and sustain our attention on them. It requires that the fieldworker dispense with research methods and seek out the ways in which members methodically organise and accomplish their own activities. Another way of putting is that the fieldworker should seek to address the 'unique adequacy requirement of methods'. This is not an abstract idea either, like professional indifference it is a requirement of action, something that the fieldworker *does*.

5.3   The Unique Adequacy Requirement of Methods

The unique adequacy requirement of methods is an instruction, to be followed throughout fieldwork, to arrive at a position where one can recognise the methods that members' use to organise and accomplish the setting's work. The requirement means that in place of devising and/or applying research methods, a key part of ethnographic study is to develop vulgar competence in the work of the setting and thus to see the work as others in the setting see it, particularly those who do it (Garfinkel and Wieder 1992). By 'see', we do not mean how they understand work after the fact or how they reflect upon and rationalise it. We mean what it looks like to members in the actual doing of work and in the methodical details of how it is done. The requirement is one that would have the fieldworker understand how the work is done in the doing of it in the same ways that the parties to it understand it to be done in the doing. As Garfinkel (2002a) puts it,

> This is work in which a study's author is uniquely and adequately competent, *NOT* necessarily to produce the *things* described, but certainly to describe and instruct [others] . . . without incongruities, errors, absurdities . . . faking, passing, or hiding out.

If you can develop sufficient competence in the work you will, then, be in a position to identify the specific or 'uniquely adequate' methods that members employ to organise and accomplish the setting's work; that is, the *situationally specific* methods that members use to conduct their work and make it accountable to *one another in situ* (see Chap. 4, for concrete examples).

Developing vulgar competence in a setting's work, rather than busying oneself with research methods, is what fieldwork is all about. It is not as difficult as it might at first seem. Take the discovery of the pulsar, for example. It is unlikely that a great many astronomers are reading this book, yet the chances are that most people see what is going on in the night's work, what the astronomers are doing, and even how they are doing it. Granted that is partly to do with the work of presentation (i.e., the work we have done to present the example), but it is also in far more important respects down to the fact that we speak the same language as Cocke and Disney and that their night's work, while containing some technical terms, is nevertheless conducted in ordinary language which we are well acquainted with and which enables us to see the methodical ways in which the setting's work is being done by the parties to it. The work of a great many settings gets done through ordinary language. It is a resource that we too are familiar with as ordinary members of society, one that enables us to understand what is going on in a setting and, if we attend carefully to it, one that often reveals the methodical ways in which the work of a setting is organised and accomplished.

This is not to say that vulgar competence or members' methods can be reduced to language, only that much may be learnt by attending to it (Boden 1994). Language also presents its difficulties. A great many settings have specialised languages – astronomy, legal work, medical work, steel work, etc. – each have different vocabularies and learning them can take a good deal of practical effort. It is also important to take the use of equipment, tools, and artefacts into account, and again some of these (such as word processing) you may be familiar with and others (such as telescopes) you may not. Then there is the embodied character of work to take into account as well. The simple truth is that there is no recipe for developing vulgar competence in the work of a setting and no collection of research methods is going to help, as nothing prior to a study can tell you what the relevant vulgar competence will consist of or how to develop it. That will wholly depend on the setting. It is for this reason that our studies insist on the unique adequacy requirement of methods; i.e., that you go and learn from the experts in a setting's work – those who actually do it – what on earth the appropriate methods could be. Unfortunately there is no substitute for hard work and for going and getting your hands dirty as it were: if not literally doing the work (as some ethnographers have been known to do) then at least spending time on the 'shop floor' and attending carefully to the work that goes on there and the ways in which it is done. Another way of putting it is that the only research method that matters is that of immersing yourself in the 'phenomenal field' or the day-to-day doing of the setting's work.

5.4 Immersion in the Phenomenal Field

Going and looking at what people do does not actually equate to a research method, even if you have adopted a distinct analytic orientation of one kind or another. Just how you get into a setting so that you can look, just what you record, just what kinds of conversation you engage in and more all lack prescription. Fieldwork is essentially contingent and it is therefore more useful to think of *approaches* to fieldwork and of *tools and resources* that support it, rather than of research methods. Indeed, having dispensed with research methods, we think it important to offer advice, borne of our collective experience, on such matters as how to approach fieldwork and the kinds of tools and resources that may help you address the unique adequacy requirement of methods. At the same time it is also worth bearing in mind what the point of fieldwork is here, namely to inform the development or design of computing systems and applications. We state the obvious because it is important: we are not engaged in anthropology or sociology but in the research and development of computing technology. The nature of the enterprise we are engaged in shapes how we approach fieldwork settings and provides us with a *practical orientation* to the conduct of fieldwork.

In anthropology and sociology, fieldwork is closely allied with particular commitments, notably ones that seek to champion social groups that are perceived to be marginalised in some way or ways and that are otherwise under-represented, disenfranchised and dispossessed. Laudable as this may be, it has to be remembered and taken seriously that these are not primary concerns in a design context, whereas building computing systems is. It may be that issues of gender, sexuality, poverty, social exclusion, etc., are salient features of the work we study, but it may also be the case that they are not. The point is that we should not ally our studies with particular commitments in the social sciences, as what is relevant should be determined by the setting's work and not by *a priori* decisions taken by the fieldworker (Sharrock 1995). One should keep an open mind then. Indeed one should be professionally indifferent to the commitments of social science regardless of personal inclination, and remember what fieldwork is being undertaken for: not to inform anthropology or sociology or any other social science discipline, but to understand the sociality of a setting's work for the practical purposes of systems design.

The fieldworker should adopt professional indifference not only to the social sciences but also to the management and business sciences too. Like the social sciences, they offer a wide range of off the shelf accounts of the organisation of work. Designers have and continue to be tempted by ready-made accounts of human activity and its organisation, dipping into them and cherry-picking as befits their particular needs. We caution the fieldworker against doing the same however, for while it may be fashionable to treat the work of a setting in terms of the latest trend, and may even appear to lend a certain kudos or cachet to your work, it needs to be remembered that an *a priori* account cannot tell you how the work of a setting is organised by the parties to it in incarnate details of the methods members actually employ to accomplish it (Rouncefield and Tolmie 2011). You should dispense with such accounts then as well as the research methods that accompany them. In doing this it may appear that we are surrendering our powers of thought. The point the fieldworker should appreciate, however, is that one should not so much think about the fieldwork setting as go and look, and do whatever thinking you have to do *in context*. So in approaching the fieldwork setting suspend the use of research methods and *a priori* accounts and set out to see what the setting's members can naturally and accountably tell you about its work. Consult the setting's members, rather than theorists who have never been to the setting and have never seen the work, let alone done it (Garfinkel 1996).

5.5   Approaching Fieldwork in Design

When approaching fieldwork it is very important, as noted above, to bear in mind why we are doing it and what it is for. Traditional versions of ethnography – that is, ethnography as it is understood and practiced in the social sciences – treat fieldwork as a prolonged endeavour: immersion in the phenomenal field is something that takes years to do. This is not a viable option in a systems development context, where things advance if not quite by the day then very rapidly indeed. No designer in their right mind is going to sit around and wait for the results of a long-term ethnography to appear before they get on with building a system. It doesn't have to be this way, however. A little fieldwork can and often does go a long way in design, indeed in a design context it is important that you do not spend too much time in the field as the return on fieldwork can rapidly *diminish*. It is therefore important to *tie* fieldwork to design activities, rather than dedicate a great deal of time on something that may well be surplus to requirements. Rather than conduct extensive periods of fieldwork, it is often more effective and productive to conduct short periods of fieldwork that are well aligned with and respond to the needs of design. Accordingly, several distinct configurations of ethnography have emerged to support the intertwining of fieldwork with design (Hughes et al. 1994) and it is towards brief consideration of these that we now turn.

Quick and Dirty Studies
This approach towards fieldwork in design is intended to support scoping activities. The aim is to use fieldwork to *develop an overview* of the work of a setting. Such studies are 'quick' because they take a relatively short period of time to do, the relativity of the matter turning upon the scale of the setting to be studied and the scope of the design task. Even in very large organisations, such as multi-national companies, an overview of the different working units that make up an organisation and their constituent activities can be developed in a very short time. They are 'dirty' because they are not well coloured. They do not elaborate in detail the rich tapestry of work in a setting, but then they are not intended to. Rather, they are intended to inform strategic decision-making within the design team. It is an iterative approach that maps out the discrete activities that occur in the setting, the interdependencies between them, and the working division of labour. Quick and dirty studies provide designers with an informed sense of what the work of a setting looks like 'on the ground' and enable them to *identify areas of work that are relevant* to systems development.

Concurrent Studies
Concurrent studies 'follow on' from quick and dirty studies and run in parallel with design work. This approach aims to *elaborate the overview* of work developed through quick and dirty studies. It is a directed approach in which each stage of the fieldwork addresses particular interests and issues raised by the designers. It is also iterative in nature and builds on quick and dirty studies in mutually elaborative cycles of fieldwork and design work. It is a very flexible approach which may be undertaken as and when required and for as many iterations as required, and it is an approach that ensures that fieldwork is tied to the practical concerns of systems development, particularly requirements specification. Concurrent studies *drill down into particular activities* that are deemed relevant to design and furnish detailed studies of work with which to derive requirements for future systems. The use of concurrent studies is particularly well suited to the development of prototypes, whether they are proof of concept prototypes or, following on from that, production level versions of new computing systems.

Evaluative Studies

This approach is concerned with the evaluation of design ideas or 'concepts' and developed systems or prototypes too. In either case its role is essentially one of providing a *sanity check* on design by consulting the work a system or proposed system is intended to support in order to establish if the solution actually supports, resonates with, and/or enhances that work. In both cases, the results of ethnographic studies are employed to identify the pros and cons of the design – both the ways in which it works or might work and any mismatch that exists – and thus contribute to its evaluation. It is worth noting that evaluation, like requirements specification, is a complex business and fieldwork is not the only approach that one should adopt. What evaluative studies offer design is insight into a system's 'workability' – i.e., its ability to support the real world, real time character of a setting's work.

Our purpose in reviewing different configurations of ethnography for design is not only to provide some practical insight into how to approach fieldwork and use ethnography for the practical purposes of systems design, but also to make it clear that *ethnography plays different roles in the design life-cycle.* Any approach to ethnography in design needs to respect the need to configure the approach for design purposes. Going out into the wild and living with the 'natives' for years on end is all well and good for anthropologists, or at least rubbing shoulders with them for a period of time on the sociologist's part, but a more structured and directed or focused set of relationships is required of the fieldworker in a design context. It is important that the fieldworker is aware of the different configurations of ethnography in design and the different roles that are required of it, so that an approach which is appropriate to the design circumstances you find yourself confronted with may be adopted.

5.6 Tools and Resources

A common requirement cuts across different approaches to doing fieldwork for design and that is the need to *assemble an ethnographic record* that captures and conveys the distinctive character of a setting and its work. The ethnographic record is what the fieldworker takes away from a setting. It evidences the fieldworker's observations and provides resources for producing an account of the setting and its work. The ethnographic record is assembled through the use of various tools and resources. We have found fieldnotes, interviews, audio and/or video recording, and more recently, system logs to be of particular value. We describe these as 'tools and resources' rather than methods as there is no prescription for their use. How you use them will be contingent upon the setting and how they become useful to you will depend on the work being studied (Button and Sharrock 2009).

5.6.1 Fieldnotes

Making fieldnotes is an indispensable part of fieldwork. It may seem like a prehistoric practice in the age of the cheap, portable, high capacity camcorder but it is a place where you can document the things you see and hear and jot down your thoughts on the setting and its work. You will find it useful to keep notes from the outset, when a deluge of information that you are unable to absorb will undoubtedly hit you. Keeping a good set of fieldnotes will help you keep track of what you are being told and help you organise your thoughts. Your notebook need not be a loose connection of disjointed comments. It may appear that that is all it is at first, as you scribble down snippets of conversation, brief descriptions of work, questions you have about it, and so on, but there are ways in which you might use your notebook to structure your thoughts and develop a coherent account of the work of a setting.

Diagrams of the ecology of work. Work is situated, which means that it always takes place somewhere, in some environment or 'ecology' of work. A useful way of organising your thoughts is to make diagrams of the ecology of work. Draw plans of it, indicate the people who inhabit it, their roles or responsibilities, and the artefacts that they use in doing the work. This frames your inquiries into the work of a setting and enables you to represent the setting to others.

Formal organisation of work. By 'formal organisation' we mean such things as plans, procedures, processes, routines, etc., that the setting's members invoke to account for the organisation of their work. Wherever relevant, describe how the setting's work is 'formally organised' across a division of labour (e.g., describe the process of work and the interrelationship of different roles and responsibilities within it) and how it is 'formally organised' at an individual level (e.g., describe the contribution of individual roles and responsibilities to the process of work).

Flow of work. By 'flow of work' we mean to draw attention to the unfolding character of work: it starts somewhere, with someone doing something and proceeds to some end. Drill down then into the particular activities done by the incumbents of particular roles. Focus on how the work moves across them, how it flows from one activity to another and one person to another. Try and start at the beginning or at least assemble a set of notes that cover all the various stages involved. Watch the work being done and develop your description on that basis.

Discrete sequences of interactional work. Flesh out your description of the flow of work by focusing on the discrete sequences of interactional work that are involved in the accomplishment of particular activities. If the work starts with a telephone call, for example, describe what it is about, if it involves the use of a computer, describe what is done on it, if notes are taken, describe what they are about and where they are placed, and so on until you understand the particular sequences of interactional work that articulate the flow of work.

Cooperation and collaboration. Focus on the cooperation and collaboration that takes place between people in the accomplishment of discrete sequences of interactional work. This may well be quite different to the 'formal' or official organisational portrait of work and the division of labour. Describe who is actually talking to whom then, what they are talking about, what they do together, the transactions that take place between them, the hand-over of tasks, and what others do in response.

Your fieldnotes provide a record of what you observe, what you hear, and what you are told. Taking notes in the field not only allows you to reflect upon the work of a setting at some later stage, more importantly it makes you *attend to the work as it occurs*. Taking fieldnotes is an active process then, whereby you can come to know the work of a setting and develop vulgar competence in it. Fieldnotes may be used not only after the fact to convey the work of a setting to others but also during the course of your observations to elaborate and verify what you are seeing and hearing. Thus, when describing the flow of work, discrete sequences of interactional work, cooperation and collaboration, etc., you may (and probably should) use your notes in various ways to recap your understanding and have it confirmed or corrected by those who do the work. When things occur in the work that you do not understand, note it down and go over it with the study participants when it is timely to do so. Taking notes helps sharpen your focus on the work and in turn will help you develop a detailed understanding of it. As your understanding of the setting's work develops, just what you note down as going on comes to reflect more and more what any other member of the setting might say is going on. In other words you increasingly account for the work of a setting in the same terms as others in the setting account for its work and increasingly speak of its methodical conduct and organisation in the same kinds of ways as well. This is an important step on the road to the uniquely adequate description of the social machinery you are seeking.

5.6.2   Interviews

A great deal of credence is given to interviews in the human sciences, but we advise that the fieldworker treat them with caution. The basic problem is this: what people say they do and what they actually do are not the same. It's not that people are lying, at least not necessarily so, but that the accounts they offer in an interview are often removed from and gloss their work. The best way to conduct an interview is in the actual flow of work, as it unfolds and as the situation permits (Beyer and Holtzblatt 1999). Interviews divorced from the work of a setting may be indexical to work practice, telling you something of what people do and how they reason about what they do, but little of how they actually do it. This is not to say that interviews removed from the actual circumstances of work are of no use, only that we need to be careful about their use and what we might expect from them. The primary value of 'decontextualised' interviews – i.e., interviews that do not take place from within the flow of work – is that they may be used to provide an overview of the work of a setting as a series of members' glosses articulating topics for further inquiry. You might engage sponsors, gatekeepers, and those who show you around the setting in such interviews to get a feel for the work and identify areas that are relevant to your project. This kind of interview is, characteristically, unstructured, driven by little more than the scope of your research and an interest in what people do in the setting. The same also applies to interviews you might do within the flow of work, which is to say they should not be driven by a *pre-formulated* set of questions but by the unfolding circumstances of the work that one is witnessing. Interviews should be 'informal' then and contingent on the work of the setting, not planned in advance. This is not to say that that you cannot ask questions about the work having re-read your fieldnotes, for example, only that you should not seek to administer a pre-formulated schedule of questions removed from the actual doing of the work. Beyond developing an overview, ask any questions you have in the flow of work, so that you can see how they are addressed in practice.

Whether done to get an overview or to drill down into the work of a setting, interviews should be conducted in the manner of a conversation taking place between the fieldworker and the setting's members, rather than in terms of a research method administered by the fieldworker. When used to drill down into the work of a setting, they should also be highly directed, which is to say that they should be concerned with the *just what and just how* of the work. Interviewing people in the field is not about being impartial – unbiased, yes, but definitely not impartial. We do not want people to tell us whatever they want – what they think of the boss, or the state of the workplace or of the nation for that matter. While such conversations may be important in terms of developing a relationship with a setting's members, they are not what we are after. We want people to tell us about the work that they do. More than that, we want them to *tell us and show us what they do* so that in turn we can identify the methods they use to organise their work as a real world, real time social accomplishment. Interviews are a tool that can help us arrive at that point. They are not an end-point, not something that stands on its own and provides a distinctive set of results. They complement direct observation, the development of competence, and the careful recording of work in your fieldnotes. Indeed, beyond engaging in an interview to get an overview of a setting's work, you are unlikely to write the details of your interview down. Rather, what will appear in your notebook is a set of observations of work relating to the questions you asked. The questions might not even be there, only the observations, and that is what counts.

5.6.3 *Audio-Visual Resources*

Our primary interest in doing fieldwork is to uncover how people do their work, not abstractly but as an actual, embodied, equipmentally-affiliated, and interactionally achieved phenomenon. If we can see how members do their work, we can then identify the methods they use to organise it. Audio recorders and video cameras are valuable resources that enable us to capture work *as it happens* and to subsequently review the recordings to examine *how it happened*. Using an audio or video recorder will enable you to flesh out your fieldnotes in real world, real time details of work's accomplishment. They have become extremely cheap, reliable, and mobile and are an invaluable addition to the fieldworker's toolkit. There are some important issues involved in their use that you should bear in mind, however.

Permission to record. Even if you have secured permission from someone in authority, it is important that you obtain permission from the individuals whose work it is that you actually want to record. It is important that you make it clear to them why you want to record their work, what the recording will be used for, who will have access to it, and how it will be stored. It is also important to make it clear that the recording is for your use only and that any extracts that you use from it to illustrate the work to designers will be anonymised. You must make it clear also that they will be anonymised in any reports you produce.

Participant control. It is equally important that the person or persons you want to record are in control. That they can have you turn the recording device off at any time or have you delete certain events from the record. You need to respect this; if a participant wants something removed from the record even if it interests you, delete it and make it clear that you have done so. You should be prepared to offer your study participants a choice of recording as well. Some people do not like the idea of being videoed, or take time to get used to the idea, so ask if you can use audio instead. If they aren't happy with that either, then so be it.

The limitations of audio. As noted above, language is a great resource and a great deal of the work of a setting is conducted through talk. Audio recordings offer us a rich resource and enable us to drill down into the work of the setting and identify many of the methodical ways in which work is organised and accomplished as an interactional matter. Audio clearly has its limitations, however – you cannot see what people are doing alongside of the talk and there are circumstances where this may matter. Never assume in that case that audio is sufficient. Always be prepared to elaborate with notes the surrounding action that envelops the sequence of talk you are recording.

The limitations of video. It is all too easy to treat video recordings as definitive – that what occurs on tape is the work in its entirety. However, it is important to recognise that video has a limited field of view. That it only captures what you point it at and that what it captures is necessarily partial. Furthermore, it is a mistake to presume that what unfolds on the recording is simply self-evident. Try watching the videos someone else has captured some time and see. Video, then, is no replacement for competence in the work of a setting and the ability to see what is going on that goes with it. Video is merely an adjunct to membership which, when used in accompaniment with the understanding of someone who has grasped the methods in view, can elaborate the work and assist in making it visible to others. Video is not a solution in and of itself. The best it can do is provide the field-worker with insight and instruction into the embodied actions and uses of material equipment that articulate a setting's work by offering the researcher opportunity to re-inspect the work at their leisure.

The limitations of audio-visual resources make it very important that you keep your fieldnotes in good order. Audio and video recordings are only resources. They are not the be-all-and-end-all of fieldwork. By their nature, audio and video recordings only provide partial records, and while they are extremely useful it is imperative that you develop a thorough written record alongside them. Audio and video recordings should *complement* your fieldnotes and allow you to drill down into particular aspects of the setting's work to develop a uniquely adequate view of it. You may also find it useful to take photographs of the setting. These can be used to elaborate your diagrams of the ecology of work, for example, or to create a record of the artefacts and tools that are employed within it. Photographs are particularly useful when it comes to report writing. As the adage goes, a picture can speak a thousand words. Maybe not a thousand in practice, but if used judiciously they may serve to illuminate settings and salient features of their work to others.

5.6.4 Physical Resources

Members' activities and the interactional work involved in doing them are replete with physical or material resources. These include resources that members themselves draw upon to account for the work that they are doing and the ways in which they are doing it, such as plans, procedures, job descriptions, etc. Such resources – call them organisational accounting devices – are extremely useful. They sensitise us to the work that goes on in a setting. They direct our focus. They put us onto salient topics. However, and perhaps more importantly, physical or material resources also include the very 'objects of work' – i.e., the things a setting's members are working with, working on, fashioning, *making*. That a setting's members are thus occupied really ought to grab and sustain our attention, but it is not the product of their labour that is particularly interesting as much as it is the use of material resources to *make* the product. Selling space on a container is a product, for example, one that enables millions of people to ship goods all over the world. The container and what is put in it – the product of sales work here – is not what is of analytic interest though. Rather, it is how the selling is done. Were we to look we not might only find a host of officially unrecognised collaborations but also a host of officially unrecognised uses of paper, including 'cheat sheets' that sales operatives prepare each week to provide quick and easy access to costs that are relevant to their product line and paper notes made in the course of enquiries that describe the salient features of particular quotes issued to particular and potential customers (Crabtree 2001). All of this when the sales operative could have issued the quote online! But then, if they had, their 'performance' would have become a far more accountable matter than any competent member would wish.

This is not a story about how people work around systems for whatever reason, though they do and the reasons are legion, but about the practical indispensability of material resources to a setting's work. Even with a new more 'user friendly' system in place,[3] you can bet a pound to a penny that members still make cheat sheets, because that limited set of information is all they need to know, and still take down notes, because not every customer is a definite sale. Physical and material resources of all kinds are crucial to the practical accomplishment of work. Without them members could not do their work and it is hard to understand what the product of work could be or could amount to in a great many cases. We are not all reduced to delivering services as yet and even if we were, we would still rely on and use physical and material resources to deliver them. They are integral to work, whether it be selling containers or forging steel or simply standing in line to buy coffee. There is much to be had then in attending to the physical and material resources that are implicated in a setting's work and that members use to conduct it. The fieldworker should look at them, should take note. Of particular import is the need to consider the work that physical and material resources are put to. Simply put, ask yourself "what are they and how do members use them?" It is essential to look at their life-in-action and to describe the work they are accountably embedded in.

5.6.5 *Digital Resources*

By digital resources we mean resources generated within computational environments. These have been used for a long time within research labs, where such things as keystroke logging or gaze tracking have been used in an attempt to better understand human-computer interaction. They are of no interest or relevance to us as we are after interaction *in the wild*, as it naturally occurs in actual settings of work. In this respect, software currently exists that enables screen recordings that capture interaction on the desktop to be made, but getting permission to install this in a setting is often a lengthy, difficult, and frequently unrewarding process. The same applies to other kinds of computer-based recording devices, though recent developments have seen the use of 'digital records' in evaluative studies of mobile and location-based experiences, and efforts are afoot to extend this approach. Digital records couple the logs generated by computers with representations of their content. Thus, and for example, it becomes possible to record the audio and text messages sent via mobile phones along with GPS data. The times and places where messages were sent and received can then be viewed on a digital map and the content of the messages be replayed alongside other recordings made by the fieldworker. Digital resources provide another complementary resource for the fieldworker. They are still largely confined to research labs but, just as audio recording and video recording were once but distant possibilities, it is likely that

---

[3] http://www.cit.dk/COT/case5-eng.html

they will become much more available over the coming years and software packages are beginning to emerge that allow fieldworkers to exploit them alongside traditional resources.[4] While something of a distraction for those working outside advanced research labs at this point in time, digital resources will undoubtedly become part of the fieldworker's repertoire in due course, if for no other reason than that everyday life is increasingly permeated with and conducted through digital means. If we want to get *within* the work of the digital society, we will in time add digital resources to the fieldwork armoury.

5.7 Practical Guidelines

There is no prescription for doing fieldwork and finding members' methods, no cookbook, no recipe, no set of methods for you to use. In their place we can only offer practical advice and recommend tools and resources that we have found useful in our own studies.

Adopt an Approach Which Is Appropriate to the Design Task
Fieldwork in design is different to fieldwork in anthropology and other social sciences. It is done over much shorter time frames, is directed towards specific design tasks, and is constrained by them. It is important to choose an approach that resonates with the design task or else the value of fieldwork will quickly diminish. Accordingly, you may use quick and dirty studies to scope settings, concurrent studies to drill down into the work and inform particular aspects of design, and evaluative studies to assess the veracity of design concepts and actual systems development.

Dispense with Research Methods
Our lack of research methods is not an inadequacy, not something that we stand in need of that should be amended at a later date. There are already lots of research methods for the fieldworker to use but we reject them. We do so because research methods lose the interactional work of a setting and the methodical ways in which members organise it. We recommend, then, that the fieldworker exercise professional indifference to research methods and set them aside in favour of immersion in the phenomenal field. In short, go and look at the work being done and develop your competence in it.

Adopt a Practical Orientation to the Field Setting
Dispense with *a priori* accounts of human action too. No matter what the business, management or social sciences say about the organisation of human activities in textbooks, and no matter your personal allegiances and commitments, each and every setting's work is particular and unique. Your job is to uncover the work of the

---

[4] See, for example, the Digital Replay System (DRS), http://sourceforge.net/projects/thedrs/

setting, not as a version of the latest approach or theory, but as a particular ensemble of activities done by just these members, in just these places, with just these tools and resources to hand. *What do they do? How do they do it?* That is what we need know.

Address the Unique Adequacy Requirement of Methods
The point of immersion in the phenomenal field – in the what and how of a setting's work – is to develop 'vulgar competence' in the setting's work: i.e., to develop an understanding of the particular methodical ways in which the work is done that is commensurate with members' understanding of its conduct. The unique adequacy requirement of methods replaces the concern with research methods with the concern to develop and convey to others (e.g., designers) a members' competence in work's methodical accomplishment. That does not mean that you have to do the 'job', only that you can see how it is done in the accountable details of its actual real world, real time accomplishment.

Assemble an Ethnographic Record of the Setting's Work
You are going to have to provide an account of the setting's work to others at some point, whether in a design debrief or on some other occasion. Assembling an ethnographic record will support that. The record is primarily composed of fieldnotes, photographs, and audio-video recordings detailing observations of the setting, its ecology, the work that occurs there, the tools and resources used, the procedures and processes at work, the flow of work, division of labour, and the actual constellations of cooperation and collaboration that articulate it. It is a rich collection of materials or 'data' that enables you to inspect and provide an analysis of the work of the setting and it may be used to instruct others in the work and its organisation as well.

Before you get to the point of being able to furnish anyone with an analysis of a setting's work however, you are first going to have to go and develop your competence in it *and* also in the job of gathering materials to assemble the ethnographic record. Prior to any discussion of analysis, then, we are going to have to look in much more detail at the job of doing fieldwork and assembling the ethnographic record.

References

Beyer, H., & Holtzblatt, K. (1999). Contextual design. *ACM Interactions, 6*(1), 32–42.
Boden, D. (1994). *The business of talk: Organisations in action*. Cambridge: Polity Press.
Button, G., & Sharrock, W. (2009). How to conduct ethnomethodological studies of work. In *Studies of work and the workplace in HCI: Concepts and techniques* (pp. 51–82). New Jersey: Morgan & Claypool.
Cocke, W. J., Disney, M. J., & Taylor, D. J. (1969). Discovery of optical signals from pulsar NP0532. *Nature, 221*, 525–527.
Crabtree, A. (2001). Doing workplace studies: Praxiological accounts – lebenswelt pairs. In M. Rouncefield (Ed.), *TeamEthno online*, Issue 1. www.teamethno-online.org.uk/Issue1/Crabtree/Crabtree.html.

Garfinkel, H. (1996). Ethnomethodology's program. *Social Psychology Quarterly, 59*(1), 5–21.

Garfinkel, H. (2002a). Tutorial problems. In *Ethnomethodology's programme: Working out Durkheim's aphorism* (pp. 145–168). Lanham: Rowman & Littlefield.

Garfinkel, H. (2002b). Ethnomethodological indifference. In *Ethnomethodology's programme: Working out Durkheim's aphorism* (pp. 170–171). Lanham: Rowman & Littlefield.

Garfinkel, H., Lynch, M., & Livingston, E. (1981). The work of a discovering science construed with materials from the optically discovered pulsar. *Philosophy of the Social Sciences, 11*, 131–158.

Garfinkel, H., & Wieder, D. L. (1992). Two incommensurable, asymmetrically alternate technologies of social analysis. In G. Watson & S. M. Seiler (Eds.), *Text in context: Contributions to ethnomethodology* (pp. 175–206). New York: Sage.

Hughes, J., King, V., Rodden, T., & Andersen, H. (1994). Moving out of the control room. *Proceedings of the Conference on Computer Supported Cooperative Work* (pp. 429–438). Chapel Hill: ACM.

Husserl, E. (1970). *The crisis of European sciences and transcendental phenomenology*. Evanston: Northwestern University Press.

Husserl, E. (1999). *The idea of phenomenology* (L. Hardy, Trans.). Dordrecht: Kluwer.

Lynch, M. (1993). Ethnomethodological indifference. In *Scientific practice and ordinary action: Ethnomethodological and social studies of science* (pp. 141–147). Cambridge: Cambridge University Press.

Merleau-Ponty, M. (1968). *The visible and the invisible*. Evanston: Northwestern University Press.

Rouncefield, M., & Tolmie, P. (Eds.). (2011). *Ethnomethodology at work*. Farnham: Ashgate.

Sharrock, W. (1995). Different kinds of ethnography: Ethnomethodology and constructionism. COMIC Deliverable 2.4. (pp. 159–177). http:// www.comp.lancs.ac.uk/computing/research/ cseg/comic/deliverables/D2.4.ps

Chapter 6
Doing Fieldwork

The important thing about the ethnographer is not that he or she brings particularly arcane skills to the collection of data, but that they bring the willingness to pay attention to people's activities, to attend in detail to how people actually go about their affairs, however ordinary and otherwise unremarkable these affairs might be.

John Hughes & Wes Sharrock

Abstract Our aim in this chapter is to elaborate some of the key issues involved in actually doing fieldwork – i.e., in going and looking at what people do for yourself and developing competence in their work. We focus particularly on a range of practical matters involved in getting into a setting, getting on with a study, and gathering resources sufficient for you to be able to provide a rich account of its work. This includes securing access, gaining acceptance in the setting, the need for informed consent, figuring out where to start your studies, developing vulgar competence in the work and, quite crucially, assembling a corpus of data or an 'ethnographic record' with which to develop an analytic account of work that reveals its real world, real time organisation.

6.1 Getting Access

The first issue you are going to have to address when doing fieldwork is what setting are you going to study and how you are going to get into it? There are a great many settings in everyday life where one can simply walk into them unhindered and observe what goes on there. Ethnography sometimes gets taught in this way, with students being asked to go and observe action in public settings or settings that they themselves are members of, and this is a good way of proceeding for training purposes as it reduces the burden of *securing access*. However, the practical use of ethnography in design more often than not requires that research be conducted in settings that the fieldworker is not a member of and does not have open access to. Wherever research is conducted the chances are that *permission* will have to be obtained to conduct fieldwork, and this often falls to the fieldworker to secure. As a general rule of thumb the smaller the research setting the easier access is to obtain, though access is always framed by the sensitivity of a setting's work and what the research seeks to explore. Consequently, securing access can take a great deal of time, weeks and even months on occasion; more than the fieldwork itself may take. This also applies in situations where research has been invited, as it can take time to work out what it actually entails: where it is to be conducted, what it is to look at, who is to be involved, what outcomes it seeks to produce, and so on, are all important matters for the members of research settings to consider. It may require that the fieldworker go through official vetting procedures and, occasionally, that contracts be drawn up specifying the remit of the research, how it will be conducted, and what its findings will be used for, or even how they may be used.

Securing access often means that the fieldworker has to go through official channels to obtain permission from those within the setting that have the authority to grant it. This is not always as straightforward as it might seem, especially where large settings are concerned. The larger the setting, the more 'chiefs' there are likely to be. This means that securing access becomes a matter of finding the relevant authority, which can be a job of work in itself even when the research is invited by someone with 'clout' within a setting. In cases where the research is uninvited, it is also about finding someone in authority who will sponsor the research. What this really requires is a so called 'C class sponsor' or someone with the seniority and clout to champion your case, open doors, and bring other relevant authorities on board. Whether talking to sponsors or relevant authorities, securing access invariably consists of a round of meetings, conversations and exchanges. This is a critical part of the research, though rarely acknowledged as such: get it wrong and you don't have a fieldsite. It is important that you seize the opportunity then and make good use of it.

It is safe to say that those whose permission you seek will not give a hoot about ethnography *per se* – i.e., they will not care about the ethnographic tradition or the analytic orientation you employ. What will concern them is what the research is about, what it entails and what, if anything, is in it for them. It is therefore essential to focus upon and explain the purpose of the research, what it seeks to achieve, how it seeks to achieve it, its intended results, and its relevance to the parties involved. It may be that the research has no relevance to the setting or not immediate relevance anyway. In all cases it is important to be candid. If the outcome is your PhD thesis, a deeper understanding of organisational phenomena, or a concrete system that may enhance the work of the setting, be sure that those who might make the research possible understand this from the outset. Explain to them the practical issues that motivate the research and those that make the setting one that is relevant to understanding them. Describe what the fieldwork will entail and how you propose to do it. Describe the kinds of work you want to observe and understand, your fieldwork practices, what immersion in the work of the setting practically amounts to and what sorts of data you hope to capture to support your analysis.

Provide them with examples of relevant ethnographic work so that they might see for themselves the kinds of things you do and the kinds of outcomes the research might produce.

The purpose of your opening meetings, conversations, and exchanges with sponsors and relevant authorities is not only to gain access. It is also to *define expectations* as to how the research will play out in the field. This is not a one-sided endeavour. It is not simply about the fieldworker setting expectations by laying out the ways in which they would like to do the fieldwork. It is about the fieldworker and relevant parties arriving at *mutual* expectations of the research exercise. It may well be, then, that conditions are attached to the research: certain areas may be ruled out of bounds, for example, or it may be that documents cannot be taken from the fieldsite, or video recording might not be allowed, or reports of the setting's work might not be open to being published. It is also important to define what results might be expected from the fieldwork, particularly on occasions where the research is seen to be relevant to the setting. It may be, for example, that fieldwork reveals nothing new to your sponsor or relevant authorities: that what a study shows of the work of a setting is already known by them. However, it is also important to have them recognise that designers and other parties external to the setting will not know this. Here, then, the research may be news to others; useful news that develops our understanding of design settings and may be exploited to shape the development of new systems. It is also the case that the more divorced a person is from the actual doing of a setting's work, the higher up the organisational food chain they are as it were, the less they know about how the work is actually done. They may understand the processes and procedures at work in the setting but they are unlikely to be aware of the actual work practices that provide for their accomplishment. That fieldwork can reveal how work is actually done on the ground is one of the key things that appeals to sponsors and other senior members in a setting. There is every chance then that the research may be of some benefit, though it is important that it is understood that the degree to which ethnography might illuminate actual work practice is conditional upon the duration of the fieldwork, the size of the setting, and the scope of the task to hand.

6.2 Gaining Acceptance

It is important to recognise that permission is not the same as *acceptance*. Even if you are successful in getting access to a setting that does not mean that those who inhabit it will accept you or what you are doing just because a senior member said you could study them. The members of a setting may not have the power or authority to grant you access, but they certainly have the ability to frustrate fieldwork. It is important that you seek to gain acceptance of the research and your presence in the setting by those who are involved in the work that you are studying. This is not simply a matter of good manners: the conduct of fieldwork relies upon goodwill and cooperation. You will need to explain to the setting's members what you are doing, why and what it is for. Senior members of a setting are not the only people who may have expectations about ethnography. Those whose work you actually study may do so as well. In the workplace these often revolve around issues of productivity and automation.

As most members know, work is often studied to improve efficiency and, where the design of computers is concerned, to deskill and even replace people. In that case one of the chief concerns members often have in the workplace revolves around the purpose of your studying them and the consequences this might have for their jobs. You need to be sensitive to this and provide an honest account of your job and its function. Doing a presentation to the setting's members which lays out the research, its aims and conduct is a good idea if it can be arranged, and it often can. A key point to convey, whether in a group presentation or in one-to-one conversation, is that ethnography is not some kind of time and motion or ergonomic study. It is not concerned to improve efficiency – that is for other members *of the setting* to address – but instead seeks to identify the 'seen but unnoticed' work practices that the work relies upon, practices that are not specified in job descriptions, workflow descriptions, process descriptions, etc. Make it clear that it is your job to convey this to the designers of new computing systems and that this often serves to shape the design of systems that support and even enhance the skills and competences that work actually relies upon, rather than to deskill work and replace people. Make it clear too that it is the work that you are interested in rather than the member who performs it *per se* – that your job is not to report on the ways in which particular individuals do their work but to understand how the work of the setting is conducted and that you will protect the identity of those who are involved in the study by making them anonymous. Protecting the identity of your 'informants' is a fundamental principle in ethnography and it should always be exercised whatever the setting. An informant's identity should never be divulged no matter the reasons proffered by those who would have you do so. Make sure that the members whose work you will be studying understand this, and keep to your word within the boundaries of the law.

Gaining acceptance by a setting's members is not always such a serious business. As design moves out of the workplace it leaves concerns with productivity and efficiency and commercial sensitivities behind and seeks to open up new, more playful possibilities instead. Leisure, entertainment, and cultural pursuits are increasingly the focus of IT research and systems design and studying these kinds of activities is much less threatening to members. You will still have to gain acceptance by the setting's members, but it is likely to be far less challenging. This isn't to say that fieldwork beyond the workplace is unproblematic. Getting access to people's homes, observing the journeys they make, looking at how they use mobile devices and share digital media, for example, is at root a significant intrusion into their everyday lives and one that relies just as much on their goodwill and cooperation as fieldwork does in the workplace. People are less likely to be concerned about deskilling and redundancy, however, as they are about *privacy* in these kinds of settings. This is a grand topic in design literatures but from the point of view of fieldwork it is a mundane concern for members and something that plays out in practical ways. Thus, protecting members' privacy during fieldwork extends beyond anonymity to ensure that they actually exercise control over what is observed and recorded and that they define the boundaries of the research. It can be especially important in personal and private settings to develop a good relationship with members of the setting. For this reason involving friends and family can be a good strategy: not because they are likely to give you unfettered access, but because they are more likely to be candid about the limits of your enquiries. In turn, this opens up the landscape of the ordinary activities that are available to ethnographic study beyond the workplace. It is worth noting that incentives – whether paying a small fee or giving a setting's members some new equipment – is often a good way of compensating participants for any disruption the fieldwork may cause and ensures that they get something tangible out of the experience too.

6.3 Informed Consent

Whatever kind of setting fieldwork is conducted in, it is important that you discuss data collection with the setting's members. In workplaces and similar organisations, restrictions may be placed on what kinds of data you can collect. Even in more informal settings, members may have concerns about data collection. If you intend to use recording devices – audio or video or even systems logs – it is important that you say so from the outset and explain how these will be used. In our own practice we tend not to make data public – i.e., we do not put it on the internet or share it in other ways. We recommend as a matter of good practice that you maintain *informant confidentiality*. This is not just a matter of anonymity but of ensuring that the data members supply you with is also protected. This is not to say that you cannot show anybody the raw data you gather in the field. There are occasions when you will want to involve other members of the design team in discussions about your findings, and using data gathered in the field is a good way of fostering that discussion. There are also occasions when it may be useful to show extracts from the data to others beyond the design team: presenting findings to the wider organisation in which you work or at academic conferences, for example. However, it is important that those who you study understand the various uses of the data you intend to gather and that they consent to it in writing.

Good practice today requires that you obtain consent from the participants involved in your studies. The specific requirements for this change from country to country, organisation to organisation, and professional body to professional body. Nonetheless, there are three basic principles of consent that arguably apply across the board. Accordingly, consent must be:

- *Informed* – i.e., consent is given on the basis that the participant understands the purpose of the research and relevance of the information or data to be gathered from them to the aims and objectives of the research, and also how the data will be handled and stored.

- *Voluntary* – i.e., consent is given freely and not as a result of coercive pressure, real or perceived.
- *Competent* – i.e., consent is given by somebody able, in virtue of their age, maturity and mental stability, of making a free, considered choice.

These principles should be embodied in an informed consent form that participants sign. Again, there is enormous variety in document formats but we would suggest that, as a matter of good practice, your consent forms include the following basic elements:

- A description and explanation of the purpose of the research.
- A description of who is conducting the research, including the researcher and funding organisation or agency.
- A description of any foreseeable risks of the research or possible discomfort to the participant.
- A description of the research methods to be used.
- A description of the types of data to be gathered and the option to agree or refuse to data types being gathered.
- A description of the intended uses of the data.
- An option to reuse the data in other research, including options to agree, disagree or request that informed consent be asked for again.
- A description of the procedures for storage and disposal of the data, including an option to agree or disagree with these procedures.
- A statement describing to what extent records will be kept confidential, including a description of who may have access to research records and an option to agree or disagree with these procedures.
- A statement that participation is voluntary and that the participant may refuse to participate or discontinue participation at any time.
- A statement of whom to contact for answers to pertinent questions about the research.
- An option to agree or refuse to participate, including signature of participant, date, and signature of witness (which may include the researcher).
- Where the participant is a minor, it is also essential that parental consent or the consent of a legal guardian is sought in addition to the participant's.

Informed consent is not only about addressing legal and ethical requirements of data gathering but also, and importantly, of data storage and use. Research is increasingly regulated by legislation governing the gathering, storage and use of personal data.[1] Legislation such as this places binding responsibilities on the conduct of research and even if they don't apply in your own country the underlying

---

[1] See, for example, the 1998 Data Protection Act in the UK, the EU Data Protection Directive 95/46/EC, and in the US the Department of Health and Human Services, Office for Human Research Protections *Human Subjects Research* (45 CFR 46, Sub-part A, Sec. 116).

principle of 'do no harm' is one enshrined in the development of contemporary computing itself (Greenfield 2006).

6.4 Finding a Place to Start

Many of the issues that are involved in gaining acceptance in a setting will actually be played out and addressed in the course of doing the fieldwork. In other words, having secured access to do the research you will need to weave gaining acceptance into the conduct of fieldwork. Obviously the first thing you are going to have to do is make concrete arrangements to visit the setting. You will also need to identify the particular individuals who will be involved in the study and go through issues of confidentiality with them. Identifying people to study is intimately connected to the question of *where should you start your study?* While you may have a very good idea what the research is for, this will probably not mean much to the setting's members. They have their own preoccupations and business to get on with and are unlikely to be able to tell you where you should start. This should not be considered a problem, however. The aim of fieldwork is to uncover the work of the setting, which is to say that although the fieldworker may have a well conceived research plan the task is to find out how the issues it speaks of play out on the ground in the course of, and as an interactionally achieved and organised feature of, members' work. That the work and its organisation is not already known occasions the research in the first place and means that the fieldworker cannot, at the outset, have a clear enough understanding of what is or is not relevant. This is not to say that we cannot define the scope of the research in advance or determine that X or Y activities are what interest us. It is to say that within the scope of the research we have no idea of what is or is not relevant as we are not in a position to make such a determination at the outset. This means that you should not worry about where to start: you should start *anywhere* you can.

'Anywhere' means start with anyone who is willing to be involved in the research and is prepared to have someone alongside them observing, recording, and querying whatever it is that they are doing. This may sound like a rare achievement, but it is surprising just how amenable people are to 'being observed', at least with the appropriate caveats in place. In over 50 years of combined experience in doing fieldwork we have only encountered a handful of people who were unwilling to be observed. It is more often the case that people are happy to talk to you about their work and show you what they do. In practice we find that the opportunity to discuss the skills and competences involved in doing a setting's work with someone who is keen to hear about them in detail is an exceptional one for many people and one that more often than not seems hard to resist, even if it cuts into their time and requires some additional effort on their part. Furthermore, the willing participant is in a good position not only to illuminate their own work but, to some extent, that of the people they work with too and to introduce you to them as well. So start anywhere in a setting you can with anyone who is willing to help you and you will soon find that your network of contacts and informants rapidly expands At the same time, your understanding of the work of the setting will become increasingly elaborate and you will start to be able to determine what of the setting's work is or is not relevant to the research and what requires further study.

6.5 Fieldwork Demeanour and Effect

A key issue involved in gaining acceptance and the conduct of fieldwork over the course of the research is *fieldworker demeanour*. If people are to open up to you, and open doors too, it is important that you are attentive to your conduct in the fieldwork setting. Nothing particularly special is required beyond what common sense would dictate of a guest prying into the intimate affairs of their host. Be courteous then and conduct yourself in a reasonable and unthreatening manner. Show your respect for the setting's members and the work that they do. You may not approve of it or like them, but that is neither here nor there, and your personal opinions should remain so. So be polite in your dealings with a setting's members. Do not deliberately offend people, be curt, short, off-hand, or criticise them. As a guest it is important that you are on your 'best' behaviour, that you do not treat people in overly familiar ways, that you do not gossip, tell tales about others in the setting, or take sides. Rather, and demonstrably, you should show a professional interest in the setting's members' and their work. Obviously this will involve asking questions of them and what they do, but remember also to shut up and listen to what they have to say and to take note of the things that they show you. Constantly talking and being inattentive to the practicalities of their work is unlikely to get you very far. The requirements of good conduct do not mean that you cannot ask difficult or probing questions of a setting's members, only that you be sensitive to the fact that you are at all times a guest and that your actions may be of consequence to them. This sensitivity is not something that should be in the 'back of your mind' so much as it should be manifest in your conduct and thus something that the members of a setting see and recognise. In turn, your fieldwork demeanour will help mitigate the effects of what after all is a disruption to the fabric of their everyday lives.

We do not mean that fieldwork demeanour will manage the so-called "Hawthorne effect" (Mayo 1933), where the presence of an observer is said to change the ways in which people work. In our experience this is something of a straw man. In fact it's a complete and utter shibboleth (Parsons 1974), borne of rationalistic (especially cognitive) perspectives on work and its organisation. Regardless of your presence, members inhabit social settings and are accountable to one another for their conduct. It may be that they do things a little differently as they get used to having a fieldworker around, and it may not, but as they come to accept you the ways in which they ordinarily and accountably do their work will become apparent. How do you know? It is a condition of doing fieldwork that the fieldworker develop competence in the work under study. This is not simply an outcome of fieldwork. The actual *conduct of fieldwork* depends upon it. Thus, doing fieldwork relies on the fact that you can and do display to members that you understand what the setting's work is and how it is done *as the fieldwork progresses*. The 'display' consists of such things as raising recognisable topics for discussion, asking appropriate questions in the unfolding flow of talk about the work, and exploring issues that build on and elaborate your evolving understanding of it. If the fieldworker cannot display his or her increasing understanding of the work as the fieldwork progresses, then their studies will not get very far. Members will come to the conclusion that the fieldworker is wasting their time and cease to entertain them. The issue is not whether or not members change their work practices because a fieldworker is present then, but whether or not the fieldworker will be privy to the setting's work at all. That will require that he or she develop and display competence in the work to the setting's members.

So forget about the Hawthorne effect: settings of all kinds have their daily business to get on with, with or without the fieldworker. It is the fieldworker's task to fit into the setting and develop competence in its work. In ethnomethodological terms, the fieldworker is required to develop 'vulgar competence'. It is all too easy to get hung up on the first part of this phrase and think that a crude understanding of work or competence that lacks sophistication is being recommended. Nothing could be further from the truth. It means that the fieldworker needs to develop his or her own competence in the competences that are in use in the fieldwork setting: members' competences through the methodical elaboration of which the setting's work ordinarily and accountably gets done. Having found someone who is willing to have a fieldworker observe them, fieldwork therefore focuses on the mundane 'day-to-day' character of the setting's work.

It may seem at first sight that what people are doing is trivial: talking to one another, making calls, sending emails, working on documents, etc. Things one might see anywhere. However, this is the stuff – the work – of everyday life in the setting, which is to say that the work of a setting is done in unremarkable ways. The fieldworker's task is to understand the occasioned character of these ordinary, unremarkable accomplishments. To uncover what it is about talking to colleagues, making calls, sending emails, working on documents, etc., that is distinctive and makes it the work of this particular setting. Thus, the fieldworker should ask, *what work is being done* when colleagues talk to each other, make calls, send emails, work on documents, etc.? This is an omnipresent issue during fieldwork, something we always ask and something you should always ask no matter the setting. Don't discount what you see then, no matter how trivial you think it may be, as the work of the setting invariably consists of and turns upon what for members appear to be unremarkable details. You may be tempted to focus on the unusual, on exceptional events that members do remark upon. While these are interesting, insofar as they illuminate the ways in which members handle contingencies, it is the 'run of the mill' that demands our attention as contingencies must be brought into accord with the day-to-day work of the setting if its day-to-day business is to proceed, and proceed it must. It is therefore important that you attend to the routine character of work. In turn, the competences members ordinarily exercise and which the work hinges upon will become apparent, along with the methodical ways in which they ordinarily exercise them.

6.6 Developing Vulgar Competence

Developing vulgar competence in a setting's work doesn't just mean that you should attend to the 'routine' character of work, it means that you should attend to the ways in which a setting's members *make* their work routine. Whatever passes as the routine doesn't just happen. People aren't slaves who blindly follow rules and procedures, even though they may do things without a second thought. That they can do their work without a second thought testifies to their competence. The important thing to appreciate is that the routine is not a precursor to work but an *outcome* of it, and an outcome that is done on a daily basis, moment-by-moment in the work of a setting's members. When asking what work is being done by members in their actions and interactions, it is important to ask how this makes the setting's work routine – i.e., how they make the work into something which is recognisably 'the same business as usual' which 'anyone around here knows'. Take, for example, the following fieldwork extract detailing routine work between library users and help desk staff (Crabtree et al. 1997).

> User: It's . erm . its . like information . information about . er . these particular products and services – market intelligence and leisure intelligence etcetera etcetera.
> Staff: Is . er . is it a serial?
> User: No . it's not a journal.
> User: Basically it's a reference book . and it tells you about particular market products and services and what to look for.

The work of asking staff at the library help for help desk consists in library users and library staff working together to identify the type of item being searched for. This can take a great deal of work (see Chap. 3 for further elaboration) but, as can be seen in the extract above, the work is essentially concerned to transform what are typically 'vague' descriptions – i.e., accounts that don't make sense in terms of the library catalogue's organisation (e.g., "information about particular products and services, etc.") – into accounts that do make sense in terms of the library catalogue's organisation and thus into objects that may therefore be searched for (e.g., " a serial" "a journal" "a reference book"). The transformation of library users accounts into accounts that are identifiable in terms of the library catalogue routinely provides for the finding and retrieval of sought after items and constitutes the routine work of help giving at the library help desk. The routine is done through the cooperative work of formulating increasingly precise and organisationally recognisable search categories that provide for the identification of a specific item or items. Thus, by attending to the mundane work that users and staff ordinarily engage in, and by asking what work is being done in their actions and interactions together, we come to see how the parties to the work *make* help-giving into a routine activity (again, see Chap. 3 for further details if needed). The fieldworker's task is to do the same in the setting's he or she studies – i.e., it is first to attend to the mundane work of the setting and then to explicate how that work is accomplished by members in their actions and interactions. In doing so, the fieldworker will develop competence in the work and develop insights into the methodical ways in which the setting's work is accountably organised by the people who actually do it as a routine 'run of the mill' matter known in common by 'anyone around here'.

The identification of members' methods or work practices is of course an outcome of fieldwork: you have to do it to see them. While you don't have to look particularly hard to find them – they are in plain view and there for anybody to see – it is important to appreciate that it takes work on the fieldworker's part to get at them (Button and Sharrock 2009). Essentially, you have to be in a *position* to see work practice. Positioning yourself is more than a matter of demeanour work, it also involves working out where in the setting to go and look. Members see a setting and its work in different ways, and no one sees all of it in its entirety. Senior members may provide you with an overview of the setting as a whole, but their view is necessarily coloured by their own responsibilities and concerns. As we have already indicated, what this means at a practical level is that you will probably end up spending some time just finding where you should go and what you should look at, especially if you are doing fieldwork in a large setting. The critical thing is to start somewhere. After all, whatever the setting, you will have to develop an overview of it for yourself, which will entail talking to a range of members anyway. So don't think of this as a waste of time but rather as a way of sharpening the research focus. There is no time out from it, no possibility of evasion, and by going through it you will arrive at a better sense of what could be of relevance to the research, where you should go and what you should look at. It may be that what you find transpires not to be relevant and that you need to move to another position, but there are no shortcuts. Furthermore, it is important to appreciate that fieldwork is an *iterative and elaborative process*, which means that what you see in one place may build on and elaborate what you see in another, so much so that what at one time seemed irrelevant turns out to be extremely salient. So be prepared to shunt around a setting without prejudice as to what, within the scope of your research, is or is not important. By doing the fieldwork and developing competence in the work you will come to see its routine character and the methodical ways in which the routine is observably and reportably accomplished.

6.7 Unpacking Work

There are various resources in a setting that you might appeal to that will help you develop an overview of work and its routine character. In workplaces and similar organisations you will find that work is elaborated by a setting's members in terms of distinctive 'accounting devices' – i.e., rules, procedures, processes, workflows, scripts, etc. One of the first things the fieldworker might do when entering the fieldwork setting is elaborate the accounting devices that are said by members to govern, regulate or organise their work. These will not explain how the work of the setting is done but they will sensitise you to the work of the setting and illuminate areas that are salient to your research. Even in less formal or constrained settings, such as the home, accounting devices may be appealed to, particularly domestic routines or 'what we usually do'. The point of fieldwork is to move beyond accounting devices and uncover the methodical ways in which the phenomena that accounting devices index and point to are actually accomplished by the setting's members in their work. Whatever accounting devices are used in the setting by members to describe their work, the fieldworker needs to attend to and explicate *how* they are accountably accomplished and thereby made into routine achievements of the setting that 'anyone around here knows'.

It is important that the fieldworker keep an open mind regarding the accounting devices that members invoke and use to describe their work, which is to say that while useful in developing an overview of the setting's work he or she should *treat them with caution*. It is all too easy to treat them as a setting's members may treat them, as descriptive devices that adequately account for the ways in which the work is done. The fieldworker needs to be particularly mindful that accounting devices may be seen and treated by members as devices that prescribe a series of steps through which the work is accomplished, whether in terms of the component parts of a process or the particular tasks those component parts are made up of. Take the lending procedure at work in a major high street bank in the UK, for example, which was summed up by the mnemonic "CAMPARI & ICE" meaning Character, Ability, Means, Purpose, Amount, Repayment, Insurance & Interest, Commission, Extras (Hughes et al. 1996). The mnemonic lays out a set of decisions to be taken in order to avoid accruing bad debts. The use of the procedure in actually making lending decisions is rather different however, as the following fieldwork extract makes perspicuous:

> Business manager: I've been to see some doctors who have a business account with the bank. They asked for an additional £6000 for a computer. Chris was asked to sanction the purchase but it's outside her discretionary power. The business is entirely satisfactory – GPs with a turnover of £300k, profit £150k. It's not reasonable to tell them to wait for such a paltry sum.

In practice, the lending procedure was not followed, let alone in a stepwise fashion, and the mnemonic does not actually characterise the decision-making process. This is not to say that the mnemonic was not used. It was, but *retrospectively*, to assemble an organisationally defensible case to support the lending decision.

Accounting devices of all sorts are used by members to provide organisationally defensible accounts of the ways in which the work of a setting is organised and accomplished. However, they do not account for the ways in which the work they govern and regulate is actually done and organised in practice. *In practice*, in distinction to reflecting on practice, members orient to and treat accounting devices

under the practical auspices of the 'gambit of compliance' (Bittner 1965), which is
to say that they orient to accounting devices as devices that describe the *outcome* of
work: what it should amount to, and where it should arrive (at a defensible lending
decision, for example). This is not to say that members have no respect for the
accounting devices that regulate their work or that they fake things to make it look
like the requirements of the device (the rules, the regulations, the procedures,
the process, etc.) have been complied with. It is to say that there is more to
work's accomplishment than accounting devices provide for or describe.[2]

A key feature of work that is missed by accounting devices, as the above extract
makes visible, is that the actual accomplishment of work relies upon *working
knowledge* (Button 2000) – on knowing what the work should amount to and how
to bring about the intended result and on being able to demonstrate 'compliance'
with appropriate procedure. It is important that the fieldworker recognise the
limitations of accounting devices then and attend to the working knowledge
members rely on and use to get the work done. That knowledge is embodied in
the practical reasoning and the occasioned judgements that members make
in particular circumstances. It is not something that stands independently of their
work but something that is embedded in its conduct and exercised in methodical
ways. Take, for further example, the case of two members of an accounting office
who are responsible for making payments to the suppliers of goods but cannot find
all of the paperwork related to a particular order (Suchman 1983); a not infrequent
event in any organisation:

Rachel: There's another payment somewhere?
Kate: Yea, there's got to be another. Let me go get the whole folder and maybe if I go
        through the control numbers (goes to the paid invoice file).
Kate: (Returns with the folder). The only thing I really was goin' on was the P.O.
        number, cause I didn't have any invoice numbers, or really any dates, to go to
        find out when it would have been paid.
Rachel: (Looking through folder contents). What purchase order are we dealing with?
Kate: 36905.
Rachel: (Leafing through folder). That tells you this is the third invoice for this P.O.
Kate: But if that's true – this is one [invoice for item 3], that's two [invoice for item 8],
        and this is three [invoice for items 6 and 7] – then there might not be another bill.
Rachel: Is that in that problem pile up there anywhere?
Kate: No, I don't recall seeing it, but I'll double check on it.
Kate: (Searching through problem pile). Huuuh.
Rachel: (Searching through paid invoices) Hmm?
Kate: This is page two [invoice for item 8]. Okay. We got three of these items for $156,
        but all of the tax on them does not equal $117, so the page one items [items 1, 2, 4,
        and 5] go with this invoice [for item 8].
Rachel: But you don't have page one.
Kate: No. Page one isn't there.
Rachel: This one [for item 8] is already paid?
Kate: Yea, this one's paid.

---

[2] Just as there was, you may recall, more to Cocke and Disney's discovery of the optical pulsar than
simply pursuing 'proper' scientific method as we elaborated in the previous chapter.

Rachel: And that's the check for it?

Kate: Yea, that – these two packing slips [for items 1, 2, 4, 5, and 8] were attached to the receiver. So that was – according to them, we've paid the full amount [for items 1, 2, 4, 5, and 8],

Rachel: We've paid the full amount, but we don't know where page one is.

Kate: 'Cause this, times tax, just don't equal up.

Rachel: I want you to call that lady and tell her you want page one of this invoice. Now at least we have a number to go on. Tell her that you're gonna do her something [pay for items 6 and 7] – we're gonna do her something, we want her to do us something [provide the missing invoice page for items 1, 2, 4, and 5]. We need page one for this invoice. Alright? That explains why all those other things [1,2,4 and 5] are not there.

Kate: Okay.

This fieldwork extract shows the ways in which work goes beyond the prescriptions of accounting devices and relies on working knowledge for its accomplishment. Procedurally, the accounting office's work is ordered (1) by the procurement office issuing a purchase order, which consists of distributing one to the supplier, one to the receiving department, and one to accounting; (2) receiving marks off ordered items on the purchase order when they arrive and passes it on to accounting; (3) accounting place the receiver's copy of the purchase order alongside their own in a temporary file; (4) the supplier's invoice is matched with the purchase order and receiver's copy and the order is audited to ensure that everything is correct; (5) after auditing payment is approved, issued, and the purchase order, receiver's copy and supplier's invoice is placed in a paid invoice file. Clearly this procedure describes the work of the accounting office, but it does not describe how the work is done and, like accounting devices everywhere, *cannot do so* as it cannot provide for every single *contingency* that may effect the work: contingencies occasioned by multiple page invoices, for example.

Contingencies inhabit work, they are not occasional visitors but constant companions to it and they are resolved through the methodical use of working knowledge. In the case above contingency is occasioned by the absence of an invoice for four out of eight items. The members involved do not know that at the outset, only that the paperwork doesn't add up. They address the contingency by exercising their working knowledge. That is, by knowing where one might look to establish what the problem is: in the paid invoice file or problem pile, for example; by knowing what to look for to identify the problem: invoices, control numbers, purchase orders, packing slips, etc.; by knowing how to work out what's wrong: by calculating figures, costs, taxes, payments, etc.; and by knowing how to work out solutions to the problems that have been identified: requesting another invoice for particular items, and promising partial payment to sweeten the request. In turn, the methodical ways in which contingencies are handled work to make them into a routine job of work: such as completing the audit so that full payment may be issued.

This is the kind of work that you never find mentioned when accounting devices are used to describe it. The working knowledge upon which a setting's work relies elaborates the real world, real time skills and competences through which the work gets done and the requirements of the particular accounting devices that govern it are met. Recognition of the *gap* between organisationally defensible accounts of work as provided by setting specific accounting devices and the ways in which work is actually accomplished on the ground is essential to effective fieldwork. It not only reveals how a setting's work actually *gets done* but, with that, the unrecognised working knowledge, collaborations, teamwork, and arrangements of cooperation that the work's achievement relies upon. This means that the fieldworker should not only think about the 'division of labour' in terms described by accounting devices (e.g., roles, job descriptions, procedures, workflow, etc.) but also in terms of how it is *actually manifest* on the ground among the parties to the work (Randall et al. 2007). Attend then to who is talking to who, working together, and assisting one another. Look at how the work actually gets done by the setting's members in their observable and reportable actions and interactions. In turn, this will provide the fieldworker with a view of the incarnate organisation of the setting and its work, conducted and organised moment-by-moment through the locally and contingently accomplished work practices of its members. It will also enable the fieldworker to speak with confidence about the setting and to relate this to designers, as this view of everyday life within the setting reflects the competence he or she has developed in its work.

6.8 Assembling the Ethnographic Record

Relating your findings to design often involves more than telling others what you have seen. While this is important, others may well expect that you ground what you say in *evidence* that they too can see and reason about. An important part of fieldwork is to assemble an evidential base or 'ethnographic record' and to use this to elaborate the work of a setting. In more prosaic terms, you will need to 'gather data'. In doing so it is important to bear in mind that you are researching particular phenomena in relation to particular design issues or problems. This means that your data gathering activities are constrained. That you are not trying to capture everything or to understand the whole setting and its organisation, only to gather data that is sufficient to your enquiries. It may take a matter of hours or it may take weeks to gather sufficient data. It is not the scale of the setting that determines what counts as 'sufficient' however, but the scale of the design problem. There may well be a relationship between the two – e.g., designing a customer service system for a large multi-national company – but it is not a necessary one as no pre-determined amount of data can satisfy a design problem. The whole point of gathering data is to develop insight and on some occasions that may come in a flash with the minimum of effort and on others it may require a sustained and prolonged effort to understand the work of a setting and what it means for design.

The same applies to the kind of data you gather to develop such insights, which is to say that in doing fieldwork there are no specific kinds or types of data that one should gather. What you gather in any particular setting and in researching any particular phenomenon will depend upon what kinds of data are actually gatherable, not only in terms of what the setting's members allow a fieldworker to gather but also in terms of what the work being studied permits the fieldworker to gather. You are not going to gather conversational data, for example, if you are studying the social organisation of newspaper reports, as the phenomenon is a textual one (e.g., Jayyusi 1991). Granted, this is an unusual example but it serves to remind us that the kind of data we gather on any occasion of enquiry will depend on the *phenomenal properties and modality of the work* we observe. If people are talking, gather talk then. If they are writing, gather texts. If they are using tools, gather data that documents tool use. Indeed, gather whatever it is about the work that its situated accomplishment observably and reportably consists of. Gather whatever is in plain view. Focus on the situational details of the work, even the passing conversations, jokes, asides and interruptions that routinely accompany collaborative activities. The *minutiae* of work may at first glance appear trivial and irrelevant. However, such fleeting occurrences are the *glue* of social interaction everywhere. The work of a setting turns upon and surrounds them, and it is more often than not elaborated by them.

The basic point to appreciate about data gathering is that it is the least of the fieldworker's problems. 'Data' is everywhere insofar as the work of a setting is replete with it and consists of whatever data could be. It requires no special tools or research instruments to see or gather. You might use a video or audio recorder to document what you see and this will enable you to go back over the work and help develop competence in it, but there is nothing exceptional about that: people everywhere make video's of other's activities and it does not make them into fieldworkers let alone ethnographers. Video or audio recording will help you capture the conversations that take place in the setting and the situational uses of tools and technologies. You might also take photographs of the various objects and artefacts that populate the setting, make diagrams of its ecological arrangements, and collect documents from within the setting that help elaborate its work: e.g., process descriptions, workflow charts, job descriptions, training manuals, emails, memos, etc. – indeed anything that the setting's members use to make their work accountable. That said, it is important to recognise that the data you gather has no intrinsic value. Its value lies not in itself but in what you make of it and specifically in your use of it to *display* the incarnate organisation of a setting's work.

In this respect, and as elaborated in the previous chapter, the notebook is one of the most important tools in the fieldworker's data collection armoury. It may seem out of date, especially when we consider the increasingly sophisticated array of data collection tools available to us, but it is still one of the most valuable. Unlike the video or audio recorder, or even sophisticated computational recording devices, the notebook is a place in which you document *your observations and thoughts*. The notebook is a site where you document what is important about the work of a setting: contacts, events, snippets of conversation or descriptions of work, reflections on what has been witnessed, etc. The notebook is still an invaluable resource then. Every fieldworker should keep one. Treat it like a diary, date entries, and leave space around field observations for future comments and analyses. Fill it in every time you visit a setting and take time after the event to think through what

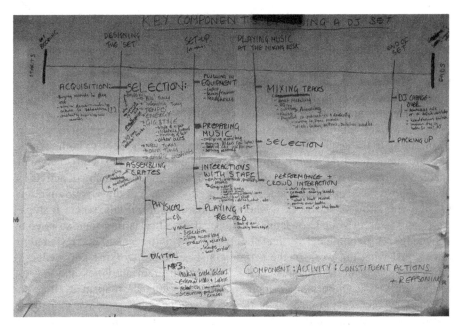

Fig. 6.1 Mapping the sequential order of nightclub DJ's work

you have seen and found before it escapes you. At first your notebook will appear to consist of little more than random notes and comments about things seen and heard in the field. However, as the fieldwork progresses your notes will become much more coherent. As you get to know the setting and its work, your notes will reflect this. More than this, as you get to know the setting, what you note in your notebook will increasingly reflect your developing competence in its work. As you move to analysis this will provide you with an invaluable resource for further reflection and explication. If you have done a good job of making notes you should find within them both the use of members' glosses and other accounting devices, and the work that underpins their use as adequate characterisations of work.

In our own experience we have found that a particularly fruitful way of getting to know the work of a setting consists in what might be called "horizontal and vertical slicing". Through the use of fieldnotes and other resources to hand this entails creating a record of the sequential order of work and the sequential accomplishment of the particular activities in and through which that sequential order is animated and produced. An example might help here. The photograph below elaborates the sequential order of a nightclub DJs' work (Fig. 6.1). The order of working consists of (1) getting a booking, (2) designing the 'set', (3) setting up, (4) playing music at the mixing desk, and (5) ending the set. Each component part of the sequential order of work is produced and accomplished through discrete sequences of activity. Designing the 'set', for example, is produced through selecting music. This involves choosing which tracks to play and relies on a diverse body of practical reasoning about the venue, the audience, the style of the gig, other DJ's who will be playing at the event, the type of music to play, what's 'big', interesting, new, full of energy, etc. It also involves assembling 'crates' – i.e., collections of vinyl and digital music, each of which are put together in different ways (e.g., the contents of vinyl crates are arranged to reflect the order of play, whereas digital content is arranged in discrete folders to reflect types and styles of music) (Ahmed et al. 2012).

Assembling the ethnographic record need not be a haphazard affair in which you bounce from pillar to post without really knowing what you're doing. The fieldworker might instead develop competence in the work of a setting by orienting to the sequential order of work from the off and seek to both unpack and document a setting's work through horizontal and vertical slicing. This will enable you to *map out in detail* the discrete sequences and sequencing of activities that compose the sequential order. Assembling the map will draw your attention to what you know of the work – where it starts, how it unfolds, where it stops, etc. – and gaps in your knowledge: in short, if the slice is thin then so is your knowledge. Horizontal and vertical slicing allows you to see, and make visible to others, just what the work of the setting consists of, the working knowledge it relies upon, and the interdependencies between different activities and parties to the work. It is important to appreciate that a sequence map in itself is an abstraction, one very much akin to those produced by process modelling approaches which have a particular kind of purchase in systems design, and that these are not sufficient for ethnographic purposes in and of themselves. What is also needed is the work that articulates the sequence map. We need to be able to see the activities that produce sequential order in the 'lived' details of their production – i.e., in details of the particular things that members *do* to accomplish the component activities of a sequence (Bowers et al. 1995). Sequence maps stand in need of elaboration then and the ethnographic record should be assembled to display the work involved in producing them.

6.9 Getting Out

Naturally there will come a point when your excursion into a setting comes to an end. It is important that you do not just disappear. There are several reasons for this. One is that courtesy demands that you express your thanks to those who have helped you, at the very least to those who have made the fieldwork possible. This is not only good manners, you may want to go back one day and do more fieldwork. Leaving properly will help. It is also a good idea to present your findings to the setting's members if they are interested in finding out what you have found out, and they usually are. 'Presentation' is a gloss on various activities, notably 'show and tell' talks to a setting's members and written reports. Show and tell talks, where you present an overview of the work you have done and of your understanding of the setting's work and its organisation, are of particular value as they enable the setting's members to comment on the accuracy of the fieldwork. Members, being the actual experts in a setting's work and its accomplishment, can tell you if you've got it right, or wrong, and what more you may need to consider. There is no better sign off on fieldwork (Hughes et al. 1994).

The fieldworker's primary task is to assemble a report that describes the incarnate organisation of a setting's work in empirical detail and this too may be of interest to members of the setting and certainly to the designers you are working with. The report must enable others to see the work of a setting and the methodical ways in which the work is organised by the parties to it. The ethnographic record is your primary resource for providing such an account or 'fieldwork report'. Fieldwork reports are substantial documents. They describe in fine detail – i.e., in details of sequential orders of work, activities done, words said, conversations had, actions accomplished, tools used, etc. – the work of a setting and its organisation. You will spend many hours assembling your report, writing rich or 'thick' descriptions of work. In doing so you will assemble 'vignettes' that elaborate particular actions and interactions by combining small pieces of these descriptions of work and transcriptions of talk with photographs and other images to elaborate the setting, its work and organisation. Every hour of audio or video, should you document work in these ways, will take up to eight to transcribe. The outcome will be an account that portrays the 'real world, real time' nature of work – i.e., an account that describes what the work looks like as it is done as a practical sociological enterprise by those who actually do it. Your report will contrast the ways in which work is said to be done by members with the ways in which the work is actually done, not ironically but in observable and reportable details of the seen but unnoticed work practices upon which the work relies and actually turns. Your report will contrast organisational accounting devices – processes, procedures, workflows, etc. – with sequence maps that elaborate the actual production of working order. It will contrast organisationally defined divisions of labour with actual constellations of collaboration and assistance. And it will describe the activities of work that take place in the setting in details of the specific machineries of interaction through which those activities are methodically made into routine accomplishments in the face of local contingencies. As we shall be discussing later however, you should not presume that the provision of a fieldwork report and various kinds of show and tell activities amount to 'job done'. Often, and most especially in the context of design, these are just starting points that will lead to a whole series of further elaborations as you work to make the ethnographic record accountable to the job of building computing systems.

6.10 Practical Guidelines

Our purpose in this chapter has been to move beyond the theory of fieldwork as it were to convey some key features of its practice; hopefully enough to get you started. Key issues here include:

Securing access to a setting
This is the first challenge that confronts the fieldworker. Addressing it entails finding people with the authority to permit the research and open doors in

a setting. It is a matter of finding the right people to ask and of even finding a sponsor to promote the work, of negotiation, of being open about the research, of defining its remit and what (if anything) the setting might expect to get out of it.

Gaining acceptance by the setting's members
Securing access is not the same as gaining acceptance by those whose work is the focus of the study. Gaining acceptance is a matter of persuasion and reassurance, of fitting into the setting, respecting participants and conducting oneself in a circumspect way, of protecting their identities, maintaining confidentiality at all times, and ensuring that the research is conducted with informed consent.

Start anywhere
There is no perfect place to start a study. The beginning – i.e., where the work itself starts – is good but you don't necessarily know where the beginning is at the outset, so start anywhere, with anyone who is happy enough to have a stranger follow them around and query whatever it is that they do. This will inevitably bring you into contact with others in the setting and expand the network of participants involved in the study.

Develop vulgar competence in the setting's work
Attend very carefully to the ways in which the setting's work gets done. Focus especially on the ways in which members assemble their routines and the working knowledge they employ to handle contingencies and thereby make the work into what is once again a routine achievement.

Assemble an ethnographic record of the work
Gather a corpus of data that documents the work. In particular, assemble a sequence map which describes the sequential order of work (where the work starts, what comes next, what follows, etc., until the work ends) and the discrete sequences of activities that animate and produce the sequential order. Make sure you gather data that elaborates the work involved in actually doing the particular activities implicated in discrete sequences of work.

Once you have assembled the ethnographic record you will need to produce an analytic account that displays the work of a setting and its incarnate organisation to designers and other stakeholders in the development process. It is towards the work of analysis that we turn next.

References

Ahmed, Y.A, Benford, S., & Crabtree, A. (2012). Digging in the crates: An ethnographic study of DJs' work. *Proceedings of the CHI Conference on Human Factors in Computing Systems* (May 5–10). Austin Texas: ACM.

Bittner, E. (1965). The concept of organisation. *Social Research, 32*(3), 239–255.

Bowers, J., Button, G., & Sharrock, W. (1995). Workflow from within and without. *Proceedings of the 4th European Conference on Computer Supported Cooperative Work* (pp. 51–66). Stockholm, Sweden: Kluwer Academic Publishers.

Button, G. (2000). The ethnographic tradition and design. *Design Studies, 21*(4), 319–332.

Button, G., & Sharrock, W. (2009). Making observations. In *Studies of work and the workplace in HCI: Concepts and techniques* (pp. 83–89). New York: Morgan & Claypool.

Crabtree, A., Twidale, M., O'Brien, J., & Nichols, D. (1997). Talking in the library: Implications for the design of digital libraries. *Proceedings of the International Conference on Digital Libraries* (pp. 221–228). Philadelphia: ACM.

Greenfield, A. (2006). *Everyware: The dawning age of ubiquitous computing*. Berkeley: Peachpit Press.

Hughes, J., O'Brien, J., Rouncefield, M., & Sharrock, W. (1994). An ethnography handbook, COMIC Deliverable 2.4 *CSCW Requirements Development* (pp. 115–158). http://www.comp. lancs.ac.uk/computing/research/cseg/comic/deliverables/D2.4.ps

Hughes, J., Kristoffersen, S., O'Brien, J., & Rouncefield, M. (1996). When Mavis met IRIS' – Ending the love affair with organisational memory. In: B. Dahlbom et al. (Eds.), *Proceedings of IRIS 19* (pp. 767–787). Gothenburg Studies of Informatics, Report 8, June 1996, Gothenburg.

Jayyusi, L. (1991). The equivocal text and the objective world: An ethnomethodological analysis of a news report. *The Australian Journal of Media and Culture, 5*(1). http://wwwmcc.murdoch. edu.au/ReadingRoom/5.1/Jayyusi.html

Mayo, E. (1933). *The human problems of an industrial civilization: Early sociology of management and organisations*. New York: Macmillan.

Parsons, H. M. (1974). What happened at Hawthorne? *Science, 183*, 922–932.

Randall, D., Harper, R., & Rouncefield, M. (2007). *Fieldwork for design: Theory and practice*. London: Springer.

Suchman, L. (1983). Office procedures as practical action: Models of work and system design. *ACM Transactions on Office Information Systems, 1*(4), 320–328.

Chapter 7
Analysing the Ethnographic Record

*Notice that in each case there is a thinnest description of what
the person is doing, e.g., penciling a line or dot on paper, and
that this thinnest description requires a thickening, often a
multiple thickening, of a perfectly specific kind before it amounts
to an account of what the person is trying to accomplish, e.g.,
design a new rigging for his yacht.*

Gilbert Ryle

Abstract In the previous chapter we elaborated a range of practical issues involved
in doing fieldwork and the assembly of an ethnographic record that documents and
elaborates the practical sociology at work within a setting. What we want to
consider here is how you might then go about producing analytic accounts of the
intersubjective or social organisation of a setting's work. In short, how do you
analyse the 'data' contained in the ethnographic record and make it visible to others
how the work of a setting is assembled as a naturally accountable matter by and for
the parties to it? Below we consider the nature and role of data in ethnographic
analysis, the purpose of analysis, some analytic practices you should avoid, and
others that are essential to elaborating the accountable organisation of a setting's
work and conveying it to designers.

7.1 Data

Collecting data is not difficult. It requires that you develop competence in 'doing
fieldwork' as discussed in the previous chapter but nothing is hidden: everything
you need to develop an analytic account is in plain view and pretty much anybody
can take fieldnotes and operate a recording device in order to capture and document
the lived work of a setting. So data is relatively easy to get but it is, as a thing in
itself, *not the point of fieldwork*. As Bannon et al. (1993) put it,

> [It is] misleading to think of ethnography in terms of 'data' or the 'materials' it generates.
> The 'materials' generated by ethnography consist mainly of field notes, audio and video

A. Crabtree et al., *Doing Design Ethnography*, Human-Computer Interaction Series,   111
DOI 10.1007/978-1-4471-2726-0_7, © Springer-Verlag London 2012

recordings, together with other displays of the setting's life. These materials are used to provide vivid exhibitions of the activities which generated them. But data in this sense is not the critical thing which ethnographic work generates. It is the ethnographer's *understanding* of the setting from within which the exhibits are extracted which is crucial.

Data is indexical to a setting's work and it is our understanding of that work, particularly our disciplinary understanding, that is important. In and of itself 'data' – i.e., the stuff we collect during fieldwork – is meaningless. It has no value until we make it into something that illuminates a setting's work and its organisation. At best, the stuff of the ethnographic record – our fieldnotes, photographs, audio and video recordings, diagrams, documents, etc. – is an *aide memoir*, a collection of 'vivid exhibits' that helps us recollect what we have seen, helps us work through the work in detail after the occasion of seeing it, and helps us elaborate our understanding of work to others as well.

The key issue, then, is not so much to gather data as it is to make sense of the data, to make something of it, without, at the same time, making too much of it – that is, without 'making stuff up', without making up an account of it that is of our own erudite fancy. Just as ethnography is bounded by the work of a setting, by what goes on there and what of its work you can capture, so your analysis is bounded by the limits of your data. Once you go beyond this to say things that are not clearly supported by the data – where, for example, you cannot easily point to sections in the data to support what you are saying – then you are in the business of 'making stuff up'. The problem with 'making stuff up', even under the auspices of supposedly very clever theories, is that it negates the whole point of ethnographic study in the first place and the painstaking work that has necessarily been involved in doing this.

7.2   Analysing a Setting's Work

We are not saying that you don't need data to produce an analytically defensible account of practical sociology and the particular ways in which a setting's members assemble its work and make it accountable. Obviously you need something to work with, something to make an analytic account out of, and a great deal of the ethnographic enterprise is directed towards getting that. What we *are* saying is that you should not fetishise data, as it is meaningless in and of itself. Nor should you exercise blind obedience to scientific tropes which suggest that one first gets data, then analyses it. If you have been doing fieldwork in anything like the way we suggest – immersing yourself in the work of a setting, developing vulgar competence in it, doing so by mapping the sequential order of work and the activities that produce and animate it – *then you have already been doing analysis*. Analysis is not something that comes after fieldwork then, but something that permeates it. It is something that we do from the off, something that occurs as soon as we walk into a setting and start looking at what is going on there. Analysis is inseparably intertwined with going and looking at what people do. It is something that we do as we seek out the accountable character of work not as an afterthought but as something that the work we are looking at is already possessed of as we do the looking. The data we gather – the 'vivid exhibits' we collect – document the accountable character of work and our evolving analysis of it.

It is not that our analytic understanding of practical sociology simply 'drops out' of our observations. We need to develop it. There comes a point, often fairly soon after fieldwork starts, when the data we have collected needs to be made sense of, needs to be thought about, and thought through. So in the *in vivo* course of doing fieldwork we often find ourselves sitting down somewhere quiet and pausing for thought to make sense of the things we have seen and the data we have gathered to record what we have seen. Analytic work starts in the field and can be rather more difficult than actually collecting the data in the first place. At least part of the difficulty is the knowledge that collecting ever more data, getting more of the same, is unlikely to be of much help. At some stage you have to resist the strong temptation to go and collect even more data and instead sit down and try and make sense of the data you have already got. Analysis generally proceeds through a number of stages or refinements as the account you are developing becomes clearer and more definite. Sometimes, especially when working within an interdisciplinary design team, a number of different analytic cuts will be made through the data as well, as different people ask a range of different questions of the researcher and the data. But it all starts off in a relatively straightforward way, by trying to carefully describe and to make sense of what you have observed. The key to analysing or 'opening up' the data is to grasp how the people doing the work you are studying make sense of it, and specifically how they make the work they are engaged in accountable to one another in the actual or *in vivo* course of doing it because that is where practical sociology resides and is to be found.

At first glance, the ethnographic record we assemble will appear idiosyncratic, messy and confusing to anyone else. Like those who we study, we need to make our analysis accountable to others so that they understand our work and can gear it into their own. We need to move beyond a fragmentary corpus of vivid exhibits to provide a coherent analytic account. Whilst collecting the corpus of exhibits is relatively simple, producing a coherent analytic account is hard work. It involves thinking about the data that you have already collected as it does not, on its own, provide you or anybody else with an informed understanding of the setting and its work. Your 'thinking' requires that you exercise sociological imagination, not of the kind advocated by C. Wright Mills (1959) and broadly practiced by social scientists today, but a more mundane and situationally relevant order of imagination practiced by the members of the setting whose work you are studying. An order of imagination that elaborates the taken for granted nature of work and the methodical ways in which it is done as an unremarkable social enterprise by *these* members, in *this* place, *here and now*. This kind of sociological imagination does not require flights of fancy, no matter how inspired they may be, but careful and detailed description of the particular ways in which work is done as an observable and reportable matter: as something that the members of a setting see and recognise, as something that you can see and recognise as well if you develop the appropriate competence, and as something that you can instruct others in too. Your task in producing a coherent analytic account is to develop an account that makes the social character of a setting's work *instructably observable* to others (Garfinkel 2002b), including systems developers and other stakeholders in the design process so that they, through your analysis, can also see what a setting's work looks like and what it consists of as an accountable matter for the parties to it.

7.3 Producing Analytic Accounts

The conventional way in which to go about producing a coherent analytic account is to leave it until later. To treat it as something that follows fieldwork, as something you 'make up' afterwards as you go about the business of constructing a representation of the social character of a setting's work. We are not being pejorative in saying that social scientists 'make things up'. As Clifford Geertz (1973), a renowned ethnographer and anthropologist put it,

> . . . anthropology exists in the book, the article, the lecture, the museum display, or the film . . . its source is not social reality but scholarly artifice.

On this view, the production of coherent analytic accounts depends on scholarly artifice, and scholarly practices of 'constructive analysis' in particular (Garfinkel 1996). Constructive analysis, or formal analysis as it is sometimes called, refers to the practice of constructing analytic accounts through the use of a theory, any theory, be it a ready made one or one you develop for yourself from the ground up (Glaser and Strauss 1967). In either case, theory is used to 'codify' practical action and practical reasoning in order to make it available to professional account – i.e., to represent practical sociology and make it into something that is professionally accountable. An example might serve to clarify what we mean here.

Eric Livingston elaborates constructive analytic practice in his unpublished primer for students, *The Ordinary Society*. By way of example he elaborates the late Robert Merton's theory of deviance and how it functions to enable society to adapt and evolve through 'structural strain'. Society, for Merton, is inhabited by members who share similar values or 'shared goals', which we strive individually to achieve. We normally pursue these through acceptable means, which is to say that we normally 'conform' to expected pathways of goal attainment and in doing so we 'structure' social life. However, this is not universally the case. Some members are cut off from the pathways by which shared goals are normally obtained; in various ways they are disadvantaged, dispossessed or disillusioned. When this happens, individuals may adopt different means towards achieving shared goals. Merton calls such people 'innovators', which is to say that social deviants are not limited to criminals. Far from it, innovators, like the nonconformist acts they engage in, come in all shapes and sizes. There are 'ritualists', for example, who have become disillusioned with shared goals but still go through the motions, 'retreatists' who have become disillusioned not only with shared goals but also with their means of attainment, and 'rebels' who reject current means and values and seek to implement alternate ones. Subsequent theories have identified other types of deviance and others again have disputed the theory and offered alternative views.

What does any of this mean for us? Well, were you to do an ethnographic study of deviance you could use Merton's theory to describe your participants and their activities: thus members will become 'ritualists', 'retreatists', 'rebels', etc. In doing this you will be assigning people and their actions to theoretical categories – you will codify the things they do – and you will do so on the basis of the perceived correspondence of member's activities to the theory that you are using. In turn, your account will make the social character of deviance instructably observable by attaching theoretical categories to real world referents – to drug users, environmental activists, terrorists, etc. – and the nature of 'strain' on the 'structure' of society will become apparent. Through codification you will be able as Livingston puts it to "grab onto little bits of the observable society" and use them as a resource to construct or elaborate a theory that accounts for observable and reportable patterns in social life. This work practice – this method that members of the social sciences use and that their analyses rely upon – is ubiquitous, not just amongst professional social scientists but amongst laymen as well. It is properly called *the documentary method of interpretation* (Garfinkel 1967c). Its use consists, as Garfinkel puts it,

> ... of treating an actual appearance as 'the document of', as 'pointing to', as 'standing on behalf of' a presupposed underlying pattern. Not only is the underlying pattern derived from its individual documentary evidences, but the individual documentary evidences, in their turn, are interpreted on the basis of 'what is known' about the underlying pattern. Each is used to elaborate the other.

The layman interprets documentary evidences on the basis of 'what anyone knows' about society and social life. The professional social scientist does so on the basis of theories of society and culture and their use to codify the ethnographic record. In either case, the method loses sight of what people do and the ways in which they do it as a real world, real time social enterprise:

> The documentary method of interpretation is a convenient gloss ... The gloss is convenient and somehow convincing. It is also very powerful in its coverage; too powerful. It gets everything in the world for practitioners/analysts. Its shortcomings are notorious: in any actual case it is undiscriminating and just in any actual case it is absurdly wrong .... in any case where [it is] administered as prescribed codes the result can be lucid, perfectly clear analytic ethnographic description, but the description will have missed the subject matter, its probity, and the point of the description, with no accompanying sign that [it is] misunderstood. (Garfinkel 2002a)

If you code up your findings you will only succeed in replacing the naturally accountable character of practical action and practical reasoning with a professional sociological account, a theoretical account essentially, that makes social organisation instructably observable by associating 'little bits' of the real world with itself (Baccus 1986).

The social sciences have shown little analytic interest in understanding how ordinary life is accomplished as a practical sociological matter, choosing instead and at best to treat it descriptively as a precursor to 'real' analysis. There are several alternatives to theorising practical sociology, however. Conversation analysis (Schegloff 2007) and interaction analysis (Jordan and Henderson 1995) make use of audio and video recordings respectively and are closely allied, historically at least, with ethnomethodology. Both have their limitations, however, and we need to be cautious about relying on them to develop coherent analytic accounts. Conversation analysis, in particular, has come under serious criticism from ethnomethodologists, including Harold Garfinkel:

> Let me give you a story. Gail Jefferson once tried transcribing Sacks lecturing using her notation [Jefferson 1978]. She told me she was confounded by not being able to hear him lecturing when she was transcribing his lectures. Given my interests, her admission was catastrophic. She was not able to listen for the technical sociological things he was talking as the matters that conversational structures could be but was able to listen for and hear her notationally indicated conversational structures. Instead of hearing him talk sociology in just the way he was talking-it-really-and-evidently and ordinarily, the details of Sacks talking conversational structures were exhibited in established conversational indicators. She detected properties that exhibited his lecture as the details of talking conversationally. So what? A conversational analysis of persons talking chemistry or talking law will have to respect the fact that they are talking chemistry or talking law. Say that between us, at the blackboard, we are talking chemistry. What does that look like in conversational structures? Right now the answer is nothing, zilch, it can't be done in C.A. (cited in Crabtree 2001)

Ethnomethodologist Michael Lynch has elaborated the issue in cogent detail. The nub of the matter is that we need to be mindful of what it is that people are *doing* when they talk if we want to develop coherent analytic accounts, and by 'coherent' we mean accounts that make instructably observable the work of a setting and its accountable organisation for the members who do it, not what that work and its organisation looks like after it has been transformed into a professional account of a "context free machinery" of talk at work (Lynch 1993).

We need to be careful when using video to conduct analysis as well (Heath et al. 2010). As discussed in Chap. 5, it also has its limitations: it only captures what you point it at and even then it provides a partial and incomplete record of what is happening. As Jordan and Henderson (1995) remind us,

> No matter how elaborate and sophisticated the recording set up is, the record will always be impoverished in some way or other and it is important for the analyst to be aware of that ... What for a human observer may be at the periphery of attention but still appreciable, may be altogether off screen in a video recording ... Another concern is the relationship between the record and the event ... What the analyst may see or hear via the tape may or may not be what the participants hear and see.

Video is a tremendous *aide memoire* to the analyst. It provides truly 'vivid exhibitions' of work being done but it needs to be treated with respect. It is not the be all and end all of fieldwork. You cannot just go into a setting, capture a load of video, and think that what is on the tape will be sufficient for your purposes. Even if we set the practical troubles of video aside, if you have not developed competence in the work your recordings will make very little sense. Try looking at video someone else has made of a setting's work and you will see that it does not speak for itself, and ask yourself who an earth are you going to ask 'what is going on' to find out? You can't turn to those in the know – the members who do the work – if you have left the setting behind. So do not reduce fieldwork to just pointing a camera at people, it is *no replacement for competence in the work* and the ability to see what is going on that goes with it. Video is merely a tool or resource that you can use alongside the understanding of the work you have developed through your immersion in it to elaborate its naturally accountable organisation. There is no substitute for competence. The purpose of the data you gather is to help you develop and convey that. Do not treat audio or video recordings as objects of analysis *per se* then, only as resources that will help you develop your analytic understanding of work and make its accountable organisation instructably observable to others.

7.4 Thick Description

So how *do* you produce a coherent analytic account? You need to orient to a setting's work from the perspective of those who do it and you need to provide a 'thick' description of what you see being done. This notion has frequently been invoked by ethnographers following Clifford Geertz's assertion that "ethnography is thick description" (Geertz 1973). The term was not coined by Geertz, however, but by the philosopher Gilbert Ryle (1968), who wasn't remotely interested in ethnography but with a "curious feature" of what is involved in "doing something":

> Two boys fairly swiftly contract the eyelids of their right eyes. In the first boy this is only an involuntary twitch; but the other is winking conspiratorially to an accomplice. At the lowest or the *thinnest level of description* the two contractions of the eyelids may be exactly alike ... Yet there remains the immense but unphotographable difference between a twitch and a wink. For to wink is to try to signal to someone in particular, without the cognisance of others, a definite message according to an already understood code ... A mere twitch, on the other hand ... has no intended recipient ... it carries no message ... The winker can tell what he was trying to do; the twitcher will deny that he was trying to do anything ... there is one element in the contrast that needs to be brought out ... Unlike a person who both coughs and sneezes, or both greets his aunt and pats her dog, he [the winker] had not both contracted his eyelids and also done a piece of synchronous signalling to his accomplice. True, he had contracted them not involuntarily but on purpose, but this feature of being on purpose is not an extra deed; he had contracted them at the moment when his accomplice was looking in his direction, but its being at this chosen moment is not an extra deed; he had contracted them in accordance with an understood code, but this accordance is not an extra deed. He had tried to do much more than contract his eyelids, but he had not tried to do more things. He had done one thing *the report of which embodies a lot of subordinate clauses* ... (our emphasis)

Thick description is an invitation to explicate a "curious feature" of doing something, namely its *accountable* character. Not professionally accountable, not accountable philosophically or anthropologically, but naturally accountable, accountable as a naturally occurring feature of some setting's work, and thus accountable to the members who do that work. The wink is a "definite message", something tell-able and report-able for the parties to it. It is, in short, account-able. If we want to provide an adequate description of it – i.e., if we want to see what for members is done in the doing, in contracting the eyelid, in winking not twitching, in doing so as an accountable matter – and if we want to provide an adequate description of other accountable actions too, then we need to report the "subordinate clauses" that accountability turns upon. Don't get hung up on the notion of subordinate clauses. It can, no doubt, be read in a variety of ways but it might also be treated as a simple turn of phrase that would have us attend carefully to *what is done in the doing* of action and have us 'thicken up' the thinnest level of description to make its accountable character visible and available to others.

Take the following fieldwork extract, taken from a study of work in a steel mill (Clarke et al. 2003), as thin a description as you are ever likely to see:

The slab of steel bashes against the mill and fails to go through.

RT mic: [inaudible].

Operator: Oh it's fucking barmy Nige! Fucking two and a half metres. It's longer than what it is the width and it wants you to get it from a metre wide. Fucking barmy.

This is the kind of thing that people actually do, the kind of thing you see them do and what you hear them do in the actual accomplishment of work, and this is what your fieldnotes may well look like when you describe what you see and what you hear. You may even have photographs to accompany your descriptions, and taken at face value they are about as much use as well. The thinnest level of account does not elaborate what is happening, let alone what is done in the doing. You cannot see what is being done here, and there are two reasons for that: one, you don't have the competence to see what is being done, and two (even if you had) the description is not sufficient to see what is being done. You might develop the former by developing the latter. That is, by 'thickening' up the description so that you can see the sense of what, accountably for those who are involved in the work, is being done and what is so "fucking barmy" about doing it.

How do we do that, how do we go about 'thickening' up our accounts so that they elaborate what is done in the doing as a locally accountable matter? In the first instance we need to be able to see what is going on in the extract above as part of an *ensemble of activities*. That whatever is being done is being done as something occurring within a sequential order of activities. It is not something that occurs alone but 'hangs together' with a range of other activities, even the inaudible 'RT mic' utterance tells us that much. Whatever is going on and being done, it is part of an ensemble of ordinary activities that occur in a steel mill. An ensemble that consists when we look at it of the 'furnace' where raw materials are transformed into steel slabs, the 'roughing mill' where the slabs are rolled into steel plates, the 'finishing mill' where the plates are rolled to their final tolerances, and the 'shear lines' where plates are cut down to the specific sizes ordered by customers. Then there are the purchasing, sales, job specification and 'build rule' activities that also preface the actual making of steel, not to mention backend activities, deliveries, invoicing, and the rest that go to make up the sequential order of work. The extract above documents a fragment of work in the roughing mill.

'Rolling' a slab that emerges from the furnace consists of reducing the slab in thickness, and increasing it in length, by 'passing' it backwards and forwards through a set of rollers until is reaches the required dimensions. It may sound simple but as Clarke et al. (ibid) describe it "like many unfamiliar work activities, the process of rolling a slab of steel appears complicated beyond belief." The work described in the extract takes place at the roughing mill 'stand', a physical structure that consists of a turning table and a 'mill', two large steel rollers driven by electric motors (which you can see on the right of the photos above). The distance between the rollers – the 'roll gap' – is adjusted by 'screws', which are set and recalculated by computer as a slab passes through the rollers. However, while aspects of the work are supported by a computer, the job is accomplished by an operator who is responsible for feeding slabs centrally and squarely into the rollers and for passing them through the rollers until the required dimensions are achieved. This is done from the 'pulpit' or control room where the stand operator works (the photos show the view the Roughing Mill operator in the pulpit has of the process).

The pulpit is furnished with various kinds of equipment. Some of these consist of hand and foot pedals used for controlling the slab on the rollers, through the mill, and eventually on to the finishing mill. Others are monitoring and measuring devices, including the furnace monitor; a mill light, which is used to control the supply of slabs to the roughing mill; temperature gauges, amp meter, load measure, screw levers, and spray thermometer; the main control pad and monitor, which tells the operator the quality of the slab, its present width and length, the required width and length, the 'turning point' or measured point at which the operator should turn the slab to roll for final length, and the 'finish point' or the point at which the operator should send the slab through to the finishing mill; a head level display providing reference points for the slab currently being rolled; and a 'RT link' or microphone that allows the operator to communicate with the furnace and finishing mill. Outside the pulpit, above the rollers, the roughing mill clock (top right of the photos above) shows the 'gauge' or thickness of a slab at each pass and measuring lights provide turn and roll instructions to the operator. The length and width of a slab can also be measured by the 'kelk' or 'accuplan', another optical gauge, while it is on the turning table. In addition, the operator can also see lights on the finishing mill, which enable him to see when the finishing mill has done with the current plate and is ready for the next.

The work of rolling steel proceeds as steel is transported from the furnace on roller tables, which are controlled in sections to give more delicate control over the movement of the slab. The roughing mill, which does the initial work on the slabs that emerge from the furnace, uses the turning table, which consists of a pair of tapered rollers that can rotate in opposite directions, to manipulate the slab into position and 'moving side guides' to square it up and centralise it in order to pass it through the rollers. The slab must be aligned each and every time it is passed through. A 'pre-broadside pass' is done first and the slab is sprayed to remove scale. The operator then 'goes for width', rolling the slab to produce the desired width up to the 'turning point'. Measurement of the slab is displayed by the kelk in the pulpit. The mill lights provide further information and instruction. One red light indicates that measuring is taking place. Two red lights that the slab has achieved width. Green lights instruct the operator to turn the slab and roll for length. Each pass of a slab through the rollers reduces it in thickness by the 'draft'.

The operator seeks to maximise the size of the draft in order to reduce rolling time and minimise heat loss, though the size varies as the slab is rolled and becomes more pliable. As the volume of a slab remains the same, its dimensions must increase as it is passed through the rollers. Most of the increase appears as extra length in the rolling direction and is quite easy to predict. There is also some 'spread' outwards and this is difficult to predict, though the thickness of the slab can at any stage be inferred from the screw position the last time the slab passed through the roll gap and the operator can take control of the screws if needs be. The roughing mill operator's task is to elongate a slab until it reaches the required measurements. A slab may be rolled in both orientations until this is achieved. It is then turned through $90°$ and rolled in the same orientation until the finish point is achieved. The final pass is a reverse pass. The rollers are then lifted and the plate sprayed as it is sent on its way to the finishing mill, where more rolling takes place until a slab reaches its final dimensions and is sent down to the shear lines for cutting into individual steel plates.

The work of rolling steel is fraught with problems. The operator is working with white hot slabs of steel that weigh a great many tons and a range of contingencies impact upon the work. The slabs themselves may suffer from 'thermal cracking', which will ruin the quality of the daughter plates that are cut from it. The work of the roughing mill critically depends upon 'slab quality' and the proneness of various metals to 'turn up' or form a U or W shape that makes a slab impossible to work with. This also occurs if a slab is too cold. The size and shape of a slab can also be problematic where and when something other than an 'ideal' rectangle is delivered from the furnace. Even the rollers can cause problems as they expand and wear with the tremendous forces that are exerted upon them and that they, in turn, exert upon the slabs. This can cause 'fishtailing', where the rollers go hollow in the middle and produce a fishtailed shape at either side of a slab (rollers are replaced once a week). Operators handle these run of the mill problems by over-riding the computer and going into manual mode, rolling slabs with thermal cracks so that the crack appears at the end of a rolled plate and may be discarded in the waste, rolling slabs faster and not cooling them to handle roll up, relying on the mill clock to handle slabs of unusual size and shape, and off-setting the rollers to handle fishtailing. Operators not only have to handle problems with steel slabs but also with the computer. It routinely fails to update, provide accurate reference points, slab sizes and processing instructions, for example, all of which occasion further over-rides and reliance on manual skill to get the job done. The job *is* done when the rolling of a slab reaches its 'finish at' measure, which is to say that it has been rolled to a specified thickness, length and width. This is provided by the computer and also ignored by operators as occasion demands so as to ensure that a rolled plate is sent through to the finishing mill in a workable state.

The operators' orientation to the finishing mill reflects the coordinated character of work. In short, a slab cannot be 'parked' for any time until the roughing and finishing mills are ready for it, otherwise it loses heat and becomes unworkable. The furnace has to coordinate its activities with the roughing mill, and the roughing mill with the finishing mill. The coordination of slabs from the furnace to the roughing mill is done through the use of the mill light, furnace monitor, and RT link. The mill light indicates whether or not the roughing mill is ready to receive the next slab from the furnace, and the RT link enables both parties to communicate directly as and when they have need (e.g., and as in this particular case, when the operator is experiencing problems with a slab and wants to ensure that the furnace does not prematurely push another slab out onto the rollers). Coordination with the finishing mill is done through the use of lights on the finishing mill – one red, one white, the latter when it is on indicating that the finishing mill has done with the current plate and is ready to receive the next one. The RT link is also used occasionally to quickly alert the finishing mill to problems, such as turn up, that may be impacting the rolling of slabs. Similarly, since the mills are next to each other, both the roughing mill and finishing mill make use of the RT link to warn each other when rolling especially long plates.

Clearly there is a great deal more to steel-making than meets the eye at first glance but, as Gilbert Ryle would have us ask, what is our stand operator doing? The thinnest level of description provided by the fieldwork extract does not tell us. What is required is a 'thickening' of the description, indeed a "multiple thickening ... before it amounts to an account of what the person is trying to accomplish" (Ryle 1968). Multiple thickening of the fieldwork extract consists in reporting the 'subordinate clauses' that furnish what the operator is doing with its locally accountable character. In short, accountable features of doing the work that make it visible to us what is done in the doing of something that is accountably "fucking barmy". The thickening up of the description relies, then, on seeing what the operator is doing as part of an ensemble of activities that are sequentially ordered and related. That the operator is doing a particular activity within the sequential order of work, namely 'passing' a slab of steel through the roughing mill. That he is doing the activity through a particular course of interactional work, proceeding from the roller tables to the turning table to the rollers themselves, to a pre-broadside pass and spraying the slab to remove scale, rolling it for width up to the turning point, doing so through the use of foot controls, computer and mill lights, handling contingencies through over-ride and the manual adjustment of slab, screws and rollers as needs be, and coordinating the work with the other activities that preface and follow it to ensure that the slab remains workable through the use of lights, monitors, and microphone. So what's so "fucking barmy" about that? The required dimensions of the slab are. The roughing mill operator is telling 'Nige' (who is the finishing mill operator) and any one else listening, (especially the furnace) that he is having problems rolling this particular slab because of its unusual dimensions and that this accounts for why he's switched on the mill light to prevent any more slabs coming from the furnace and why the finishing mill will have to wait, and observe some unusual 'rescue' attempts from him, before he can send the slab through. Clearly this is a difficult job to do and we can see that the operator is trying his best to handle it as we thicken up the fieldwork extract through the competence we have developed in the setting's work.

The production of coherent analytic accounts – i.e., accounts that make instructably observable the work of a setting and its accountable organisation for the members who do it – relies on the development of competence in a setting's work and thick description. As noted above, analysis is not something that happens after fieldwork, but runs through it. There is a particular feature of a setting's work, any setting's, that you will encounter in the *in vivo* course of analysis, both in the field and wherever it is that you sit down to think through the things that you have seen there, and that is the *retrospective-prospective* sense of action:

> Many expressions are such that their sense cannot be decided unless one knows or assumes something about the biography and the purposes of the speaker, the circumstances of the utterance, the previous course of the conversation, or the particular relationship of actual or potential interaction that exists between speakers. The sensible character of an expression requires that we wait for what a speaker or speakers say next for the present significance of

what has already been said to be clarified. Thus, many expressions have the property of
being progressively realised and realisable through the further course of the conversation.
This property of common understandings stands in contrast to the features they would
have if we disregarded their *temporally constituted character*. However, for the purposes
of conducting their everyday affairs persons refuse to permit each other to understand
"what they are talking about" in this way. The anticipation that persons will understand the
occasionality of expressions, the specific vagueness of references, the *retrospective-prospective* sense of a present occurrence, waiting for something later in order to see
what was meant before, are sanctioned properties of common discourse. They furnish a
background of seen but unnoticed features of common discourse whereby actual utterances
are recognised as events of common, reasonable, understandable, plain talk. (Garfinkel
1967b, edited and abridged)

The same applies to embodied actions and interactions as well and not just talk,
which is to say that the accountable character of the particular actions that someone
is doing depends on the *temporally constituted* character of those actions, and thus
on their retrospective-prospective relationship to other actions. We can see that
(now) in the field extract – the accountable character of what is being said and done
clearly depends upon the temporally constituted character of the particular actions
the operator is engaged in and their retrospective-prospective relationship to
other actions.

In the *in vivo* course of doing analysis you will run up against the retrospective-prospective character of action. This is not some kind of nuisance that you could
well do without, or that you could get rid of even if you tried, but indispensable to
the work of analysis. It gears you into the particular actions in and through the
temporal accomplishment of which work is assembled and conducted. In doing so it
makes visible how particular actions are paired with one another – adjacent pairings
of action (see Chap. 4, for further elaboration) that reveal the methodical ways in
which work is accountably organised by the parties to it: e.g., the methodical way
in which the movement of slabs from the furnace mill to roughing mill is done
through the use of the mill light, or the methodical way in which thermal cracks are
handled by over-riding the computer and manually turning the slab so that the crack
appears at the end of the rolled plate, or the methodical ways in which roughing mill
operators know that the finishing mill is ready to receive a rolled plate by looking
out for the white light on the finishing mill or calling them on the RT mic if they
can't see it, etc. Attending to the retrospective-prospective character of action opens
up its accountable character and enables you to explicate the work practices and
machineries of interaction that members use to conduct and orchestrate their work:
e.g., machineries of interaction for *working* steel as a real world, real time social
enterprise. Pay very careful attention to the retrospective-prospective character of
action when *doing* analysis, then. It is the key to understanding what is done in the
doing of work.

Analysis is, typically, an iterative business. It gets done in the field, it gets done
in the office and it gets done in other locations too. As you work through the
ethnographic record it occasionally requires that you revisit the fieldsite to gather
more data as well. This is especially true in a design context, where your studies
will be geared into different stages of the design process and seek to elaborate

different aspects of a setting's work and dig deeper into it as particular design problems emerge (see Chaps. 5 and 8, for further elaboration). Nonetheless, making sense of the data you have gathered and making something out of it is all about making out the methods that member's use to make their work accountable to one another. This does not require that you 'make stuff up' – you should not be engaging in scholarly artifice when doing analysis and offer cultural interpretations to design. You should, instead, be explicating through thick description how it is that members do their work and make it accountable to one another. In doing that you will make it visible – instructably observable even – how members make sense of and interpret their work and do so in recognisable detail. As Sacks (1992) put it with reference to the instructable observability of his own analytic findings,

> I take it that lots of the results I offer, people can go and see for themselves. And they needn't be afraid to. And they needn't figure the results are wrong because they can see them.

Sacks was working with conversational materials that just about any competent member of society, being a master in natural language, can recognise. You may be working with materials that require the development of more specialised competences. Nonetheless, you need not be afraid to make the accountable character of the work you are studying instructably observable. You needn't figure that your results are wrong because your descriptions are not dressed up in a garb of scholarly ideas that obfuscate the real world, real time character of work and its organisation. However, if you are to be successful in your efforts there is one further requirement that needs to be placed on your analytic work, and that is the requirement that thick descriptions furnish *praxeological* accounts.

7.5 Praxeological Accounts

If you are to make the work of a setting instructably observable, if you are to make it visible and available to others, and available to design reasoning too, then your thick descriptions of work need to provide 'praxeological accounts' – i.e., accounts that convey the local accountability or situated intelligibility of work-as-it-is-accomplished in terms that the setting's members know and recognise. While the accountable character of practical action and practical reasoning is central to the notion of thick description, thick description is not a solution to the problem of analysing the social character of a setting's work in and of itself. The idea of 'subordinate clauses' is one that we need to be particularly mindful of, as it opens the door to the 'etcetera problem' (Sacks 1963). Simply put, this means that any description of the social character of work may be indefinitely extended – there is always something more to say. As Ryle (1968) puts it subordinate clauses "pyramid indefinitely". We might ask, for example, what more there is to working in a steel mill: what goes on beyond the pulpit, what are worker-management relations like, what is it to be a member of a steel working community, etc.? The description of subordinate clauses might lead us, in other words, to consider the broader context of the work. This is what social scientists usually do: tell us that we need to appreciate the broader context in which ordinary activities take place and then proceed to elaborate it for us. In doing this, and as Richard Harper points out in Chap. 2, they lose sight of the work itself; what they tell us "is not the work – *not* the thing that you would actually observe if you were doing ethnography – but the stories people tell about the political arrangements at work." We need to be careful when doing thick description in that case.

We need to remain focused on Ryle's 'curious' feature of doing something, namely its accountable character. To reiterate, that does not mean philosophically accountable or anthropologically accountable, etc. It means, locally accountable, accountable to these people here and now, to the parties to whatever it is that is being done in a setting. This analytic move reclaims context. It makes context into a members' problem and something that will therefore be elaborated in the doing of work (Button and Sharrock 2009). The purpose of thick description as we understand it is to elaborate *work-in-context* (Garfinkel 1967a). Thick description is not an end in itself but a means to an end, one that enables us to provide 'praxeological' accounts of a setting's work. Praxeological accounts show us how particular activities are done in real time by the local cohort. They are, in ethnomethodology's curious terminology, first segments of 'lebenswelt pairs', which is to say that they *display* how particular activities are done as a social enterprise, that they are paired with those activities and provide corrigible 'sketch accounts' of them that are open to correction, revision, and reform (Garfinkel and Wieder 1992). Praxeological accounts enable you to see how work is done as an accountable matter and make it instructably observable or visible and available to others (Garfinkel 2002b). The purpose of thick description is to enable you to provide these corrigible sketches of work and in doing so to explicate, as Benson and Hughes (1991) put it, the methods that the setting's members could have used to produce "what happened in the way that it did."

We have sought to give you some advice on how you might go about doing this, not only in the current chapter but throughout this book. At every turn we have sought to elaborate a distinctive *analytic orientation* that you might adopt when doing fieldwork. An orientation to the achieved ordinariness of everyday activities in a setting; to the practical action and practical reasoning that is implicated in their achievement; to the interactional work in and through which practical action and practical reasoning gets done; and the methods, procedures, or work practices that members use to make their work accountable in the doing, which in turn elaborate the machineries of interaction members use to conduct and organise their work (Chap. 3). We have sought to provide practical analytic advice as to how you might locate members' methods by attending to the building blocks of interaction and how it is assembled through the adjacent pairing of the particular actions it is composed of (Chap. 4); by mapping the work of a setting through horizontal and vertical slicing to elaborate the sequential order of activities making up the work of a setting and to drill down into the actual sequences of interactional work that those activities are accomplished through (Chap. 6); and by conducting analysis through thick description of particular activities-being-done and attending carefully to the retrospective-prospective character of action to elaborate its locally accountable character. In turn, you can use thick descriptions to provide praxeological accounts that display the work of setting in methodical detail and make it instructably observable to others.

In saying this we are mindful of Erving Goffman's refusal to provide advice on the conduct of fieldwork:

> This was a principled refusal ... He felt very strongly that you could not elaborate any useful rules of procedure for doing field research and that if you attempted to do that, people would misinterpret what you had written, do it (whatever it was) wrong, and then blame you for the resulting mess. He refused to accept responsibility for such unfortunate possibilities. (Becker 2004)

We entertain similar reservations though our own experience is that for all the work involved and the sensibilities it requires fieldwork is relatively easy and, for those that manage to develop a reasonable level of competence in a setting's work, analysis is not unduly difficult either. Nonetheless, our advice does not constitute a set of rules of procedure or cookbook of recipes; it is not some kind of 'painting by numbers' approach to ethnographic analysis. You cannot simply follow our advice in a stepwise fashion. You will have to figure out, in the circumstances in which you are working, how to make use of it – how to apply it to the work you are studying. No amount of advice we could offer can tell you how to do that. You will have to *work-it-through* and *work-it-out* for yourself. What we can do, however, is give you some insight into how you might make use of praxeological accounts to convey your analysis to others.

7.6 Making Use of Praxeological Accounts

As we noted earlier in this chapter, it is sometimes necessary to provide different analytic cuts through the data, as different people ask a range of different questions of it. There is always an element of 'recipient design' when we present our analyses to other people. Emmanuel Schegloff explains what we mean in describing a meeting that occurred between himself, Harvey Sacks and a cousin of Sacks' -

> I had come to Los Angeles for a few days so we could have some time to work together. It was the afternoon of the first or second day and we were settling down to work when a cousin of Harvey's showed up, visiting from out of town – a young woman in her late teens ... She ended up staying for some 2 h – in any case, longer than expected, and, for the last half hour or so, was asking Harvey about 'his work', about which she knew nothing. When it was time for her to go, we took her to the place she was staying (not too far away), and in the car on the way back Harvey apologised to me for the intrusion on our limited time together. I replied that it was alright; given her un-informedness and naiveté, Harvey had had to explain things to her that he and I ordinarily took for granted and referred to in inexplicit ways, and I had found it interesting to hear his account of such shared-by-us matters to an uninformed person. To which Harvey replied, 'Oh, that's interesting' ... We spent the next hour or two talking about that – about how 'designing-the-talk-for-the-current recipient' would have to figure in subsequent work. (cited by Lerner 2007)

Recipient design is not restricted to this particular occasion or to talk more generally, it is a feature of embodied activities of all kinds (see Chap. 4, for example) and of the texts that we write as well. In short, our actions are designed with respect to the particular recipients that are also implicated in them. Conveying an analysis of work is no different. We have to design it and design it in particular, situationally relevant ways for its recipients.

Even when conveying the results of our work to those we have been studying, we need to design our analytic account for them in order to convey our findings in an effective way. We wouldn't just 'chuck' a praxeological account at them. Rather we would do a presentation, and possibly write a report as well if that was required, designed specifically for them. We wouldn't be talking about 'praxeology' then or 'achieved ordinariness' or 'machineries of interaction', etc. We would talk in mundane terms of how members reason about the setting and its activities and how it is that the people there do them. In doing so, the workings of our analytic craft will disappear from view to some large extent, it will become *invisible work*, as we orient ourselves to the outcomes of it or the 'results' instead. If we design our analytic report well we might even get something out of it too, particularly an appreciation of whether or not it is correct or whether it needs revising or reforming in some way or other. In short, a well-designed analytic report will enable the members of a setting to validate your study findings and we recommend that you do this as a matter of good practice whenever and wherever possible.

You are also going to have to convey the results of your studies to systems developers and this may require that you design your report, both a verbal and a detailed textual report, in a different way in order to address the practical concerns that developers have about building computing systems and working out how your studies impact upon that particular job of work. While the analytic task remains the same – to make the accountable character of work instructably observable – the practical demands of systems design may shape the ways in which you go about conveying your results. As an outcome of working with designers over the years we have found a small number of concepts to be of reoccurring use when designing our analytic reports, concepts that help us frame our analysis of a setting's work and present our results. They include 'distributed coordination', 'plans and procedures', and 'awareness of work' (Hughes et al. 1997).

Distributed Coordination

A commonplace feature of ordinary activities is that they are embedded within an ensemble of activities. Specific activities are performed as operations within a division of labour, as steps in a protracted series of operations, and contributions to larger processes that implicate multiple parties. Both the activities and the people who perform them are interconnected. They are not isolated activities and persons but part of an organisation of activities and persons. Distributed coordination draws our attention to the organised character of ordinary activities, to their place within larger processes of work, and the manner and means by which a setting's members concert their activities with others in the division of labour. Distributed coordination is a framing device that allows us to elaborate the division of labour, the activities that compose it, and how those activities combine to articulate larger processes of work. It provides a vehicle to present and articulate to designers the various ways in which the coordination of people and tasks is practically accomplished as a routine feature of the real world, real time work of a setting, including the equipment (tools, artefacts, material resources, etc.) that members use to gear their activities into one another and accomplish coordination.

Plans and Procedures

Plans and procedures are commonplace means by which distributed coordination is supported by a great many organisations. They are designed to coordinate work across the division of labour in order that the separate work activities it consist of combine and cohere to meet organisational goals such as productivity and efficiency. Plans and procedures often specify work's activities as things done in step-by-step stages, though there is more to following them than the steps specify. The successful accomplishment of plans and procedures is dependent on members' appreciation and practical understanding of what the plan specifies in particular circumstances, with the particular equipment, people, and contingencies to hand. This framing device allows us to elaborate how plans and procedures are practically accomplished in the course of work. It provides a vehicle to present and articulate to designers the local skills and local knowledge that a setting's members utilise to achieve the objectives laid out by plans and procedures and, in doing so, to elaborate the practical distinction between plans and procedures and what is actually involved in 'getting the job done'. Illuminating this distinction is key to avoiding design decisions that may reify plans and procedures within a computing system.

Awareness of Work

It is commonplace, too, that in the course of doing their work, members make what they are doing 'visible' or 'intelligible' to others involved in the work. The various ways in which awareness is developed, in which work is made public and available to others, are essential ingredients in 'doing the work' as part of a socially distributed division of labour. The ways in which awareness of work is conveyed are not necessarily designed or planned as a formal part of work's organisation. More often than not it turns upon informal mechanisms of interaction and interactional subtleties that make the work visible at-a-glance so that it can be 'taken note of', 'reviewed', 'queried', and so on, by others involved. These mechanisms put work *on display* so that others may be aware of it and constitute a major aspect of the means through which the coordination of work tasks is achieved as a practical matter. Understanding these 'displays' relies upon knowledge of the work itself and how the awareness mechanisms are embedded within the work as an instrument of the work. Accordingly, this framing device allows us to elaborate that knowledge and the awareness mechanisms that collaboration trades upon. It provides a vehicle for presenting and articulating to designers the local 'ecology of awareness' – i.e., the particular ways in which work sites and working materials are laid out and arranged so that members can make reciprocal sense of each other's activities, can see what other people are doing, and how this fits into the pattern of work which they are concertedly producing. In short, the awareness of work and the ways in which it is done emphasises to designers the fundamentally social and accountable nature of work.

We think, by way of concrete example, that each of these concepts can be used to characterise the work of the roughing mill that we have spent some time elaborating here; work that you will have to do in the settings you study too, there is no time out from that, no shortcuts. If you can't see how they apply to the roughing mill case then see Clarke et al. (2003). Either way, the point and purpose of these concepts is *simplification*. As Hughes et al. (1997) put it,

> ... there is a difference in the needs and vocabulary of designers and fieldworkers ... the designer is characteristically in search of ways of *simplifying* the complexity of the design situation, often by means of abstractions which will delineate critical features of that situation and of the design problem.

The above concepts and the 'framework' they collectively provide is not an analytic one. They are not analytic concepts. You should not use them to try to *do* ethnography. They are only intended as communication devices that allow you to parse the complexity of your studies of work in ways that are useful to designers and in ways that allow you to point out important features of a setting's work to them. As Hughes et al. (ibid.) put it again,

> The framework is fundamentally motivated by the demands of design. The intent is to provide some bridge between fieldwork and emerging design decisions. It worth stressing here that the framework is not an analytical device that is then applied to a setting. Rather the aim is to use the framework to highlight particular issues within a corpus of fieldwork material.

In elaborating these framing devices we are not saying that you *have* to use them to present and convey the results of your studies of work. Even in our own experience they have limited utility being, as they are, derived from ethnographic studies of workplaces. If you are studying what goes on in workplaces they may well be useful to you. They may turn out to be useful in other settings too (you'll have to see what works for you), but design is reaching ever outwards and evermore into diverse areas of everyday life. The usefulness of these devices will depend on the kind of work you are studying, the design task, and the design team. It is also the case that over the years we have built up a working relationship with designers that stands upon *shared understandings* of what ethnography is, what it does, the kinds of results it produces (if not the work involved in producing them), and how these may be leveraged into design. Consequently, we find that presenting studies of work in mundane terms of how the setting's members reason about the setting and its activities and how it is that the people there do them often works as well for designers as it does for those we have been studying, at least as a precursor to building or refining computing systems: a precursor that enables designers to "grasp 'what is really going on' in the course of a piece of work, 'what is really the problem' about doing it, and what instruments might be devised to help resolve these problems" (Hughes et al. 1992).

7.7   Practical Guidelines

Analysis, as you might expect, is a complicated business. You are doing it for yourself, you may well be doing it for the members of a setting, and you will be doing it for system designers. Nonetheless, there are a number of key issues that you should attend to if your analysis is to be successful and provide designers with the insights they need to develop systems that meet the real world, real time demands of work and its organisation.

Analysis Starts with Fieldwork

Analysis is not a separate activity from fieldwork. Fieldwork is not about going out and looking at what people do, gathering some 'data', and then analysing it when you get back to the ranch. Analysis is part and parcel of fieldwork. It permeates fieldwork. When you go into the field – into a setting – you should be doing analysis. You should be applying the precepts and sensitising concepts that underpin the ethnomethodological approach to ethnography. You should be seeking out from the start what the work of a setting consists of, how it is assembled, and how it is organised as an accountable matter by the parties to it for the practical purposes of their work.

Do Not Use Constructive Analytic Practices to Do Analysis

Conventional approaches to ethnographic analysis would have you make your data into something that is accountable in terms of professional social science. In particular they would have you construct an analytic account through the codification of your data to produce a scholarly interpretation of a setting's work. In doing so you will loose the work's local accountability: loose what it looks like for the parties to it, loose its recognisable intelligibility to the parties to it, and lose how it is done by them as a practical sociological enterprise. In place of the work's real world, real time social organisation you will put what is, essentially, a theoretical account of work and its organisation. That's a choice you make. We caution against it if you would understand work as a naturally accountable accomplishment and develop systems that are accountable to how the work is actually done.

Develop Thick Descriptions of Work

In place of constructive analytic practice – in place of codification and the production of theoretical accounts – you might develop thick descriptions of work in and over the course of doing fieldwork and in working through what it is that you have seen. To do that you will need to develop your competence in the work of a setting so that you can arrive at position where you can see *what is done in the doing* of the particular actions and interactions that make up specific activities of work. It means that you will need to develop your understanding of the ensemble of activities involved in work's accomplishment and the particular actions that elaborate those activities and make them accountable to the local cohort. You might attend to a ubiquitous feature of action in the actual course of analysis to grab onto and explicate the accountable character of the activities that make up a setting's work, namely its retrospective-prospective character. This will reveal how members piece their actions together and in doing so organise their work as a social enterprise.

Use Thick Descriptions to Provide Praxeological Accounts

Thick descriptions of work are indefinitely extendable. There is always something else to say. To ensure that you do not go off track and get lost in extraneous considerations it is necessary to provide praxeological accounts of work. These may be produced from the thick descriptions you assemble in the course of developing your competence and your analysis of the work of a setting. Praxeological accounts make the accountable character of work 'instructably observable' or visible and available to others by *displaying* what is done in the doing of work and how it is done as a social enterprise by the local cohort. Praxeological accounts are the primary output of ethnographic work. They sensitise us to the real world, real time character of work and its organisation as a practical sociological achievement.

Design Your Results for Your Recipients

It will do you no good to talk about thick descriptions and praxeological accounts, or the work that goes into producing them, to the people you would have take notice of your findings or results. You can't dispense with them but the recipients of your analyses are only interested in what you have found, in what you have to say about the work of a setting. The art and craft of doing fieldwork and producing analytic accounts necessarily becomes invisible work. In its place is put the practical requirement that you pull out and convey the key features of the work that you have been studying. This, in turn, requires that you design your analysis, or at least what you would have a particular set of people understand of it, for the particular recipients who want to make use of it. You might trade in mundane reasoning to do so or you might exploit the concepts of distributed coordination, plans and procedures, and awareness of work to convey your results.

In either case, in a design context at least, the ethnographer's job is not done. If we've got it right, if we've managed to convey the accountable character of work to designers, then we need to help them *leverage it in* to the actual design of computing systems. We turn towards understanding some of the ways in which we might go about doing that in the next chapter.

References

Baccus, M. D. (1986). Sociological indication and the visibility criterion of real world social theorising. In H. Garfinkel (Ed.), *Ethnomethodological studies of work* (pp. 1–19). London: Routledge.

Bannon, L., Bowers, J., Carstensen, P., Hughes, J., Kuutii, K., Pycock, J., Rodden, T., Schmidt, K., Shapiro, D., Sharrock, W., & Viller, S. (1993). COMIC deliverable 2.1. *Informing*

CSCW System Requirements, http://www.comp.lancs.ac.uk/computing/research/cseg/comic/deliverables/D2.1.ps

Becker, H. (2004). On the value of ethnography: Sociology and public policy. *The Annals of the American Academy of Political and Social Science, 595*(1), 264–276.

Benson, D., & Hughes, J. A. (1991). Method: Evidence and inference. In G. Button (Ed.), *Ethnomethodology and the human sciences* (pp. 109–136). Cambridge: Cambridge University Press.

Button, G., & Sharrock, W. (2009). How to conduct ethnomethodological studies of work. In *Studies of work and the workplace in HCI: Concepts and techniques* (pp. 51–82). New Jersey: Morgan & Claypool.

Clarke, K., Martin, D., Rouncefield, M., Sommerville, I., Hughes, J., Gurr, C., Hartswood, M., Proctor, R., Slack, R., & Voss, A. (2003). Dependable red hot action. *Proceedings of the 8th European Conference on Computer Supported Cooperative Work* (pp. 61–80). San Diego: Kluwer.

Crabtree, A. (2001). Harold Garfinkel in conversation with Benetta Jules-Rosette. *Wild sociology: Ethnography and design*. University of Lancaster.

Garfinkel, H. (1967a). What is ethnomethodology? In *Studies in ethnomethodology* (pp. 1–34). Englewood Cliffs: Prentice-Hall.

Garfinkel, H. (1967b). Studies of the routine grounds everyday activities. In *Studies in ethnomethodology* (pp. 35–75). Englewood Cliffs: Prentice Hall.

Garfinkel, H. (1967c). Common sense knowledge of social structures: The documentary method of interpretation in lay and professional fact finding. In *Studies in ethnomethodology* (pp. 76–103). Englewood Cliffs: Prentice Hall.

Garfinkel, H. (1996). Ethnomethodology's program. *Social Psychology Quarterly, 59*(1), 5–21.

Garfinkel, H. (2002a). Central claims of ethnomethodology. In *Ethnomethodology's program: working out Durkheim's aphorism* (pp. 91–120). Lanham: Rowman & Littlefield.

Garfinkel, H. (2002b). Two propaedeutic cases. In *Ethnomethodology's program: Working out Durkheim's aphorism* (pp. 149–162). Lanham: Rowman & Littlefield.

Garfinkel, H., & Wieder, D. L. (1992). Two incommensurable, asymmetrically alternate technologies of social analysis. In G. Watson & S. M. Seiler (Eds.), *Text in context: Contributions to ethnomethodology* (pp. 175–206). New York: Sage.

Geertz, C. (1973). Thick description: Toward an interpretive theory of culture. In *The interpretation of cultures: Selected essays* (p. 3). New York: Basic Books.

Glaser, B., & Strauss, A. (1967). *The discovery of grounded theory: Strategies for qualitative research*. Chicago: Aldine.

Heath, C., Hindmarsh, J., & Luff, P. (2010). *Video in qualitative research*. London: Sage.

Hughes, J., Randall, D., & Shapiro, D. (1992). Faltering from ethnography to design. *Proceedings of the Conference on Computer Supported Cooperative Work* (pp. 115–122). Toronto: ACM.

Hughes, J., O'Brien, J., Rodden, T., Rouncefield, M., & Blythin, S. (1997). Designing with ethnography: A presentation framework. *Proceedings of the Symposium on Designing Interactive Systems* (pp. 147–158). Amsterdam: ACM.

Jefferson, G. (1978). Explanation of transcript notation. In J. Schenkein (Ed.), *Studies in the organisation of conversational interaction* (pp. xi–xvi). New York: Academic Press.

Jordan, B., & Henderson, A. (1995). Interaction analysis: Foundations and practice. *The Journal of the Learning Sciences, 4*(1), 39–102.

Lerner, G. (2007). *Languse posting*, April 30th, http://www.list.hum.aau.dk/pipermail/languse/Week-of-Mon-20070430/002753.html

Lynch, M. (1993). Molecular sociology. In *Scientific practice and ordinary action: Ethnomethodological and social studies of science* (pp. 203–264). Cambridge: Cambridge University Press.

Mills, C. W. (1959). *The sociological imagination*. Oxford: Oxford University Press.

Ryle, G. (1968). The thinking of thoughts: What is 'Le Penseur' doing?, *University Lectures No. 18*. Saskatoon: University of Saskatchewan.

Sacks, H. (1963). Sociological description. *Berkeley Journal of Sociology, 8*, 1–16.

Sacks, H. (1992). On sampling and subjectivity. In G. Jefferson (Ed.), *Lectures on conversation*, Vol. I, Part III, Spring 1966, Lecture 33 (pp. 483–488). Oxford: Blackwell.

Schegloff, E. (2007). *Sequence organisation in interaction: A primer in conversation analysis.* Cambridge: Cambridge University Press.

Chapter 8
Informing Design

Computer scientists, software engineers and system developers have a specific mastery of modeling and programming. The construction of such models is an essentially logical exercise of generic and abstract character. Ethnography counterbalances this abstract and generic disposition, highlighting the considerable difference, and often discrepancy, between the logical and the practical order of an activity.

John Hughes

Abstract The point and purpose of doing ethnography here is to 'inform' design – i.e., to help designers figure out what to build and give concrete shape to computing systems. It is worth stating the obvious, as it all too often seems to get forgotten in ethnographic discourses surrounding design that doing ethnography is not about ethnography *per se* but about design. So how can ethnography give shape to design? What practical approaches can be used to leverage ethnographic findings for design purposes? How can it be used to figure out what to build? It has often been said that it is very difficult to relate ethnographic findings to design: that ethnography produces rich or 'thick' descriptions of work whereas design is necessarily about abstraction and therefore requires some means of parsing and reducing the complexity represented by thick descriptions of work to develop computational models that may subsequently be implemented in computing systems. Over two decades of practical involvement in design a range of approaches have emerged and/or been appropriated to help ethnographers make their studies relevant to design and translate them into design resources 'telling' designers what to build. Our purpose here is to outline these.

A. Crabtree et al., *Doing Design Ethnography*, Human-Computer Interaction Series, DOI 10.1007/978-1-4471-2726-0_8, © Springer-Verlag London 2012

8.1 Implications for Design

The idea of deriving 'implications for design' from ethnographic studies refers to the significance ethnographic findings may have for design, or what studies of work mean for the actual design of computing systems. If we take the mail handling example discussed in Chap. 4, for instance, we can say that on the basis of the sequential order of the work and the distinctive work practices or machinery of interaction that members use to articulate and organise it that the study 'implies' the following for the design of email systems for the digital home of the future: it is necessary to support the *distribution* of email *across various sites* in the digital home and it is necessary to support the ways in which mail is *methodically* distributed. As Harper et al. (2000) put it,

> ... a letter in the geography of the home is a marker of what point a job-to-do has reached. Email might support this if the screens are located in places that equate to locations within the domestic workflow.

Thus the placement of mail – at the front of the table, by someone's seat, next to the phone charger, etc. – 'marks' out what point in the handling process the work has reached and it does so for members in the methodical details of various action statuses: that mail has arrived and needs sorting, that this mail is for you, that that needs attending to now, that this one can wait, etc. The strong implication for design of the intersubjective and accountable organisation of mail handling is that email in the digital home of the future should be supported through multiple displays situated around the home that enable the distribution of email to reflect the action status of mail and the work that needs to be done. Thus, email handling is transformed from a private activity conducted at a single screen, which is busied with the reading, writing, archiving and deleting of mail, and instead becomes a public activity that also enables members to place mail at different sites around the digital home and allows them to take action on mail items displayed at those sites.

It has long since been noted that detailed implications for the design of particular classes of computing system or application such as email are rare. As Plowman et al. (1995) put it,

> One of the precepts of ethnographically oriented ... studies, and part of the rationale for favouring such approaches over more experimental methods, is that every work environment is unique, work practices are highly situated, and specific design solutions are needed for specific situations. Papers describing design guidelines for *specific* systems ... may therefore be expected to constitute the largest of our categories. However, such detailed design guidelines are typically absent from ... conference or journal papers, which tend to offer a description of a case study, followed by an 'implications for system design' section at the end ... in which a number of highly generalisable or semi-intuitive recommendations are made.

It has subsequently been suggested that attempts to evaluate ethnography's worth in terms of its ability to provide detailed implications for design are misplaced. As Dourish (2006) puts it, for example,

> The call for 'implications for design' I would argue, drawing upon the notion of requirements in traditional software engineering, is a request for empiricism. It is a request

that ethnography provide 'facts' – when people work, how they talk to each other, what they do when they sit down at the computer, and so forth … What has traditionally been more complicated has been to establish a deeper, more foundational connection between ethnography and design – to look for a connection at an analytic level rather than simply an empirical one.

While we would not dispute the need for the ethnographer to adopt a distinctive analytic orientation, and for designers to develop an appreciation of this distinctive orientation, it is important to appreciate that the findings produced through ethnography ought to have more about them than analytic significance: that they really should display and ground design in 'facts'. 'Facts' matter to us as much as they do to designers. Very specifically, 'social facts' matter and not as analytic phenomena – not as ideas or concepts you might come across in textbooks or scientific papers – but *in the empirical details* of the intersubjective machineries of interaction that members know, use and recognise, and which systems may therefore be designed to support.

The need for actual empirical insight is essential to ethnography and to design. Consequently, ethnographers have been urged to move beyond 'platitudinous' implications for design and adapt to the demands of design practice (Shapiro 1994). Rather than throw a set of generic, semi-intuitive findings over the fence and leave it for designers to work out what they mean, the challenge instead becomes one of actively engaging ethnography in the creative process of design and working out what should be built. The need for adaptation is essential: just doing ethnography, especially at an analytic level, is not sufficient. Ethnographic findings need to give shape or form to particular design solutions. They need to be a formative part of the mix if the approach is to be of lasting utility to designers. That means that ethnographers are going to have to get down off the fence and get their hands dirty in real *design work*. It is no good trying to shift the goal posts by arguing that implications are not the best measure for evaluating ethnography's worth. Clearly they are very, very important and speak of ethnography's utility to systems design. Demonstrably, they are not hard to derive from particular studies for particular design purposes: attend to the sequential order of work and the work practices that articulate it and ask yourself what is critical to the continued accomplishment of the work in a novel technical environment – i.e., ask yourself what of the work a new system must support, *what is essential*, *what must be done*, and you will derive specific implications for the design of specific computing systems; implications that may subsequently be articulated for designers through a Software Requirements Specification document.

8.2 Requirements Specification

The Software Requirements Specification document or SRS provides a detailed description of a computing system or application. It is a both a specification of what should be built and a communications device between stakeholders in the design process. It spells out in detail what services a system should provide, specific system properties, and constraints on the operation of the system. While attempts have been made to provide universal standards for writing SRSs,[1] there is no uniformity in practice. Insofar as there is any commonality to software requirements specification then it revolves around a concern to specify *user requirements* and commensurate *system requirements*.

> User requirements are statements, in a natural language plus diagrams, of what services the system is expected to provide to system users and the constraints under which it must operate.
>
> System requirements are more detailed descriptions of the software system's functions, services, and operational constraints ... system requirements ... should define exactly what is to be implemented. (Sommerville 2011)

Ethnographic findings may be drawn upon to specify user requirements. They are not requirements in and of themselves but grist for 'requirements analysis' – i.e., working out what should be built. Ethnographic findings do not specify that, they only highlight important, even critical features of work that should be taken into account when making such decisions and furnish concrete empirical resources with which to go about making those decisions: they show what the work is and how it is actually organised and accomplished. There is more to requirements analysis than this, but it is an important ingredient nonetheless.

If we return to the mail handling example we can say then that user requirements consist of the following:

USER REQ1. Users need to be able to collect email and then distribute it across multiple interfaces to display various action statuses, including:

    1.1 Mail that awaits sorting and distribution
    1.2 Mail that has been assigned to a recipient
    1.3 Mail that requires immediate action
    1.4 Mail for which action is pending
    1.5 Mail that indicates a pending event
    1.6 Mail for social viewing

USER REQ 2. Users need to be able to archive mail
USER REQ 3. Users need to be able to delete mail

With a set of user requirements in hand it then becomes possible to specify a commensurate set of system requirements, e.g.,

SYSTEM REQ 1. A *displays manager* that enables users to,

    1.1 Find and name networked display panels in the local environment
    1.2 Connect/disconnect networked display panels
    1.3 Monitor the connection status between display panels

SYSTEM REQ 2. An *accounts manager* that enables users to,

    2.1 Add/delete user email accounts
    2.2 Assign add/move/archive/delete email rights to users
    2.3 Set up and organise archives (add/delete folders)

---

[1] IEEE Standard 830–1998 *Recommended Practice for Software Requirements Specification* http://standards.ieee.org/findstds/standard/830-1998.html

SYSTEM REQ 3. An *email client* that enables users to,

    3.1 Retrieve email from user accounts (mail remains unopened by default)
    3.2 Move email to named display panels on the network
    3.3 Move opened mail to archive
    3.4 Move unopened or opened mail to trash

SYSTEM REQ 4. A *database*

    4.1 Store accounts data
    4.2 Store emails

These system requirements may then be further decomposed into hardware requirements, software requirements, communications requirements, user interface requirements, and associated non-functional requirements that are essential to 'defining exactly what is to be implemented'.

8.3 Developing System Models

If particular implications for the design of particular computing systems and applications are not especially difficult to derive, and if it is equally possible to specify requirements for a system based on those implications for design, it would not be unreasonable to ask why highly generalisable, semi-intuitive implications for design emerged as the norm in ethnographic research papers and reports? The simple answer is that this is what designers initially asked of ethnographers. Designers didn't (and don't) just want solutions to particular design problems, generic design solutions are required too. Designers want solutions that can be *shared* across a community of practice. The reporting of generic implications for design was, then, an attempt to share knowledge with the broader design community and especially those members who did not have access to ethnographic expertise. It was especially concerned to identify generic features of work and its organisation that could provide a foundation for modeling socio-technical solutions. We have elaborated these in the previous chapter, but to provide a brief and salient recap they include the following:

- *Distributed Coordination*, which orients us to the division of labour, the activities that compose it, and how those activities combine to articulate larger processes of work. It focuses our attention on the various ways in which the coordination of people and tasks is practically accomplished as a routine feature of the real world, real time work of a setting, including the equipment (tools, artefacts, material resources, etc.) that members use to gear their activities into one another and accomplish coordination.
- *Plans and Procedures*, which orients us to the particular ways in which plans and procedures are practically accomplished in the course of work. It focuses our attention on the local skills and local knowledge that a setting's members utilise

to achieve the objectives laid out by plans and procedures and, in doing so, to elaborate the practical distinction between plans and procedures and what is actually involved in 'getting the job done'.

- *Awareness of* Work, which orients us to the ways in which work is put on display and others are made aware of it and can coordinate their actions accordingly. It focuses our attention on the local 'ecology of awareness' – i.e., the particular ways in which work sites and working materials are laid out and arranged so that members can make reciprocal sense of each other's activities, can see what other people are doing, and how this fits into the pattern of work which they are concertedly producing.

These generic organisational features of work provided ethnographers with a 'presentation framework' – i.e., with a way of organising their findings and articulating them to designers in terms of a division of labour inhabited by different people doing different jobs of work that are interleaved through the practical accomplishment of plans and procedures and situationally relevant displays or representations of work (Hughes et al. 1997). For designers, these generic organisational features of work provided a *method* for developing use case models of the sociality of work (Villers and Sommerville 1999).

Use cases (Jacobson et al. 1992) are used to model work. As Ian Sommerville (2011) describes them,

> … a use case identifies the actors involved in an interaction and names the type of interaction. This is then supplemented with additional information describing the interaction with the system. The additional information may be a textual description or one or more graphical models such as UML sequence or state charts. Use cases are documented using a high-level use case diagram. The set of cases represents all of the possible interactions that will be described in the system requirements. Actors in the process, who may be human or other systems, are represented as stick figures. Each class of interaction is represented as a named ellipse. Lines link the actors with the interaction. Optionally, arrowheads may be added to lines to show how the interaction is initiated.

The identification of generic features of work enabled designers to incorporate the sociality of work into these models. Thus, the mail handling example may be modeled as in Fig. 8.1 below in terms of distributed coordination between actors (e.g., mail sorters and recipients), procedures for handling mail across the division of labour (e.g., for getting mail, sorting it, passing it on to recipients, and displaying it in various ways), and mechanisms for representing the status of the work in the course of doing it (e.g., through the use of situated displays to make the action status of mail items visible). The generic features of work the use case is predicated on enable designers to model particular solutions that take the sociality of work into account. Generic 'implications for design' were not and are not intended to tell designers what to build but to draw attention to generic features of work that can be oriented to and explicated through fieldwork to develop situationally appropriate models of work. They do not dispense with the need for ethnography in that case but rather occasion it and provide *novices* with a framework to work within, both in terms of orienting the analysis of

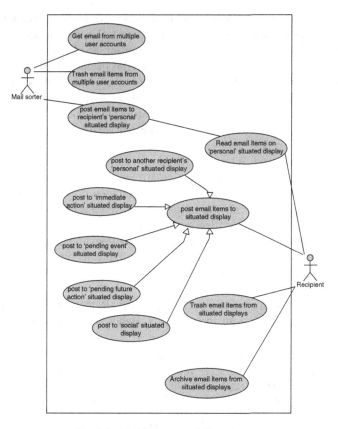

Fig. 8.1 Modeling the sociality of work

ethnographic findings to generic features of work and its organisation and developing commensurate computational models.[2]

8.4   Sensitising Studies

It is clearly possible to derive user and system requirements from ethnographic findings and to generate abstractions sufficient for developing technical solutions. Translating thick descriptions of work into concrete design resources through the production of software requirements specification documents or use cases works well in situations where the goal is well understood – e.g., building a system to

---

[2] As noted in the previous chapter, the framework does not provide concepts for conducting ethnographic analysis but for *presenting* those analyses and bridging between ethnography and design.

support a particular job of work (such as an email system for the digital home; a call centre support system; a parts ordering system; etc.). However, much of the design work that ethnography is embedded in is far 'looser' in character and concerned with novel if not blue-sky research. By definition this means that the goal is not well understood, indeed that the research is without a clear goal beyond general objectives, that the problem is ill defined and somewhat fuzzy. The challenge here is not so much one of figuring out what to build but of understanding the very possibilities for design – i.e., of figuring out what kinds of things *might* be built? SRSs and use cases do not help here, as they presume an understanding of the problems to be addressed. What is required instead is an understanding of the *play of possibilities*. There are, of course, a great many ways in which one might go about doing this, but insofar as the use of ethnography is concerned then deploying the approach to provide *sensitising studies* has proved a useful technique.

Sensitising studies do what they say on the tin: they sensitise designers to the work of a setting. They are a means of developing domain knowledge and insight into the play of possibilities for design. They are, typically, of very short duration, done over several days at most. They differ from quick and dirty studies (see Chap. 5) insofar as they are not intended to be built upon iteratively and con-currently in a requirements engineering process. Rather, they provide studies of 'perspicuous settings' – an idea initially elaborated by Harvey Sacks in an interchange with Harold Garfinkel:

> Harold, I have a distinction between 'possessibles' and 'possessitives'. By a possessable I mean you're walking down the street, you see something, it looks attractive, you'd like to have it, and you see of the thing that you'd like to have that you can have it. You *see* that of the thing. As compared with, seeing the thing you'd like to have you see about it that you can't have it. You *see* it belongs to somebody. I'll call that a 'possessitive'. Now, Harold, what do I mean by that distinction? That is what I want to find out. I don't want you to tell me. I don't want to settle it like that. I could go to the UCLA law library, I know how to use it, but I don't want to write definitions. I want to find a work group somewhere who, *as their day' s work*, and because they know it as their day's work, will be able to teach me what I could be talking about as *they know it* as the day's work. One day he came in with a great grin. He'd found such a group. In the Los Angeles Police Department are police who, in riding around their territories, as part of their work, spot cars that have been abandoned. Other cars look equally bad, but it could be found out that they were not abandoned. You call the tow truck for one of these cars; the other you ticket. As their day's work the police must make this distinction: make it fast, make it subject to supervisory review for the truth, correctness, and other adequacies of the recognition, and make it in each particular case. (Garfinkel and Wieder 1992, abridged)

Perspicuous settings are everyday settings whose work is relevant to our under-standing of a problem situation. They teach us, as Sacks was keen to pursue in his own investigations, what we could be talking about *from a members' perspective* and, in doing so, sensitise us to the work involved in addressing the problem, whether it be the work of figuring out which cars to ticket or tow or work of more immediate relevance to technological research.

The idea of addressing the problems of IT research by consulting the work of a perspicuous setting may seem absurd to many a developer, after all the future has not been built yet so how can the ordinary members of society teach us anything of what we could be talking about? Let's take a real case by way of example, however. A research project is tasked with developing mobile and location-based solutions to support and enhance interaction with rural places.[3] How might the researchers address the problem? In the first instance we might ask what, *from a practical point of view*, could we be talking about when we talk about "people's interactions with rural places"? One topic that immediately presents itself (and there are no doubt many) is that of *visiting place*, which is to say that people ordinarily interact with rural places through visiting them. We might learn more of what we could be talking about then, and what we might in turn be trying to support and enhance through the design of mobile and location-based applications, by consulting the work of visiting place. We might, in other words, consult a perspicuous setting in which members are busied with the work of visiting a place. Were we to do that we might find something very much like the following:

- *Where should we go?* Visiting a place requires that members first figure out where to go. This often involves the use of location-based resources to identify candidate places to visit and other considerations of a geographical and a personal nature (e.g., interests, novelty, risk, excitement, etc.; distance, time it will take to get to a place, cost of going there, weather, etc.), all of which may be the source of agreement, disagreement, and negotiation between parties to the decision-making.

- *Planning for the visit.* Once a particular place has been decided on, members need to plan for the visit. They need to determine how to get there, what route to follow, what things they need to take with them, when to leave, what they are going to do once they are there, how much money they will need to do the things they want to do, who they need tell about their visit and who will cover contingencies (like feeding the cats), and who should do what and when so that they can get out of the door on time.

- *Preparing to leave.* Things of relevance to a visit (clothes, maps, food, equipment, etc.) have to be brought together at timely moments. This cannot necessarily be done days ahead but often has to be done just before departure. Thus, food has to be prepared, bags packed, the house be prepared for absence, the car loaded with people and stuff before you can lock the door and get underway.

- *Going there.* Then you need to make your way there, which in addition to way-finding may well involve in-journey entertainments to pass the time and searching out remarkable sights and scenes of interest as you pass through the land around you, and then there are pit stops for fuel, toilets and snacks.

- *Arriving.* So you've made it, you're there: where do you actually want to be, where do you actually want to go? There are a host of things we need to do when we arrive in a place: find a place to park, for example, figure out what to take

---

[3] Bridging the Rural Divide EPSRC EP/I001816/1, www.bridgingtheruraldivide.com

with you and what to leave behind, figure out who should take what, and figure out where to go from here.

- *Doing visiting.* So where *do* we go from here? What does that sign say? Which way's the beach? Figuring out where to go next, and getting there, relies on our 'reading' the landscape around us and drawing on 'situated displays' which point us in the right direction and in other ways point out relevant features of the landscape (paths, sites of interest, pubs, toilets, etc.). So we follow signs and paths, guides and maps, engage in the activities that we came here to engage in, take photos of our grand day out to remember it by, stop occasionally for refreshments, and then it's back to the car and we head off home.

- *Going home.* Going back is much like leaving home in the first place, we have to load up and find our way, but now we have other things to occupy us: the things we saw, the things we did, what was good, and what wasn't, what we should do again, and when – visits beget visits and discussing our next adventure is as good a way to fill the journey home as is dissecting the one we have just had.

- *Getting home.* Eventually we return home, unlock the house, unload the car, put stuff away (our coats, our boots, rubbish from the journey home, etc.) or put it somewhere on hold where we will deal with it later. We send the kids for their baths, check on the pets, check to see if any messages have been left, etc. The household routine resumes.

- *After the visit.* The visit rapidly recedes into the past, it is done, dusted, a grand day out of little relevance to anyone else but us. It may be newsworthy to some members of our family and our closer friends. Grandma and Grandad may enjoy hearing what the kids did over the weekend, your friends of a good place to take their kids some day too. What of your remembrance of the event? What of those photos you took? You're in no rush, they're on the camera, you'll sort them out when you have time.

It might be thought that not much can be gleaned for the design of a generic solution from a single study of a single family's day out. However, if we look at the work of visiting place from an intersubjective point of view we can see that the family's work is shot through with familiar events that we recognise too and shot through with organisational features that may readily be generalised. Thus we can say that the work of visiting place is organised by members in the following ways:

- Through searching location-based resources to identify candidate places to visit
- Through assembling location-based resources to plan a visit to a particular place
- Through using location-based resources to find the way around a place
- Through capturing location-based resources to remember visiting a place
- Through sharing location-based resources with interested parties.

In sensitising us to the work involved in visiting place, a single study of a single family's day out teaches us that when we talk about developing mobile and location-based solutions to support and enhance interaction with rural places, we could be talking about developing an application that enables users to search, assemble, use, capture, and share location-based resources to support and enhance the identification of candidate places to visit, to plan a visit to a particular place, to do the visit, make a record of it, and subsequently to share the experience with others. Thus, sensitising studies *ground* us in the intersubjective organisation of human activities and put us onto real world *topics* that are relevant to the future technologies we wish to develop.

8.5   Scenario-Based Design

Sensitising studies provide an empirical focus and concrete starting point for design reasoning. That reasoning may be further elaborated through the production of scenarios. Scenario-based design is a powerful alternative to software requirements specification. In place of abstract lists of user and system requirements, scenarios provide "stories about people and their activities" (Carroll 2000). Not any old stories, of course. Scenarios are a particular kind of story having a particular kind of narrative structure:

- Scenarios are always situated in a *setting or settings.*
- Scenarios always have at least one human agent or *actor.*
- An actor always has an objective or *goal* to achieve.
- Scenarios always have a *plot* that describes the sequence of actions and events whereby actors achieve their goals.

The purpose of a scenario is to provide a concrete 'envisionment' of a design solution, one that specifies the *tasks* users of a system can or must carry out.

Thus, if we turn to the visiting place example, we might develop the following scenario based on the sensitising study of the work involved in visiting place and the core tasks it elaborates.

Visiting Places Scenario[4]
Jack lives in Manchester and wants to take his family out of the city for the weekend, somewhere in the nearby countryside where they can go for a pleasant walk. He asks his wife and kids where they might like to go: they agree on somewhere in the Peak District, which is only an hour's drive away. He opens a web browser on his desktop machine and clicks on the 'PlaceBooks' link. The link directs him to the global PlaceBooks archive, where he types in 'family walks in the Peak District'. The search returns thirty-three hits, which are displayed on a map of the area. He clicks on various items to view the PlaceBooks – small leaflet-like guides to particular places – discussing various options with the family and eventually downloading a PlaceBook describing a walk around Mam Tor near Castleton into his local PlaceBook archive.

---

[4] This is a reconstituted scenario assembled for the purposes of exposition. In practice, a variety of scenarios were constructed as our understanding of the design problem evolved. This scenario re-represents the key features of an evolving set of scenarios to provide a textually coherent elaboration of "typical and significant user activities" (Carroll 2000).

After dinner, Jack searches the Internet for further information about Castleton. He finds places to visit – the Blue John mine, Peveril Castle, and a cave system called the Devil's Arse – and various media about these places (descriptions, photos, even videos), which he downloads. He also finds places to eat and adds links to these to his local PlaceBook archive as well. He then opens the archive and the Mam Tor PlaceBook and deletes the content he is not interested in. He is left with a map of Mam Tor, which displays a route on it. He then starts to add his own content to the PlaceBook: web pages of places the family might visit, photos of Peveril castle, a video of trip through the Devil's Arse, a map that shows places to park and places to eat, text he has cut and pasted from websites about good pubs and cafes in the area, another map that shows the route to take from Manchester.

On Saturday morning, while the family get their walking gear together and load up the car, Jack gets his smart phone, logs onto his PlaceBook account and adds the Castleton PlaceBook to it. The phone caches related content and the family set off on their visit. Jack's wife checks the PlaceBook a couple of times *en route* to ensure they are on the right track, and uses it to find a place to park. Then the family set off on their walk. The route map in the PlaceBook is an active one, it exploits the smart phone's GPS to show the family where they are on the route and the position of any nearby content they have cached. Jack also uses the smart phone to take photographs and videos of his family and the various things they have done and seen over the course of their walk. The smart phone allows Jack to geo-tag content, including text and audio messages as well as visual media, and also allows him to record his own route as the family make their way back from Mam Tor via a different route to the one in the PlaceBook.

Having finished their walk around Mam Tor, the family head into Castleton to find a place to eat. They consult the PlaceBook and decide on the Bulls Head pub, where Jack can have what he feels is a well-deserved pint as well as bite to eat. After a late lunch the family stop at the visitor centre across the road and find a situated display showing official tour guides around the area. Jack launches the PlaceBook app on his smart phone and it retrieves a list of PlaceBooks available at his current location. He downloads one about Peveril Castle, which is where the family are headed next before setting off home.

One evening during the following week, Jack syncs his smart phone with the PlaceBook archive on his computer. He opens the Castleton PlaceBook and adds content he generated during the family's day out and other content from the official guide of Peveril Castle. He then publishes his PlaceBook on the global PlaceBook archive. He has the choice of sharing the Castleton PlaceBook with a group friends or making it publicly available. Jack publishes it to his 'family' group, which the kids' grandparents have access to.

This scenario addresses the topics made visible through the sensitising study of visiting's work: searching, assembling, using, capturing, and sharing location-based resources to support and enhance the identification of candidate places to visit, to plan the visit, do it, make a record of it, and subsequently share the experience with others. It does so with an eye towards articulating the design of a particular application, one called 'PlaceBooks', which enables users to accomplish these core tasks and exploit mobile and location-based devices and resources to support and enhance their interactions with rural places. The scenario moves beyond ethnographic study then to specify requirements for a novel application whose design is rooted in the intersubjective work of visiting place.

The scenario may itself be subject to further elaboration to specify just what the task or tasks described involve. Storyboards are one technique that may be used to do this (Boyarski and Buchanan 1994), providing graphical depictions of narrative scenarios. Specifically, storyboards visualise the 'plot' or the sequence of actions and events that users engage in to accomplish their goals. Storyboarding is a

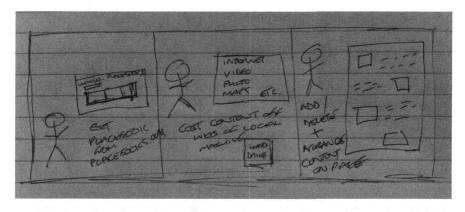

Fig. 8.2 Storyboarding the assembly of a PlaceBook

technique derived from film-making, where they are used to decompose narratives into 'sketches' that elaborate specific sequences of action and events to be filmed (Hart 1998). In a design context, those sequences of action and events are oriented to the device, application, or service to be built. Thus, storyboards are used to depict user interactions with a technical object and the events that are sequentially implicated in that interaction. They are typically drawn with pencil and paper and consist of three or four 'frames' that visualise the key features of a sequence of action and events. They need not be particularly well drawn – you do not need to have artistic talents to do a storyboard – you just need to be able to draw the key features of a sequence of user-machine interaction. If we take the task of assembling a PlaceBook, for example, we might depict it as follows (Fig. 8.2).

This is the kind of storyboard that gets produced in practice on pieces of paper or sketched out at the whiteboard in the course of design meetings,[5] though more polished versions may subsequently be drawn up and distributed. Storyboards are rough sketches that can be quickly drawn and amended to elaborate scenarios, and in this particular case, the key features of assembling a PlaceBook from the point of view of user-machine interaction. The storyboard says first that a user should be able to get a PlaceBook from the global PlaceBook archive; secondly that he or she should be able to get other content (including video, photos, and maps) from off the internet or a local machine; and thirdly that the content may deleted from a PlaceBook, new content added, and that the user can arrange it on a page as he or she pleases and annotate it as well. Scenarios and storyboards are not particularly sophisticated devices but that belies their power: anyone can use them to specify the key characteristics of sequences of user-machine interaction and thus elaborate in fine detail requirements for new computing systems.

---

[5] Storyboards are one of many 'lo-fidelity' techniques for sketching out design problems and solutions, including thumbnail sketches, wireframes, and comic strips; any and all of these techniques can be used to leverage ethnographic findings into the elaboration of user-machine interaction.

8.6   Mock Ups and Prototypes

Scenarios and storyboards are useful devices for transforming ethnographic findings into requirements for particular systems. Nonetheless, we have found that more is required by designers on occasion, particularly the specification of sequences of user-machine interaction in precise detail. In other words, and by way of example, what does assembling a PlaceBook actually look like as a sequential accomplishment of human-computer interaction: just what should the system actually *do*?

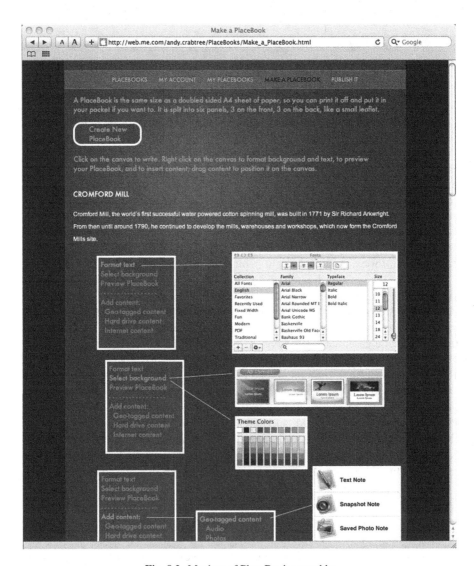

Fig. 8.3 Mockup of PlaceBook assembly

Building a mock up is a way of answering that question. Mock ups have a long and venerable tradition in computer science, enabling designers and other stakeholders to develop models of computing systems (Ehn and Kyng 1991). Mock ups are a different kind of model to use cases. They are *replicas* of a system made out of cardboard or paper, wireframes, slideshows or web pages to provide low and mid-fidelity representations of a computational system, application or service which may in turn be drawn upon by designers to develop a functioning prototype. They are, typically, very detailed and describe the *particular steps* involved in accomplishing a task or set of tasks. The PlaceBook mock up in Fig. 8.3 above shows, for example, the steps involved in assembling a PlaceBook, including formatting text, selecting background, and adding content. More steps are involved in assembling a PlaceBook and the complete mock up for the PlaceBooks application specifies step-by-step how users create accounts, get PlaceBooks, make them, manage their collection, share items, and also use them on mobile devices. Mock ups provide a concrete specification for design. They say *build this*, which is not to say that *just this* will be built as requirements change and evolve throughout the development life-cycle (Sommerville 2011). Nonetheless, mock ups provide a baseline and elaborate core functionality that a system needs to support. In that respect, they furnish a highly detailed and nuanced requirements specification, which may be built upon and elaborated iteratively through further design activities involving the use of mid-fidelity and high-fidelity prototyping techniques that enable the evolution of increasingly sophisticated solutions.[6]

8.7 Evaluation

Ethnography and ethnographers can and do play an active role in the development of mock ups and prototypes. Whilst it is a designer's business to *make* prototypes, ethnography is not redundant in this part of the design process. Early efforts to incorporate ethnography into design pointed to the use of the approach to conduct 'sanity checks', for example (Hughes et al. 1994). The use of ethnography in this role extends across several dimensions. It includes using ethnography to monitor systems in their use in order to tweak existing systems or inform the design of the next generation of system. This approach towards evaluation locates ethnography in an iterative process of "continuous but modest redesign", with systems evolving in a similar way in real world contexts (ibid.). Here ethnography is somewhat removed from the actual process of building a system first-time-through as it were. An alternative use of ethnography in evaluation is to assess the viability of design proposals. Whilst being oriented to design first-time-through, this kind of sanity check often precedes the building of mock ups and prototypes and is concerned to assess the *prima facie* viability of design ideas (see the following

---

[6] See, for example, http://www.placebooks.org/placebooks/

section for further detail), though it may extend to considering the introduction of off-the-shelf systems into a setting. Something that draws more fully upon an ethnographer's competence is the idea of 'situated evaluation'.

Situated evaluation is more closely allied to what is traditionally thought of as evaluation in design, namely an approach that provides a "significant check of a system's capacity to deliver what is required of it" (Twidale et al. 1994). In this context evaluation is understood to be either formative or summative in character, where the former is a constructive part of an iterative design process and the latter assesses the outcomes or results. Both approaches are concerned to validate systems. Typically, formative approaches do so in qualitative ways, whereas summative evaluation is concerned with quantitative measures. Situated evaluation is a formative approach to evaluation. It seeks to validate systems, including prototypes of systems, by drawing on the domain knowledge developed by an ethnographer to conduct a sanity check on a system's 'fit' with the work of a setting. 'Fit' means that a system resonates with the work of a setting or, where a completely new system is being built, that it is compatible with the work of a setting and meets the real world, real time requirements of the work. Situated evaluation extends the focus of validation beyond the functionality provided by a system, and measures of its performance, to provide a sanity check on its ability to be situated or embedded in the work of a setting. As Twidale et al. (ibid.) put it,

> The salient issue, both in principle and in practice, should be how we determine whether systems can be said to 'work' or not.

Situated evaluation has evolved since its inception from an approach that draws on the domain knowledge developed by an ethnographer to become a much more proactive feature of iterative evaluation cycles in design. Just as an ethnographic study might be commissioned to monitor the use of an existing system and identify areas for improvement or change, so you might actually conduct an ethnographic study of a prototype to understand its fit with the work it is intended to support, especially where totally new kinds of system are being developed, e.g., in the development of future and emerging technologies and blue-sky research. In such circumstances evaluation may be the very first point in the development cycle that the work of a setting is actually taken into account. This is often the case in academic research and research in advanced industrial labs and it has led to an approach of deploying prototypes 'in the wild' to better understand the socio-technical properties of future and emerging technologies. From an ethnographic point of view, such deployments may be treated as 'breaching experiments' or occasions that 'call forth' work practice and make it available to design reasoning (Crabtree 2004).

An example is probably in order. *Can You See Me Now?* is the name of a mobile, mixed reality hide-and-seek style gaming experience.[7] It was co-developed by the performing arts group Blast Theory and the Mixed Reality Laboratory at the

---

[7] http://www.blasttheory.co.uk/bt/work_cysmn.html

University of Nottingham. Technically it was one of a series of 'in the wild' explorations of the socio-technical properties of emerging mobile and location-based technologies. As ethnographers, we had nothing to do with the design of the system – we conducted no studies to shape requirements and were not involved in its development in any way. We were, however, commissioned to study its deployment in the wild and did so in a variety of settings at home and abroad.

What we found was that players of the game – who included online players (members of the public) who used avatars to roam around a virtual model of Sheffield or Rotterdam (etc.) and the artists, who assumed the role of 'runners' and used handheld devices to seek out and locate online players' avatars as they traversed physical space – had to contend with and work around *constant interruption*. This was a result of intermittent GPS coverage across the physical gameplay area, which resulted in runners not being able to get or maintain a 'fix' on online players and thereby come to 'catch' them. The runners therefore had to manage the effects of constant interruption if they were to make the game work, and they did this by building up between them a stock of working knowledge of 'good' and 'bad' areas in which to play the game, of ways of avoiding those with poor service coverage, and by developing strategies for doing diagnostic work when troubles arose in areas where service coverage was usually deemed to be good. The results of our evaluative studies led to the development of new visualisations of GPS availability to support the building up of a stock of knowledge of service coverage and the conduct of diagnostic work. See Fig. 8.4: black areas are

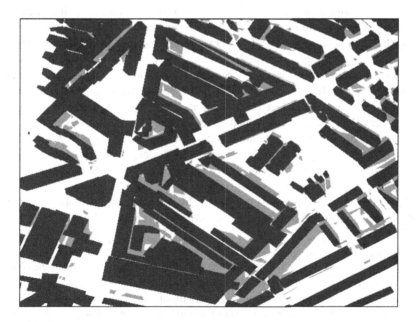

Fig. 8.4 Responding to ethnographic evaluation: visualising GPS service coverage

buildings, white areas indicate 'good' GPS coverage with line of sight to three or more satellites, and grey areas indicate poor GPS coverage (Crabtree et al. 2004).

As ethnography's engagement with design has developed, evaluation has moved beyond doing sanity checks – i.e. beyond helping designers figure out what changes to make to existing systems or whether or not their novel prototypes adequately support the work of a setting. The approach is of course still used widely for those purposes. Indeed, the use of ethnography to monitor or study existing systems is now one of the most popular ways of employing the approach in design. However, and at the same time, it has also evolved to assume a formative position in the process of *innovation*, in distinction to 'tweaking' existing systems, where ethnographic studies are done to uncover the sociality of future and emerging technologies and to factor that understanding into design through evaluation as an iterative and constructive feature of research and development life-cycles. Ethnography is not restricted to the 'up front' business of requirements specification, however it is done and articulated. The approach can assume equally diverse roles in evaluation, whether you want to monitor existing systems, do a sanity check on a prototype you have built, or understand the socio-technical characteristics of future and emerging technologies.

8.8   Assumption Testing

Assumption testing is distinctive species of evaluative work concerned with the practical sociological adequacy of novel design ideas or concepts. It is a kind of evaluative work that ethnographers often find themselves involved in and although it may occasion or be occasioned by fieldwork, more often than not it draws on prior work and the ethnographer's professional sensibility – i.e., that distinctive analytic orientation that underpins fieldwork. Specifically, assumption testing is concerned to *unravel and make explicit* the assumptions that design concepts trade on by exploring what is being taken for granted about the way the social world works within them. We can then ask whether reasonable assumptions about the social world and its organisation are being made and this, in turn, might serve as a test or arbiter of the viability of a design concept: of the capability of some projected technological solution to find its place in a pre-existing world and how well it might sit with the ways in which members order it.

Consider the following design concept, by way of example, one of a series devised to articulate the possibilities for 'intimate' computing:

> Paul is helping Anna to move into her first apartment. Before he leaves he gives Anna a house-warming present, which consists of a pot plant with a 'glow tag' stuck in it. When she asks what the glow tag is he just says she will see. Once Paul has gone Anna puts the plant in her living room and tends it and cares for it as she gets on with her life.

> One year later Anna is sat in her living room with a friend when the glow tag in the plant pot begins to glow. She remembers that it was a year ago that she moved in and later in the day phones Paul and thanks him for the plant.

> Many years later: Anna is now living in a different place and has a family. She has kept the glow tag with the plant, although the plant is now in a much bigger pot. It still glows every year and reminds her of her first apartment.[8]

Let us pause to consider for a moment how it would be, as an ordinary social act, to give someone a plant when they've just moved into a house with an unfamiliar device attached to it that the giver steadfastly refuses to explain. There are many familiar augmentations to plants – baskets, ribbons, gift cards, etc. – and if a plant comes with any of these attached one can readily understand what it is and what it's for. By definition, the same cannot be said of a plant, or any other gift, that is augmented by something wholly unfamiliar. This situation in turn begs the question as to what might become of the unfamiliar augmentation, especially in light of the ways in which we routinely treat the familiar augmentations that are attached to plants: they have limited shelf life. Thus, the plant might remain but there is absolutely no guarantee that the basket, the ribbon, the gift card, etc., will accompany it in a year's time should it survive that long. Furthermore, as the glow tag has nothing to commend it as a coherent independent object with distinct function, there is nothing to motivate the recipient to give its treatment a second thought, nothing that says it is 'special' – just giving someone something doesn't confer that status on an object – and nothing to say that it should be kept and not be thrown away. When we look at the design concept through the lens of everyday life, and the ordinary ways in which the ordinary objects it trades on are used and organised, it is clear that this projected use of 'glow tags' is untenable. That is not to say that there is no possible 'intimate' use of the technology, only that this design concept requires *revision*.

Assumption testing is all about using ethnography to revise or 'respecify' design concepts, though it is inevitably the case that many a design concept gets laid to waste in the process of formulating ideas that hold water. By 'hold water' we do not mean that design concepts have logical coherence insofar as their constitutive elements are compatible with one another, but that they have *practical coherence*. That they are compatible with the *incarnate* character of practical action and practical reasoning and, thus, with the naturally accountable, intersubjective organisation of everyday life and everyday activities as we know and experience them as members. There is no time out from the social, even in reflection or the imagination and the projection of possible futures. What is reflected upon, imagined, and projected is *always* accountable to the social order and not in some grand way but mundanely so, in passing details of the day-to-day things that people ordinarily do. You can use ethnography to grab onto ordinary, everyday life before it passes you by. Use it to assess the accountability of design concepts. It need not take long. You don't need to commission and conduct time-consuming field studies and wait upon the production of an ethnographic report. Instead, and far quicker, you might include an ethnographer in the discussion and development of design concepts or, alternatively, develop the analytic orientation and apply it yourself.

---

[8] Multiple Intimate Media Environments http://mime.cs.nott.ac.uk/content/concept3.html

8.9   The Importance of Collaboration

Demonstrably, the ways in which ethnography might *constructively* inform design are manifold, ranging from requirements specification and system modelling, to scenario-based design and mocking it up, to the evaluation of design concepts, existing systems and innovative prototypes. Clearly ethnography can move beyond providing mere implications for design and actually be leveraged into design practice. However, insofar as ethnographers are employed to do the job, in distinction to designers learning to do ethnography for themselves, then it is extremely important to appreciate that an ethnographer is not going to provide you with an SRS, or develop use cases for you, or scenarios, storyboards and mock ups in isolation. They will no doubt be more than happy to conduct field studies, tear you precious design concepts to pieces, and evaluate systems and prototypes, but when it comes to leveraging ethnography into the construction of systems it needs to be understood that the production of design resources has to be a joint endeavour; something done, something produced, *between* ethnographers and designers (Diggins and Tolmie 2003).

The different kinds of design resources discussed here are products of collaboration between ethnographers and designers. They cannot be produced by an ethnographer alone but rely upon interdisciplinary dialogue and cooperation. They are the product of collaborative work and a willingness on the part of ethnographers to respond to the demands of system design. Clearly a great many technological and creative issues are bound up with this but it may be apparent by now that a common concern cuts through the actual construction of computing systems and that is a preoccupation with the specification of *sequences of interaction*. Whatever technological components make up a system, possessing whatever technological capabilities they have, to address whatever problems may be to hand, at build time design is occupied with the construction of specific sequences of human-machine interaction. Pick up your smart phone, fire up an app, open a web browser on your desktop machine or a word processing document even. Wherever you look, whatever you use, whatever you do, you will find yourself engaging in, following, producing a specific sequence of interactions to accomplish a specific task. That is, of course, no accident. It is what systems design is all about: designing machine sequences to enable people to accomplish particular tasks. Whether it be in the dry textual details of an SRS, or in graphic uses cases, narrative scenarios, storyboard sketches, even replicas of actual systems, design is clearly 'busied' with the specification of specific sequences of human-machine interaction and the construction of systems to support them.

All manner of human activities are constructed or assembled through distinct sequences of interaction and ethnography, at least as we understand it, is foundationally concerned to elaborate their social character. So when we study the work of a setting inevitably we come to focus on the sequential order of work and the methodical ways in which the sequential order is accountably assembled or put together by members in their interactions. Our studies do not simply convey *what* activities a setting's members engage in and the work their practical accomplishment consists of, they also unpack *how* members do that work as a sequentially ordered interactional achievement. If one were to look for a foundational relationship between ethnography and design it might, then, be found in a mutual concern not only with the work of a setting or the work of using computer systems (old and new), but also with the sequential order of work and very specifically with the ways in which sequences of interaction are assembled and made accountable. As Richard Harper put it in Chap. 2,

> ... if you're doing ethnography it seems intrinsic to the observation and grasping and feeling inside the worlds of those that you're studying that you get a sense of how those worlds are *assembled* and thus you therefore also have a sense of how it can be *reassembled* ... For me, I cannot see how ethnography isn't about how the world's *made* and therefore how the world might be *made differently*.

We would suggest that core to 'assembling the world' are sequences of interaction and that helping designers 'reassemble the world' might therefore be done by paying close and careful attention to the methodical ways in which members put their work together in and through the construction of specific sequences of interaction. Furthermore, that a range of design practices exist that enable ethnographers, working in collaboration with designers, to 'factor' the assembly of a setting's activities into design by transforming the sequential order of work into design objects that enable designers to reassemble work in very fine detail, proceeding from distinct jobs of work, to specific sequences for assembling them, to precise methodical steps for doing the assembly. It shouldn't be thought that ethnography is some grand solution to 'wicked' problems of design in saying this. Only that it is an effective way of complementing design-led approaches to requirements specification and evaluation and helping designers rebuild the world (Sommerville 2011).

8.10   Practical Guidelines

We take it that all of the readers of this book have some kind of interest in using ethnography to inform systems design. We have outlined a number of ways in which you might go about translating ethnographic findings into design resources that leverage the social into the actual construction of computing systems. What approach works best for you will depend upon the nature of the project you are involved in and its objectives, the degree to which ethnographers are embedded in the design process, and the extent to which formal processes are expected to be adhered to. Whatever the particular circumstances of your work, a good way to proceed in design is to attend to the following issues.

Ask Yourself What of a setting's Work a New System *Must* Support
What does the sequential order of work, and the distinctive work practices or machineries of interaction that the members of the setting use to articulate it, 'imply' for systems development: what organisational features of work *will* a new

system *have* to support? If, for example, current work practice facilitates the marking out of things for different people and their status within a workflow through the placement of objects, this requires some kind of recognition within future design. Conveying this to designers will require more than just passing over a body of findings. You will need to become a part of the creative mix to establish what is essential and what must be supported in the future if designers are to properly recognise the implications of your findings.

Use Your Findings to Specify the Social Character of Requirements
Ethnographic findings are not requirements in their own right, but they may be drawn upon for the purposes of requirements analysis. You can exploit a rich variety of design-based practices to do that, including developing an SRS, or use cases, scenarios, storyboards, and mock ups. Use whatever approach works best for you and the designers you are working with but in each case it is essential that you explicate or make visible the social character of requirements: the division of labour, the activities that compose it, they ways in which they hang together sequentially to form larger processes, the ways in which they are coordinated with one another, that plans and procedures are practically accomplished, and that the parties to the work make one another aware so that they can concert their actions accordingly.

Where Goals Are Not Well Understood Make Use of Sensitising Studies
Systems development is not always concerned, in the first instance, with the design of particular systems, applications or services. Instead development may occasion 'research' to open up the play of possibilities for design. In such circumstances ethnography may be exploited to provide sensitising studies that elaborate something of what the possibilities for design might actually be. This involves the identification of 'perspicuous settings' or everyday settings where the work that goes on there speaks directly to what we want to understand about some problem or set of problems. The goal here is less about trying to uncover the highly specific details you might be looking for when engaged in requirements analysis or the building of use cases. It is much more about using snapshots to elaborate the intersubjective organisation of human activity and to bring into view *real world topics* that are relevant to the frequently fuzzy kinds of articulations of the future encountered in technology research.

Use Ethnography to Assist in Evaluation
The usefulness of ethnography doesn't stop at investigative studies conducted *prior* to the construction of systems, either as a means of opening up the play of possibilities for design or of specifying requirements. Ethnography, and the analytic 'mentality' that is involved in doing it, may also be drawn upon to evaluate design concepts, prototypes, and systems in use. Your analytic sensibilities can be put to good use to assess and revise the assumptions that underpin emerging design concepts, and to provide a sanity check on prototypes under development. Your observational skills may be also be exploited to evaluate a system once it is positioned in a real setting to identify areas for improvement or change. This can

then form part of an iterative cycle with ethnographic findings providing evaluation of an increasingly developed system-in-use that leads to further refinement and further *in situ* evaluation until it 'fits' with the work practices it is intended to support.

Collaborate Closely with Designers to Translate Study Findings
The creation of design resources that are attentive to practical sociology is a joint endeavour between ethnographers and designers. The successful use of ethnography in design not only relies upon leveraging results through design-based practices but, in the very course of doing so, on an active dialogue between both parties with each being willing to respond to the other's questions and demands. The important common ground shared between both sets of interests is a fundamental preoccupation with *sequences of interaction*. Recognise this common interest and elaborate it in collaborative exploration of existing sequences of interactional work and how they might be reassembled through the construction of new sequences of human-machine interaction.

At this point in the book we have gone through the chief characteristics of an approach to design ethnography that we have practiced over many years. We have given you practical guidance as to how to adopt a similar approach and how to ground that in the distinctive analytic orientation that arises from ethno-methodology. Of course, ethnomethodology is not without its critics. It can be easy to get bogged down in these criticisms and lose sight of the *practical benefits* of using the approach, however. The next chapter therefore turns to a range of common misunderstandings, objections and complaints we have encountered within the design community and the ways in which these are often founded upon misconceptions of ethnomethodologically-informed ethnography.

References

Boyarski, D., & Buchanan, R. (1994). Computers and communication design: Exploring the rhetoric of HCI. *Interactions, 1*(2), 24–35.

Carroll, J. (2000). Five reasons for scenario-based design. *Interacting with Computers, 13*(1), 43–60.

Crabtree, A. (2004). Design in the absence of practice: Breaching experiments. *Proceedings of the Symposium on Designing Interactive Systems* (pp. 59–68). Cambridge: ACM.

Crabtree, A., Benford, S., Rodden, T., Greenhalgh, C., Flintham, M., Anastasi, R., Drozd, A., Adams, M., Row-Farr, J., Tandavanitj, N., & Steed, A. (2004). Orchestrating a mixed reality game 'on the ground'. *Proceedings of the CHI Conference on Human Factors in Computing Systems* (pp. 391–398). Vienna: ACM.

Diggins, T., & Tolmie, P. (2003). The 'adequate' design of ethnographic outputs for practice: Some explorations of the characteristics of design resources. *Personal and Ubiquitous Computing, 7*, 147–158.

Dourish, P. (2006). Implications for design. *Proceedings of the CHI Conference on Human Factors in Computing Systems* (pp.541–550). Montreal: ACM.

Ehn, P., & Kyng, M. (1991). Cardboard computers: Mocking-it-up or hands-on the future. In J. Greenbaum & M. Kyng (Eds.), *Design at work: Cooperative design of computer systems* (pp. 169–195). Hillsdale: Lawrence Erlbaum Associates.

Garfinkel, H., & Wieder, D. L. (1992). Two incommensurable, asymmetrically alternate technologies of social analysis. In G. Watson & S. M. Seiler (Eds.), *Text in context: Contributions to ethnomethodology* (pp. 175–206). New York: Sage.

Harper, R., Evergeti, V., Hamill, L., & Strain, J. (2000). Paper-mail in the home of the 21st century. *Digital World Research Centre*, http://citeseerxist.psu.edu/viewdoc/summary?. doi=10.1.1.104.2351.

Hart, J. (1998). *The art of the storyboard: Storyboarding for film, TV, and animation.* Oxford: Focal Press.

Hughes, J., King, V., Rodden, T., & Andersen, H. (1994). Moving out of the control room: Ethnography in systems design. *Proceedings of the Conference on Computer Supported Cooperative Work* (pp. 429–438). Chapel Hill: ACM.

Hughes, J., O'Brien, J., Rodden, T., Rouncefield, M., & Blythin, S. (1997). Designing with ethnography: A presentation framework. *Proceedings of the Symposium on Designing Interactive Systems* (pp. 147–148). Amsterdam: ACM.

Jacobson, I., Christerson, M., Jonsson, P., & Overgaard, G. (1992). *Object-oriented software engineering: A use case driven approach.* New York: Addison-Wesley.

Plowman, L., Rogers, Y., & Ramage, M. (1995). What are workplace studies for?. *Proceedings of the 4th European Conference on Computer Supported Cooperative Work* (pp. 309–324). Stockholm: Kluwer.

Shapiro, D. (1994). The limits of ethnography. *Proceedings of the Conference on Computer Supported Cooperative Work* (pp. 417–428). Chapel Hill: ACM.

Sommerville, I. (2011). Requirements engineering. In *Software engineering 9* (pp. 82–117). New York: Pearson.

Twidale, M., Randall, D., & Bentley, R. (1994). Situated evaluation of cooperative systems. *Proceedings of the Conference on Computer Supported Cooperative Work* (pp. 441–452). Chapel Hill: ACM.

Villers, S., & Sommerville, I. (1999). Social analysis in the requirements engineering process: From ethnography to method. *Proceedings of the IEEE International Symposium on Requirements Engineering* (pp. 6–13). Limerick: IEEE.

Chapter 9
Some Common Misunderstandings, Objections and Complaints

Our studies have begun to reveal immortal ordinary society as a wondrous thing – lay analysts or professionals, with straightforward normal thoughtfulness, are able to read it out of relevance: eyeless in Gaza.

Harold Garfinkel

Abstract A great many people find ethnomethodologically-informed ethnography problematic. Not only does it have a peculiar language and talk about the world in terms that designers often find strange and hard to digest, when they do manage to swallow it then it often sits uncomfortably with their prior intellectual diet. It is not possible to do justice to the full range of misunderstandings, objections and complaints that are entertained about ethnography, but we can address some of the more common and salient ones. Accordingly, this chapter seeks to explore, elaborate and even correct some of the chief ways in which ethnography is continuously 'misread' by designers and others involved in the development of computing systems. You will find even more matters of contention in the social sciences but we wish to set those aside here and focus on the key issues that we have encountered within a design context over the years. These tend to revolve around issues of subject, method, role and scope of ethnography in design. A rounded appreciation of them relies on understanding what we have said in the previous chapters.

9.1 Method

In a design context fieldwork and ethnography are all too often taken to be the same thing, the same 'method'. A great many studies in HCI and CSCW are routinely labelled ethnographic when they merely involve 'going and looking' – i.e., fieldwork. While ethnography does require fieldwork, that is not all there is to it: *analysis* of the intersubjective or 'social' organisation of human action, including technology use, is also required. Anybody can do fieldwork, no special training is required,

A. Crabtree et al., *Doing Design Ethnography*, Human-Computer Interaction Series, 159
DOI 10.1007/978-1-4471-2726-0_9, © Springer-Verlag London 2012

though developing a practical sensibility towards 'looking' at people will help. Developing an analytic sensibility will take a little more effort, requiring that you adopt a distinctive orientation to human action: attending to the work of a setting, for example, and the methodical ways in which it is assembled and made account-able by members, for members.

The requirement for your studies to not only go and look but also to apply a distinctive analytic orientation to the naturally accountable organisation of work makes it clear that ethnography – in contrast to fieldwork – is not simply an observational method. It is about so much more than going and looking. You have to understand work from a particular *perspective*. Practically speaking, this entails learning what it is that people do and coming to see how it is that they do it, and in terms that members themselves would recognise. This requires work on your part: it requires observation, yes, but it also requires that you interact with study participants (you are not a fly on the wall), that you talk to them so that you can develop your understanding of their work, that you keep detailed fieldnotes and assemble a rich record of materials or 'data' that elaborate a setting's work, that you use that material to provide a rich account or 'thick description' of the setting's work, and in doing all of this that you apply the precepts and concepts of the analytic perspective that you are labouring under.

How you arrive at a distinctive analytic understanding of a setting's work and its incarnate organisation will very much depend on the nature of the work being studied. This belies another profound misunderstanding about ethnography: that it is a method at all. There is no *a priori* formula you can employ – no recipe – for conducting fieldwork and producing an analytic account, as what you see and what you find is contingent upon the work under investigation. To say that the work of a setting is naturally accountable and necessarily possessed of certain features (such as practical action and practical reasoning, interactional work, and work practices that reveal distinctive machineries of interaction, as discussed in Chap. 3) is not to provide a set of step-by-step instructions that you can follow to arrive at a distinctive result. It is only to provide a particular orientation to a setting's work and to attune you to features of it that are essential to ethnographic study. In each and every case you will have to exercise that orientation and discover what those features look like and consist of 'here and now' in just this place, with just these people, working with just these tools and resources to hand. You have to flesh the perspective out and how you do that will depend upon the work itself as it is made visible and accountable to you by the setting's members in the course of doing it.

9.2   Common Sense

It is not uncommon for people to remark that ethnography is 'just common sense' – i.e., that it is just about producing common sense descriptions or accounts of the world that anyone can provide. Ethnographers have had occasion to berate the design community for entertaining a conception of the approach that effectively reduces it to chatting with people and the gathering of anecdotal evidence which, of course, anyone can do (Forsythe 1999). While we do not share the view that PhD level training is required to do good ethnographic work in and for the purposes of system design, we wholeheartedly agree that such an understanding of ethnography is absurd. Not only does it propagate a view that ethnography lacks rigor, it also leads people who want to try to do ethnography for themselves to produce 'scenic' accounts of a setting's work (Button 2000) – i.e., accounts that describe observable features of a setting's work but fail to get to grips with what is actually being done or how it is accountably organised in the doing. Take, for example, the following account:

> During services screens were used extensively to accompany music, illustrate sermons, and share announcements and video. Words to hymns and Bible verse were frequently displayed over a background depicting religiously-inspired imagery. It was also common for the pastor to read selected Bible verses that would then be displayed on the screen. We observed parishioners following along and looking at screens to know what verse to turn to in their Bibles. The appearance of a new verse on the screen was followed by a flurry of paper turning. (Wyche et al. 2007)

This is the kind of common sense description that anyone might produce if they were asked to go and look at what people do in an American mega-church and, indeed, in a great many smaller churches in contemporary culture too. There is nothing unusual in it either. It is not a unique instance of bad research singled out for its lack of workmanship. Far from it: the annals of HCI and CSCW are replete with scenic descriptions offered under the auspices of ethnography. Rather, it is an instance that displays with great perspicacity the distinctive character of scenic accounts, which might usefully be described as "I went there and this is what I saw". While it is commendable that members of the design community take ethnography seriously enough to want to try to do it themselves, it is imperative that they move beyond going and looking and exercise *epistemological discipline* too.

Epistemological discipline means that one adopt, apply and *adhere* to the precepts and concepts provided by particular analytic perspectives. There is no requirement that the perspective employed be ethnomethodological in character but it is necessary to move beyond scenic orders of account that anyone can provide and to explicate or make visible *what is done in the doing* of situated action. Otherwise, you are not even trading in common sense descriptions and understandings of work. What do we mean? We mean that insofar as anyone can provide an account of situated action, even common sense descriptions require of any person that they be competent in the work that their descriptions purportedly describe: that they understand the activities that go on in church, for example, just as they must necessarily understand the activities that make up any other setting's work. In other words, even common sense descriptions require that the notion of 'anyone' be bounded and constrained in its application to 'any competent member' of a community of practice as it were, or to people who are *familiar* with and *know* a setting's work. So, and for example, people are not simply 'looking at screens', 'following along' or engaged in 'a flurry of paper turning' in the American mega-church. They are doing being at prayer, and doing so congregationally in the company of others.[1]

What anyone can say will not do, then, and it is also necessary to go beyond the common sense descriptions offered by any competent member as well. Ethnography, at least as we understand and practice it, is not about explicating what 'anyone' – i.e., what any competent member – knows: why would you need an ethnography to do that when you could just go and ask anyone? Rather, ethnography is foundationally concerned to explicate how common sense knowledge is intersubjectively provided for such that any member can see what is going on around them, hear what their fellow members are doing, respond accordingly, and tell you what is happening to boot. Our interest is not in common sense knowledge *per se* then, but in machineries of interaction that enable members to order their activities and thus make them accountable to one another and others who might inquire into them. As Sacks (1984) puts it,

> ... order is an important resource of a culture ... any member encountering from his infancy a very small portion of it, and a random portion in a way (the parents he happens to have, the experiences he happens to have, the vocabulary that happens to be thrown at him in whatever sentences he happens to get) comes out in many ways pretty much like anyone else.

Sacks is suggesting that despite all of our individual differences of personality and circumstance, we nevertheless conduct ourselves in much the same orderly ways as anyone else: we walk as others walk, queue as others queue, greet our friends and colleagues as others greet us, etc., and we do more specialised activities, including those implicated in our jobs, in the ways that our colleagues do and recognise too. Furthermore, our membership is predicated on a very limited and extremely contingent sample: none of us encounters culture or society as a whole yet we turn out 'much like anyone else' – i.e., much like any other competent member.

Order is the grounds upon which 'what anyone knows' trades. It is often treated as a grand topic created by the operation of large social forces and trends which can only be elaborated by the social sciences. We take a different view: order is a mundane feature of everyday life that a setting's members are intimately acquainted with. We are not counterposing common sense and social science knowledge in saying this – for us they are both the same, with the latter merely being an educated if somewhat ironic version of the former (Sacks 1992). Neither steps outside the natural attitude, which is to say that while both can and do offer rich accounts of order neither of them questions the grounds on which common sense knowledge

---

[1] It might be argued that the work of Wyche et al. is better understood as a species of 'contextual inquiry' (Beyer and Holtzblatt 1999), but this does not negate the problem of scenic description (Hartswood et al. 2002). On the contrary, it shows up the essential shortcomings of fieldwork approaches that lack analytic foundation and reinforces the need for epistemological discipline: just going and looking and interpreting what you see and hear is not a sufficient basis for understanding how people actually *do* their work. More is required.

is possible: it may be treated as erroneous, mere 'folklore' to be corrected by science, but that it exists is taken for granted by the man-in-the-street and social scientist alike. Ethnography provides an alternative treatment, explicating the seen but unnoticed machineries of interaction that underpin common sense knowledge. It treats what anyone knows without irony and seeks instead to uncover 'the animal in the foliage'. This requires epistemological discipline or rigor and makes it necessary to *move beyond* common sense descriptions of what anyone knows to reveal the distinctive machineries of interaction that a setting's members use to order their activities and to make their work accountable to one another.

9.3   Understanding the User

The view that ethnography is busied with the production of common sense accounts underpins the view that it is a "user's champion". Initial reports about ethnography's utility in the design process certainly encouraged this understanding of the approach, and it is one that still echoes strongly today, but it is also to some extent an unintended consequence of the language of design and talk about "understanding user needs." Clearly we are not exempt from the confusion and complaints that arise from such misunderstandings. Perhaps, the most vocal opponent of this view on ethnography is Participatory Design (PD), a distinctive design practice that seeks to develop computing systems through the direct involvement of users and other stakeholders (Greenbaum and Kyng 1991). Proponents of the approach have had occasion to charge ethnography with misrepresenting itself as a 'proxy user', which leads to a problem of one-way communication between users and designers.

Whether you care about the practical problems of PD, or not, it is important that you appreciate that ethnography is *not* a user's champion. It never has been and it never will be, if for no other reason than that the ethnographer can never arrive at an appreciation of a setting's work that 'users' – or rather members – have. In all but a handful of rare exceptions, ethnographers do not do the work they study and they certainly don't have to 'live' it, i.e., their lives do not depend upon it. From our point of view then, though we appreciate that cultural anthropologists will contest this, ethnography is not in the business of representing users. We prefer to let users speak for themselves, and Participatory Design has proved itself a highly effective approach towards realising this. Setting the users' voice aside, ethnography's job in design is instead oriented towards uncovering and representing other distinct properties of the user experience. Very specifically, we are concerned to explicate their work practices and the machineries of interaction these make visible. As these are taken for granted it is often extremely difficult for users to articulate them. They remain seen but unnoticed and it is our job to make them available to account so that the real world, real time ways in which a setting's work is actually done and organised can be addressed in design.

9.4 Subjectivity

Whatever the analytic disposition of the ethnographer – be they ethnomethodologically-oriented or prefer more fashionable cultural perspectives – they will inevitably be charged with subjectivism, which is to say that our findings are just a collection of personal interpretations of a setting's work, our results no more than what we make of what we see rather than reflections of reality. Some – indeed most labouring within contemporary cultural perspectives – are happy to accept the charge and even defend it. As Paul Dourish (2006) puts it,

> ... ethnography ... is inherently interpretive ... it is important not to ignore the role of the ethnographer as interpreter and framer of ... 'facts' rather than as a passive mirror of the site.

This is not an uncommon view and not wholly misplaced, being traceable back to the origins of social science and efforts to define what makes it distinct from natural science.[2] It is also a view "far more personalised" through the crisis of representation that beset the social sciences in the 1980s, which obliged the ethnographer to bear individual responsibility for "defining the significance of his own particular projects because the general theoretical umbrella of justification of the field no longer adequately does this" (Marcus and Fischer 1986). Thus, in place of objective facts stand subjective interpretations and 'reflexivity' – the *hallmark* of contemporary ethnographic studies across the social sciences and increasingly in design too.

Reflexivity demands that we acknowledge the essentially interpretive character of ethnography: it simply cannot be otherwise. Furthermore, that we acknowledge that ethnographic findings are essentially an individual researcher's interpretations of what he or she sees in the field. Reflexivity draws the fieldworker's attention to the unavoidable fact that whatever he or she does will shape the way in which a setting's work is perceived and the account they can offer of it. There can be no 'value free' observations, everything is coloured by one's personal perspective, analytic commitments and interactions with a setting's members. Reflexivity compels us to reflect upon *our* impact *as* fieldworker *on* the setting's members and the analytic accounts we subsequently provide about them. It puts the fieldworker at the centre of the ethnographic enterprise in an attempt to manage what might be described as the 'bias of the self' on fieldwork. As Sim (1999) puts it,

> Subjectivity is a fact of life. Since eliminating it or controlling for it is not possible, the researcher must take into account subjectivity and personal impact on the site during data collection.

We disagree, which is not to say that we think it possible for the fieldworker to be objective – to be a neutral observer, a mirror of the site or setting even, who sees and reflects reality for designers. Rather it is to say a plague on both schools

---

[2] See Wilhelm Dilthey and Max Weber, for prime examples.

of thought: machineries of interaction are neither subjective nor objective; they are *intersubjective* – known, used in common, and taken for granted by any and every competent member of a setting.

Doing ethnography need not be about the fieldworker's interpretation of a setting's work, then. It can, without issue, be about the intersubjective ways in which a setting's members make their work accountable to one another. In other words, it can be about explicating the interpretive framework of members, rather than the interpretive framework of the fieldworker (the things he or she did, the things they saw, they way they made sense of them and rendered them sociologically significant, etc.). Instead of focusing on the 'reflexivity of the actor' – i.e., the inquiring self – the fieldworker might instead focus on the 'reflexivity of accounts' – i.e., the incarnate ways in which members make sense of what they and those around them are doing (Czyzewski 1994). Those ways of making sense, of interpreting action, *of making it accountable* – the machineries of interaction of which they demonstrably consist – are known and used in common by members. They are intersubjective and thus available as intersubjective phenomena to the inquiring fieldworker too, not in his or her capacity as a 'reflexive social analyst' but as an ordinary member of society who wishes to develop vulgar or ordinary competence in a setting's work. Ethnographic findings need not be reduced to the subjective interpretation of the fieldworker. They may be rooted in and display the machineries of interaction that a setting's members intersubjectively employ to make their work accountable both to themselves and the inquiring fieldworker, should he or she elect to *see* beyond the self.

9.5 Reproducibility

The alleged, and all too often real, subjectivity of ethnographic findings leads to the charge that ethnographic results are not reliable: send another ethnographer into the same setting and you'll get a different set of results; hence the charge of subjectivism, which certainly applies if you treat ethnography as cultural critique. The 'reliability' of ethnographic findings refers to their reproducible and generalisable character. The charge reads that as ethnographic findings are subjective interpretations they cannot, therefore, be reproduced by others or be generalised to other settings in which the same sort of work occurs. This lamentable situation may be attributed to ethnography's failure to make itself answerable to the principles of scientific inquiry. No doubt this view is fostered by those who would make ethnography into cultural critique and change the rules of the game, reframing issues of reliability under the auspices of the contemporary 'crisis of legitimation' (Denzin and Lincoln 2005). For our part we would simply point out that the social sciences are foundationally different to the natural sciences and different standards are therefore required to assess the reliability of ethnographic work.

Both natural science and social science might be said to be in the business of accounting for the regularities of life. The natural sciences conduct their business in terms of general physical *causes* (X happens because of Y; the apple falls because of gravity, etc.). This 'positivist' model of account has been imported into the social sciences to elaborate and explain general social causes giving rise to regularities in society at large too. While positivism is strongly contested and underpins the crisis of legitimation in contemporary ethnography, many social scientists still labour under its yoke and offer various orders of causal account, from those that address social structures that regulate individual action, to the cultural motives that we draw upon to shape our individual identities in the face of societal constraint. The perceived need to account for causation is alive and kicking in the social sciences, arguably even in many 'post-structural' or 'post-modern' accounts as well: the topics may be different but the *explanatory* role they play maintains.

There are foundational alternatives. Most of the regularities found in social life are not of a causal variety; rather, they are 'rule-like' in nature, which is to say that the *procedural* character of human activity accounts for its regularity. As Sharrock and Randall (2004) put it,

> Taking the simple example of the counting sequence '1, 2, 3, 4, 5', one can see that these steps follow not because of causal necessitation, but because of socio-cultural convention which orders the steps in that succession. It is enumeration in this sequence that constitutes counting, and so the connection between the steps has a normative character. Counting in this sequence is a widespread regularity in our social life, but it is not one that is causally based.

The normative 'this is how we proceed' character of human action draws our attention, not to an abstract principle of scientific method with which to assess the reliability of ethnographic findings, but to what people ordinarily do and the ways in which they ordinarily do it. Furthermore, when designers ask questions of the reliability of ethnographic findings they are in the course of *doing design* asking practical rather than methodological questions. Thus, for all the talk of science, explicating the ordinary character of work is what issues of reliability actually turn upon in design. We find then that when designers query the reliability of our findings that they are asking practical questions of the order, "is what you have seen people doing what they ordinarily do?" and, commensurate with that, "are the ways in which they do what you have seen them doing how they usually proceed?" Clearly you need to know such things if you are going to develop a computing system that supports a setting's work.

You might wonder how can we possibly say 'yes' to such questions based on contingent observations of a small number or even just one case. What *legitimates* the making of generic claims? Harvey Sacks (1984) addressed the issue as follows,

> ... the fact that certain results are gotten from one informant would not necessarily be a warrant for those things being good procedures on their own terms, but evidence for an *arrangement* of the world which could be seen to be usable ... you may well find that you got an enormous generalisability because things are so arranged that you *could* get them; given that for a member encountering a very limited environment, he has to be able to do that, and things are so arranged as to permit him to.

We take it that Sacks is saying that even a single case or instance of work displays the particular procedures that members use to do it, whether it be taking turns at talk or handling the mail, sharing photographs, etc. (cf. Chap. 4). There is nothing in an instance of this or that job of work being done that says whether or not the procedures it exhibits are good or bad; that is a judgement you will have to arrive at through other means. Rather, the procedures elaborate a distinctive 'arrangement' for doing the work that is 'usable' by other members. Thus, the arrangement of procedures provides for generalisation to other instances of the same work: to other instances of taking turns at talk or handling the mail, sharing photographs, etc. It does so because particular arrangements or configurations of procedures for doing particular jobs of work elaborate particular machineries of interaction that any competent member uses to do the work. We don't all walk in different ways, or all cycle or drive differently, etc. On the contrary, we mostly do our activities in much the same ways and we do so because that is what *our culture has provided us with* – the ability to conduct ourselves in much the same ways (ibid.). If we didn't, the orderliness of our activities would disintegrate. Thus, the intersubjective or social character of work practice provides for the generalisation of ethnographic findings, even from a single instance which provides us with an empirical sample of a particular arrangement or set of work practices – a shared machinery of interaction – that members (in the plural) use to do a particular activity. Multiple instances of an activity are not required then – generalisation is not provided by numerical frequency – as the phenomenon (the social machinery of interaction) is displayed in *each* and *every* case. In saying this it is, however, important to be aware of the risks of generalising from exceptional cases. It is not that generalisation from such cases cannot or should not be done. Rather, it is incumbent upon the ethnographer to situate them in relation to what constitutes 'business as usual' and to furnish design with a detailed empirical understanding of a setting's work that elaborates what it ordinarily consists of and how it ordinarily proceeds, even in exceptional cases.

9.6   Validity

Issues of reliability are further compounded by a concern with theory which, like method, ethnomethodologically-informed ethnography firmly rejects. The view is that without theory we are merely providing descriptions of human action and its organisation, which anyone can do. Yes, we are, though that does not mean that one can forego epistemological discipline: common sense descriptions will not suffice. That we have no theory to offer is not what concerns us. Rather it is the idea that ethnographic studies are 'merely' descriptive. What this means is that they have no *explanatory power* and so lack *validity*. Newton's account of the 'motion of bodies' did not, by way of example, simply provide an explanation of falling objects but furnished a theory of 'universal gravity' explaining the 'system of the world' that was far more powerful and thus 'valid' than those that went before it.

The idea that theory is necessary is, in a great many respects, predicated on the problems of natural science. In this domain researchers find themselves confronted by phenomena that are not possessed of their own means of accountability.

You cannot ask the falling apple why it falls or the earth why it quakes. Physics, plate tectonics, and a veritable host of natural phenomena studied by the natural sciences all require theory to provide defeasible or testable accounts that explain the hidden causes of observable regularities in life. The phenomena of the social sciences are very different, however. Not only is the need for causal explanation negated by human action's normative character, the regularities of social life are also possessed of their own means of accountability. Football cannot be adequately accounted for in explanatory terms of cause and effect, for example; rather its accountability resides in the 'rules of the game' and in playing by them. Unlike the phenomena of natural science, nothing is essentially hidden from the social sciences – their phenomena are already accountable – and the need for explanations therefore comes to an end (Malcolm 1993).

Theory is *not necessary* in the social sciences then, especially in a post-structural or post-modern age, yet even opponents of positivism cling dearly to the idea that theory is required to account for regularities in social life. As John Hughes (2001) describes it,

> The aspiration to general theorising is an aspiration to novelty, to things that are not ordinary, to give new insights to people, to portray society as something different to the way it is usually experienced.

Clearly designers need to be very careful when turning to ethnographic approaches that trade on theory, at least if they wish to develop computing systems and applications that support the 'usual experiences' that members have in the various settings they inhabit. But what of the validity of ethnographic findings: if validity is not located in the power of explanation provided by a theory, where is it to be found?

The first thing we would point out is that theory *is* description: Newton's theory of gravity offers a description of the 'mechanical laws' that govern moving bodies. So theories do not stand in sharp contrast to descriptions at all: we do not have theory on the one hand and description on the other. Indeed, when we look to the use of theory in ethnographic work we see that it is used to *do* the job of describing social life (e.g., Bell et al. 2005). Furthermore, and here's the rub, we can see that descriptions reflexively provide analyses of social settings and their work, transforming something as ordinary and commonplace as the kitchen sink from a mundane technology into a rationalised site of production and consumption that constitutes a politicised object reifying gendered divisions of labour (ibid.), for example. The point to take note of here is not whether such descriptions are adequate, relevant or true, but that *to describe something is to provide an analysis of it*. There is no time out from that, not for the ordinary man in the street and not for the social analyst. So the issue comes down to this: are you going to analyse what you see in terms of its natural accountability or are you going to use theory to do the job of description instead?

Clearly that's an individual choice, but it is important to appreciate that theoretical description has no inherent advantage over atheoretical description, other than to recommend your work to other theorists who would turn ethnography into cultural critique. Nonetheless, and as John Hughes (2001) again describes the situation,

> ... ethnomethodology has particular advantages in its use of ethnography to inform system design when compared with other approaches which also use fieldwork ... It is here where I can simply point to the massive difference between ethnomethodology and constructivist sociology and the methodological decision of the former to look at the phenomena in its 'raw state' independently of the apparatus of sociological theories and methods which obscure the phenomena they presume to address. The 'raw state' of the phenomena is, of course, the 'everyday world' and the 'ordinary affairs' of the members of society.

It is the 'raw state' of the phenomena that validity turns upon for ethnography, and more specifically the *recognisability* of 'everyday life' and members 'ordinary affairs' that atheoretical ethnographic descriptions provide. In short, members can recognise the work of a setting and also, as they are known and used in common, the machineries of interaction that they employ to accomplish and organise that work too. In turn, this enables a setting's members to confer validity on ethnographic findings. Atheoretical descriptions provide defeasible analytic accounts – members can test them as it were, say if they are right or wrong and what more needs to be done to amend them. Theory is not required to produce valid results that root design in 'everyday life' and the 'ordinary affairs' of a setting. Indeed, using theory 'obscures' the day-to-day work of a setting and its real world, real time organisation and makes it into something extraordinary and unusual or strange instead. Like method, one should dispense with it then and describe human action in its 'raw state' – i.e., in terms of its natural rather than its theoretical accountability for the practical purposes of system design.

9.7 Time and Cost

Ethnography is commonly thought to be a time-consuming and costly enterprise. No doubt this view arises from anthropology, where ethnography is routinely done over months and years, and by anthropologists who propagate the requirements of their trade with little respect for the demands of system design (Jordan and Dalal 2006). As we have noted previously, ethnography *in design* is very different to ethnography in anthropology or the other social sciences. Not only does it eschew theory and method, it does not require that the ethnographer spend a great deal of time in the field either. Indeed, there is a declining rate of utility for fieldwork in relation to systems design. Prolonged periods of fieldwork lasting weeks and months are not required. Instead it is important to configure fieldwork to support design activities – scoping, elaborating, and evaluating systems and their features, for example – rather than letting the ethnographer have free rein. This way, ethnography remains focused on design problems and ensures that diminishing returns do not set in.

There is, of course, no formula that can be applied to the amount of time needed to do fieldwork for the purposes of design – that will depend on the scale of the design task – but a great deal can be learned about a setting and its work from relatively short periods of fieldwork: typically days, occasionally weeks if the setting or task is big (e.g., understanding work in a large multi-national firm), but months and years? Never, and that is because we are not trying to understand as much as we possibly can about a setting and its inhabitants. In a design context, field studies are targeted, focused; they seek to uncover and elaborate specific features of a setting's work: how air traffic controllers organise the skies, how bank tellers do sales work, how customer service staff book containers on ships, etc. Fieldwork is *constrained* in a design context by what designers need to know about the work of a setting and its impact on systems development. Furthermore, it is not the fieldwork that takes up the bulk of the time, but working through the data gathered in the field and leveraging the results into design.

The idea that any of this is any less of a 'problem' for other approaches is deeply misplaced. Diary studies, interviews, surveys, experiments, cultural probes and a host of other approaches all take a great deal of work to do, many of them as much if not more than what is involved in doing ethnography *in a design context*. Even though new technologies make it possible to conduct diary studies, interviews and questionnaires online, that does not reduce the work involved in preparing them or producing a body of findings from them. There are no short cuts. Whatever approach you use will take time and a considerable amount of effort and it will, of course, cost something too. There are no free lunches. Everything costs money and there is no evidence whatsoever that ethnography is any more expensive than any other approach. It might look like that from a designer's point view if they have to hire an ethnographer either directly or on a consultancy basis, but then it's going to cost money to employ someone else to understand 'user needs' as well. It's all a question of what you want to spend your money on – on what kind of insights into users you quite literally place a value on. If you want a certain kind of inspiration, go hire an artist to put a cultural probe together for you. If you want to know more about what users think, go hire someone to conduct some interviews for you. If you want to know about users' work practices, go hire an ethnographer. Whoever you hire, it will take them time to deliver results and it will cost you a professional fee, unless you wish to do-it-yourself but then that will only save you money, not effort.

9.8   Current and Future

A common complaint about ethnography concerns its focus on current practice. The charge reads that design is all about the future, about creating new artefacts, yet ethnography only focuses on how things are 'here and now' and in turn "privileges the status quo" (Dekker et al. 2003). No doubt such views have been encouraged by ethnographers' reflections on perceived problems of the approach:

> The ethnographer's achievement is characteristically designed to be 'appreciative' of the lives it studies, to emphasise the skill and the rationality with which activities are conducted, and to exhibit the 'unperceived' functionality with which those activities

are interrelated. Showing that a pattern of activities has the intricacy, balance and reciprocal interdependence that is found among the parts of a watch, to use this analogy, is to have accomplished an impressive ethnography. To do this, of course, in various ways militates against the idea of design intervention, an intervention which may disrupt by reorganising a well-established pattern of activities. (COMIC 2.1 1994)

The 'non-interventionist' view of the approach referred to here is not one entertained by ethnographers but by designers, however. It is no doubt compounded by ethnographers' attempts to assuage their concerns by pointing out the virtues of exercising caution. As Bob Anderson (1997) puts it,

> The point for the ethnographer is the exploration of how change at the structural level gears with change at the level of practice. Where are the sticking points? The lines of tension? . . . When called upon to draw out the implications of their analyses for explicitly engineered change, it is ethnographers not their ethnographies who are cautious . . . given our experi- ence of explicitly engineered change, perhaps we should be grateful they are.

The impetus towards caution is driven by the failures in software engineering that motivated the inclusion of ethnography in design in the first place. It is not the kind of caution that says "don't change anything" but rather "think about the consequences of what you are proposing before you implement change." That designers may think this a negative point says more about their understanding not only of ethnography and its ability to shape change but of the nature of their own profession too.

Design is not simply in the futures business as it were, it is not simply about creating novel artefacts but about redesigning the very ways in which people do their work. Design is as much about *redesigning work practice* as it is about creating new artefacts. Computing systems are not simply technological systems, they are socio-technical systems (Mumford 1985). That means that designers are not just creating new technological artefacts but new systems-of-work as well. It also means that the efficacy of design, its success if you will, is inextricably bound up with the 'here and now', with current work practice. As Mogensen (1994) puts it,

> One can focus on tradition or transcendence, but the question is always that of tradition and transcendence – we are always bound in our tradition to some degree and, at the same time, have to transcend the present in order to solve our problems.

In other words, effective design is not a matter of 'tradition' (current practice) versus 'transcendence' (novelty), not a matter of choosing to design for the status quo *or* to make something totally new, but a matter of tradition *and* transcendence: of creating something new based on an appreciation of the way things are 'here and now'.

Clearly a great deal of foundational computer science research doesn't do that, and there is no particular reason why it should, but where technology is being *applied* to real world settings then it is clearly the case that a failure to take work practice in the 'here and now' into account is one of the primary causes of failure in systems design (May 1998). Far from being inimical to change, ethnography roots transcendence (design-led change) in tradition (current practice). It does not bind design to the status quo but provides designers with insights into the real world, real time organisation of work that may be drawn upon to reason about the design of future socio-technical systems-of-work. It is an inability to see that design is as much about redesigning work practice as it is about creating novel artefacts that leads to the view that ethnography is conservative and reluctant to engage in the business of change. The view is misplaced: ethnography is deeply concerned by the business of change and seeks to inform design as to important matters that this turns upon.

9.9   Informing Design

So how is ethnography to 'inform' design and thus help designers build socio-technical systems-of-work? Ethnography produces highly detailed and nuanced accounts or 'thick descriptions' of a setting's work, which designers often find difficult to parse. As one of our own colleagues put it in the early days of working with us,

> "Look, I don't care about all this ethno babble, just tell me what to build! All you ever do is tell me stories. Why is this useful? What can I do with it?"

Obviously there is world of difference between what constitutes an adequate account of a setting's work for the purposes of ethnography and what constitutes an adequate account for design. How are designers to parse thick descriptions and develop the abstractions that are essential to the development of computing systems?

> One recourse is to abandon any such questions to the designer, having contributed to the 'pot' key additional (and previously invisible) knowledge of what is salient to the organisation of the work setting. The designer, or the design team, is saddled with the responsibility for the system and so this must undoubtedly be where all final resolutions are achieved . . . It seems odd [however] to impose the entire responsibility for the redesign of work on systems designers while those whose specialty is supposed to be the analysis of work run for cover. (Shapiro 1994)

Odd indeed, and a view again based on a misplaced understanding of ethnography's involvement in design amounting to little more than the appending of 'implications for design' at the end of its research reports. It is important to appreciate that what gets published in conferences and journals is not the business of ethnography *in* design. It is the business of researchers who seek to share knowledge about the approach and the potential significance of findings to systems research and development. In design itself, in the actual course of building computing systems and applications, ethnography has become increasingly allied to a range of design practices that have been developed over the last 20 years to support communication between a variety of stakeholders and to promote their engagement in the creative process of design (see Chap. 8).

Early efforts to exploit ethnography in the design process explored the development of tools to support concept generation, for example, and this work in turn led to the development of tools to enable ethnographic findings to be used to generate use cases. Closely associated with use cases are scenarios, descriptions of actors, their goals, and the interrelated activities involved in accomplishing them. Scenarios have proved to be a particularly powerful way of parsing ethnographic findings for design and they marry well with storyboards, enabling ethnographers and designers to articulate and visualise the sequences of user interactions (current and/or future) described by scenarios. Each of these techniques – use cases, scenarios, and storyboards – enable ethnographers and designers to bridge the socio-technical divide and facilitate the rapid generation of prototypes elaborating new systems-of-work. They place the onus for relating ethnographic findings, not on the designer or the ethnographer, but on both parties, requiring of each that they adopt *interdisciplinary* design practices to articulate the salience of ethnographic findings to the actual construction of computing systems insofar as a division of labour exists between the two. Insofar as a division of labour doesn't exist, insofar as designers do ethnography themselves, then they might also usefully go about articulating and translating ethnographic findings into system requirements through the use of these design practices.

It is also the case that, in course of doing fieldwork for particular design projects, ethnographers and designers have come across features of work that are of broader purchase and may be reused by others. These have been presented to the design community in terms of 'sensitising concerns' (COMIC 2.4 1994), 'alerting concepts' (Hughes et al. 1992), and 'patterns of interaction' that elaborate recurrent features of work (Martin et al. 2001). They focus on what we might call 'formal organisations of work' – i.e., workplaces, rather than interactional work in any domain (the home, the streets, public spaces, etc.) – as this is where the bulk of ethnographic work has been done to date in a design context. They do not provide prescriptive models for the analysis of work, but rather draw attention to some of the fundamental features of work's naturally accountable character in formal organisations – features which, instead of having to reinvent the wheel every time they wish to understand work, ethnographers and designers might use to *elaborate* a setting's work and *attend to* relevant features of it. They are 'pointers' to salient features of work in the workplace that one might find operating across a great many settings, and it is this kind of thing you often find reported in research articles so as to inform the broader community. It would be a mistake to confuse these outputs as being the only way in which ethnography 'informs' design, however. Such outputs are about sharing knowledge that has emerged from particular design-oriented endeavours but their use, their salience to the actual design of novel systems-of-work, is underpinned by fieldwork and a lively set of interdisciplinary design practices for using ethnographic findings to actively shape the future.

9.10   Beyond Work

That ethnography has largely been used to inform the design of workplace systems to date leads to the charge that it limits the possibilities for design. In contemporary contexts, workplaces are no longer the primary site for computing: the computer has moved out of the workplace and is finding its way into ever more diverse areas of everyday life. As Bell et al. (2003) put it,

> In the workplace, applications tend to focus on productivity and efficiency and involve relatively well-understood requirements and methodologies, but beyond this we are faced with the need to support new classes of activities ... Current understanding of user needs analysis, derived from the world of work is not adequate to this new design challenge.

From this point of view, what the contemporary situation requires is a new approach to ethnography that dispenses with an orientation to work and focuses instead on consumer culture and broader cultural practices. This seems like sound advice but there is far more to it than meets the eye. The turn to culture is not simply an injunction to extend the gaze from work to wider society but an invitation to ethnography as cultural critique. It very much turns upon a profound misunderstanding of the notion of 'work' in the kind of ethnographic studies that we advocate, which have by and far had the greatest impact on design to date.

As we have already had occasion to remark elsewhere (Crabtree et al. 2010), and been at pains to point out here when discussing the foundations of our approach, the notion of 'work' in ethnomethodologically-informed ethnography does not refer to what goes on in the workplace. Rather, it refers to the practical action and practical reasoning involved in accomplishing activities of *all kinds*, whether they are part of an organised system of paid labour or not. It is shorthand for 'interactional work' – i.e., the specific courses of practical action and practical reasoning that members *do* to make or assemble or put their activities together so that they turn out to be the most ordinary things in the world. The notion of work in our studies orients us to a world of 'achieved ordinariness' then, or to a world in which people actively make the activities they are engaged in into the ordinary activities that they recognisably are for themselves and the other members around them. The 'making', the 'assembling', the 'putting together' of activity is what the notion of 'work' means and refers to. If we attend to it we can, in turn, see the procedural or methodical ways in which the work is done, or the 'work practices' members use to conduct the work they are busied with. Work practice reflexively elaborates distinctive machineries of interaction that organise work. That machinery is inter-subjective in nature – known and used in common by any competent member – it is *social* or *cultural* through and through.

The turn to 'work' *is* a turn to culture then, whether it be in the workplace or any other setting. What then is the cause of confusion and ensuing calls for change? Certainly it is predicated on a misunderstanding of what work means in ethnographic studies, no doubt fostered by the fact that the bulk of ethno-graphic work has been conducted in the workplace and the names that have been attached to such studies over the years ('studies of work', 'work practice studies', 'workplace studies', etc.), but it also derives from a fundamental shift in design's focus: from the workplace to wider society. The turn to culture is not an ethnographic turn then, but a technological turn, from developing computers for use in the workplace to developing computers for much more diverse contexts of use. The 'turn to culture' is a gloss on this *technological shift*. It is treated as an invitation to engage in ethnography as cultural critique, however, under the mistaken and misleading auspices that ethnography done in the workplace is about work so (obviously) new approaches are required. However, the turn to culture has already been made in ethnography – it was made at the outset – through its studies of 'work', which root design in the intersubjective grounds of everyday life and thus in culture and cultural practice.

There is no constraint then, no limiting of possibilities for design in employing ethnographic studies of work. There may well be risks in employing ethnography as cultural critique, though. Such approaches are essentially theoretical. Thus they aspire to novelty – which no doubt has an inherent appeal – but in doing so render social life into an unfamiliar, unusual, and ultimately 'strange' phenomena that undermines any possibility of developing systems to meet user needs. Ironically, this particular consequence has been seen by exponents of alternate approaches as a virtue. As Boehner et al. (2005) put it, for example,

> ... our desire [is] to embody cultural critique in systems; i.e., systems may be designed, not to do what users want, but to introduce users to new, critically-informed ways of looking at the world around them.

All well and good for would-be ethnographers and intellectual provocateurs but it is perhaps less enchanting for customers, clients and end-users. There is no imperative for design to turn to new approaches to ethnography however, no logical or practical necessity for design to turn to ethnography as cultural critique. Indeed, there may well be good practical reasons why designers might regard such approaches with suspicion.

The turn to cultural critique – not culture *per se* – can only set the relationship between systems design and the social sciences backwards. Over the last 25 years ethnographers and designers have developed a relationship in which the practical implications for design of the incarnate social organisation of human action have been explored to determine how it may be supported, automated, or enhanced through the actual construction of computing systems. Prior to this, ethnographic studies sought to have designers recognise – through critiques of design – that cultural and social organisational features *per se* should be attended to and incorporated in the design process. This was an important step. It sensitised designers to the fact that incorporating human factors was not just about engineering ergonomic or cognitive solutions. Through an historical and ongoing interdisciplinary effort, the relationship between ethnography and design has moved on from one of general exhortation to one of practical engagement. However, new approaches raise the spectre of ethnography taking a step back to general exhortation. They tell designers that they should suspend their cultural biases, adopt new values, engage in critical reflection, build cultural critique into their systems, and so on. Instead of detailed empirical accounts of particular organised activities in particular settings relevant to systems design, new approaches offer the designer a return to a world of moral and political invective. This raises a key question for designers to consider: will that do the job – can you *build* real world computing systems on the basis of cultural critique?

9.11   Anything Does Not Go

It may seem that our invitation to ethnography – a unique one that requires you dispense with theory and research methods – amounts to saying that 'anything goes'. That ethnography opens the door to epistemological anarchy. One might entertain the thought but it would be a gross misrepresentation of our approach, with its insistence on epistemological discipline. Our rejection of research methods is not a rejection of rigor but of *rationalism* and the production of results through the development and application of *logical procedures* or 'formal methods'. While these are essential to the construction of computing machines, they are incapable of explicating the machineries of interaction that a setting's members use to organise their work. Not only do logical procedures get in the way of and lose ethnography's phenomenon, they are actually the root cause of epistemological anarchy according to the philosopher who actually coined the phrase 'anything goes'.

> 'Anything goes' is *not* the one and only 'principle' of a new methodology ... It is the only way in which those firmly committed to universal standards and wishing to understand history in their terms can describe my account of traditions and research practices ... If this account is correct then all a *rationalist* can say about science (and about any other interesting activity) is: anything goes. *Paul Feyeraband*

Feyeraband was a philosopher of science, one engaged in an argument which was concerned to show the absurdity of rationalist approaches to science and 'any other interesting activity'. We cannot do full justice to Feyeraband's case here but the gist of it is that if you impose a rationalist view on everything it looks like anything goes because nothing ever measures up to a set of universal standards, not even science itself (Newall 2005).

In other words, there is no universal Scientific Method but a veritable host of scientific activities each busied in its own unique ways with its phenomenon, producing logical procedures for their study that are in each and every case intertwined with a lively body of work practices that provide for their inter-subjective use and accomplishment. Hence the charge that rationalism degenerates into epistemological anarchy: logical procedure, including Scientific Method, dissolves into the local and occasioned work of a setting. We are not advocating 'anything goes', then, when we say that the fieldworker must dispense with method. On the contrary, we are insisting upon rigor: on adherence to an epistemological discipline that would have you recover the local work of a setting and thus make visible the methods that members use to make logical procedures work when and where they have need to do so. Whether it be the mundane work of writing computer programmes (Button and Sharrock 1995), or making scientific discoveries (Garfinkel et al. 1981), or playing by the rules of less formalised activities (Zimmerman 1973), we would have you dispense with method because members' activities are *already replete* with them. How you 'go about' finding members' methods will very much depend upon the kind of work you are studying, not upon a set of logical procedures, and on your ability to develop competence in a setting's work so as to see and recognise the methods that members know and use in common to conduct that work.

9.12 Practical Guidelines

All of the practical guidelines in this book have so far have focused upon pinpointing specific recommendations regarding things you should *try to do*. This final set of guidelines are of a different character and elaborate a set of cautions that, if adhered to, will assist you in navigating some of the more serious misunderstandings and objections you might encounter in doing design ethnography. These revolve around two key axes: design itself, and science more broadly.

Design
An aggregated set of common misunderstanding's objections and complaints suggest that ethnography is an observational method that produces common sense descriptions of users and their work, that it is expensive and takes a long time do, that it is difficult to relate findings to the design of computing systems and it is of limited utility: (a) because it's findings are very detailed and design requires abstractions, (b) because it focuses on current practice and design is all about future practice, and (c) because design is about more than making systems to support work. Our correctives to these misconceptions emphasise the following issues:

- *Ethnography is not a method.* It is an analytic perspective on fieldwork, one that requires you to arrive at an incarnate understanding of a setting's work and its organisation by developing your competence in it.
- *Ethnography does not provide common sense accounts.* It explicates the practical sociology that common sense accounts trade upon to reveal distinctive machineries of interaction.
- *Ethnography is not about understanding the user.* It is not a user's champion. It is about doing fieldwork to explicate 'users' or members work practices and the machineries of interaction these make visible.
- *Ethnography is not time consuming and especially costly.* There is just as much effort and cost involved in doing good questionnaires, or diary studies, or interviews, etc., and a great deal can be discovered in a short period of time.

- *Ethnography is not inimical to change.* The approach exploits studies of current practice to enable systems developers to reason about design as a socio-technical enterprise and create new technological systems-of-work.
- *Ethnographic findings are not unduly difficult to feed into design.* A wide range of design-based practices may be used to translate 'thick' descriptions of work into design resources that enable the construction of computing systems.
- *Ethnographic studies of work are not limited to the workplace.* The notion of 'work' that is central to ethnographic studies refers to how it is that members assemble or put activities of all kinds together in interaction.

Science

A further set of common misunderstanding's objections and complaints suggest that ethnography is not scientific because it lacks method, is subjective, and produces results that are not reproducible or valid.

- *Research methods are not necessary.* You need to dispense with research methods, but that is not the same as saying that you need to dispense with rigor. On the contrary, uncovering the local work of a setting and thus making visible the methods that members use in order to make that work an ongoingly accountable and coherent enterprise involves an adherence to epistemological discipline that an unquestioning attachment to formal methods would have you dispense with for the sake of proceeding in a formally sanctioned way. If you do that you *will* loose the phenomenon.
- *Members' methods are not subjective.* Traditional concerns about matters of interpretation and whether the ethnographer's position should be thought of as subjective or objective are irrelevant to your interests here. Your job is to explicate the observable and reportable ways in which members establish for one another an accountable understanding of what is going on. The methods they use do that and the machineries of interaction they elaborate are neither subjective nor objective but intersubjective: social through and through and available to the inquiring ethnographer as intersubjective phenomena that any competent member can see.
- *Members' methods are reproducible.* The social character of machineries of interaction provides for their reproducibility. They are not tied to actors but to activities. They provide individuals with interactional methods or work practices for doing an activity and proceeding with it in the same ways as usual. These machineries of interaction are essentially shared – known in common and recognised by members in the plural and their use provides for the production and reproduction of the activities they provide for and organise.
- *Members' methods are accountable.* Unlike the phenomenon of natural science, human activities are already accountable in situated details of the methods members use to conduct them. There is no hidden order to human activities and no need for theories to explain and validate our findings. The validity of

ethnographic accounts turns upon the making visible of the discrete machineries of interaction that members use to conduct their activities, which anyone who is a party to work can recognise and can confirm that it works in the ways that you say it does. Validity, in short, turns upon the intersubjective accountability of your studies of work.

Does this constitute a scientific approach? We do not care if it does or it does not. What we *do* care about is rigor. We do not care about science because it is endlessly contestable as to what constitutes it. The contest is a diversion here. Rigor is not. You either do rigorous studies and make it visible how members do their work as an intersubjectively accountable matter or you don't. Ethnography as we know and practice it makes no claims to be anything more or less than a rigorous discipline, an *epistemological discipline*, that sensitises designers to the real world, real time character of a setting's work and its intersubjective organisation: to the practical sociological character of work as it is known, recognised and accountably organised by the people who do it. As Tom Rodden put it in Chap. 2,

> Where's the science? Where's the big theory? There isn't one. Its contribution is very much one of working through what the doing of an activity, an endeavour, is in sufficient detail so that you can understand enough about what a technology will need to do to survive.

If that's something that you care about too, we suggest that you put whatever ideas you have about science on hold and develop epistemological discipline instead. We hope that what we have had to say here may be of some help as you go about the business of working through what the doing of this endeavour consists of in sufficient detail so that you understand what your systems will need to do to survive as well. We wish you the best and good luck.

References

Anderson, R. (1997). Work, ethnography and systems design. In A. Kent & J. G. Williams (Eds.), *Encyclopaedia of microcomputers* (Vol. 20, pp. 159–183). New York: Marcel Dekker.

Bell, G., Blythe, M., Gaver, W., Sengers, P., & Wright, P. (2003). Designing culturally situated technologies for the home. *Proceedings of the CHI Conference on Human Factors in Computing Systems* (pp. 1062–1063). Fort Lauderdale: ACM.

Bell, G., Blythe, M., & Sengers, P. (2005). Making by making strange. *ACM ToCHI, 12*(2), 149–173.

Beyer, H., & Holtzblatt, K. (1999). Contextual design. *ACM Interactions, 6*(1), 32–42.

Boehner, K., David, S., Kaye, J., & Sengers, P. (2005). Critical technical practice as a methodology for values in design. *Proceedings of the CHI Conference on Human Factors in Computing Systems*, Workshop 9. Quality, Value(s) and Choice, 2–4 April. Portland: ACM.

Button, G. (2000). The ethnographic tradition and design. *Design Studies, 21*, 319–332.

Button, G., & Sharrock, W. (1995). The mundane work of writing and reading computer programs. In G. Psathas & P. ten Have (Eds.), *Situated order: Studies in the social organisation of talk and embodied activities* (pp. 231–264). Washington, DC: University Press of America.

COMIC Deliverable 2.1. (1994). *Informing CSCW requirements.* www.comp.lancs.ac.uk/computing/research/cseg/comic/deliverables/D2.1.ps

COMIC Deliverable 2.4. (1994). *CSCW requirements development.* www.comp.lancs.ac.uk/computing/research/cseg/comic/deliverables/D2.4.ps

Crabtree, A., Rodden, T., Tolmie, P., & Button, G. (2010). Ethnography considered harmful. *Proceedings of the CHI Conference on Human Factors in Computing Systems* (pp. 879–888). Boston: ACM.

Czyzewski, M. (1994). Reflexivity of actors versus the reflexivity of accounts. *Theory, Culture and Society, 11*, 161–168.

Dekker, S., Nyce, J., & Hoffman, R. (2003). From contextual inquiry to designable futures: What do we need to get there? *IEEE Intelligent Systems, 18*(2), 74–77.

Denzin, N., & Lincoln, Y. (Eds.). (2005). The discipline and practice of qualitative research. *Handbook of qualitative research* (pp. 1–32). Thousand Oaks: Sage.

Dourish, P. (2006). Implications for design. *Proceedings of the CHI Conference on Human Factors in Computing Systems* (pp. 541–550). Montreal: ACM.

Elliot Sim, S. (1999). Evaluating the evidence: Lessons from ethnography. *Proceedings of the 5th International Workshop on Empirical Studies of Software Maintenance* (pp. 66–70). Oxford: IEEE.

Forsythe, D. (1999). It's just a matter of commonsense: Ethnography as invisible work. *Computer Supported Cooperative Work: The Journal of Collaborative Computing, 8*, 127–145.

Garfinkel, H., Lynch, M., & Livingston, E. (1981). The work of a discovering science construed with materials from the optically discovered pulsar. *Philosophy of the Social Sciences, 11*, 131–158.

Greenbaum, J., & Kyng, M. (Eds.). (1991). *Design at work: Cooperative design of computer systems.* Hillsdale: Lawrence Erlbaum Associates.

Hartswood, M., Procter, R., Slack, R., Voß, A., Büscher, M., Rouncefield, M., & Rouchy, P. (2002). Co-realisation: Towards a principled synthesis of ethnomethodology and participatory design. *Scandinavian Journal of Information Systems, 14*(2), 9–30.

Hughes, J. (2001). Of ethnography ethnomethodology and workplace studies. *Ethnographic Studies, 6*, 7–16.

Hughes, J., Randall, D., & Shapiro, D. (1992). Faltering from ethnography to design. *Proceedings of the ACM Conference on Computer Supported Cooperative Work* (pp. 115–122). Toronto: ACM.

Jordan, B., & Dalal, B. (2006). Persuasive encounters: Ethnography in the corporation. *Field Studies, 18*(4), 1–24.

Malcolm, N. (1993). The limit of explanation. In P. Winch (Ed.), *Wittgenstein* (pp. 74–83). Ithaca: Cornell University Press.

Marcus, G., & Fischer, M. (1986). *Anthropology as cultural critique: An experimental moment in the human sciences.* Chicago: University of Chicago Press.

Martin, D., Rodden, T., Rouncefield, M., Sommerville, I., & Viller, S. (2001). Finding patterns in the fieldwork. *Proceedings of the 7th European Conference on Computer Supported Cooperative Work* (pp. 39–58). Bonn: Kluwer.

May, L. (1998). Major causes of software project failures. *CrossTalk: The Journal of Defense Software Engineering, July*, 9–12.

Mogensen, P. (1994). *Challenging practice: An approach to cooperative analysis.* www.daimi.au.dk/publications/PB/465/PB-465.pdf

Mumford, E. (1985). Socio-technical systems design: Evolving theory and practice. In *Computers and democracy: A Scandinavian challenge* (pp. 59–77). Aldershot: Avebury.

Newall, P. (2005). Anything goes: Feyerabend and method. *The Galilean Library.* www.galileanlibrary.org/site/index.php/page/index.html/_/essays/ philosophyofscience

Sacks, H. (1984). Notes on methodology. In J. Maxwell & J. Heritage (Eds.), *Structures of social action: Studies in conversation analysis* (pp. 21–27). Cambridge: Cambridge University Press.

Sacks, H. (1992). On exchanging glances. In G. Jefferson (Eds.), *Lectures on conversation* (Vol. 1, Part I, Fall 1964 – Spring 1965, pp. 81–94). Oxford: Blackwell Publishers.

Shapiro, D. (1994). The limits of ethnography. *Proceedings of the Conference on Computer Supported Cooperative Work* (pp. 417–428). Chapel Hill: ACM.

Sharrock, W., & Randall, D. (2004). Ethnography, ethnomethodology and the problem of generalisation in design. *European Journal of Information Systems, 13*, 186–194.

Wyche, S., Medynskiy, Y., & Grinter, R. (2007). Exploring the use of large displays in American mega-churches. *Proceedings of the CHI Conference on Human Factors in Computing Systems* (pp. 2771–2776). San Jose: ACM.

Zimmerman, D. H. (1973). The practicalities of rule use. In J. D. Douglas (Ed.), *Understanding everyday life: Toward the reconstruction of sociological knowledge* (pp. 221–238). London: Routledge.

Chapter 10
Design Ethnography in a Nutshell

> *The prime objective is not so much ethnography as such, but ethnography as a means of uncovering the real world character of work for systems design.*
>
> John Hughes

Abstract This chapter may be read as both an introduction to and summary of our account of design ethnography. By turns we outline the 'turn to the social', which occasioned ethnography's initial involvement and its ongoing use in design, and the foundational nature of 'studies of work' that ethnography provides. We outline basic concepts that underpin ethnographic studies of work and practical tips for applying those concepts and 'finding the animal in the foliage' or the real world, real time organisation of human activities. We also consider a range of practices that have evolved over the last 20 years for incorporating ethnography into the design process, and a number of myths that have emerged along the way. In a nutshell, our purpose here is to outline what is involved in doing ethnography for systems design so that you might develop your awareness and learn important aspects of doing the job yourself.

10.1 The Turn to the Social in Systems Design

Ethnography came to prominence as a design resource in the 1990s as the computer moved into the workplace. The move required that designers rethink their assumptions about computer users (Suchman 1987) and develop their appreciation of the real world, real time character of work and its organisation. Of particular issue was the need to move beyond prevailing cognitive models, which provided reified understandings of computer users and obscured the actual context of work (Grudin 1990). It was recognised that work is essentially a social endeavour, something done by multiple parties and not by individuals working alone: even the

A. Crabtree et al., *Doing Design Ethnography*, Human-Computer Interaction Series, 183
DOI 10.1007/978-1-4471-2726-0_10, © Springer-Verlag London 2012

lone individual has to gear their actions into that of others and is accountable to them. Design therefore took a 'turn to the social' and sought out new approaches that were capable of understanding and conveying the sociality of work so that designers might better respond to the challenge.

Ethnography was one of many candidates that seemed to be of some promise to design (Crabtree 2003; Randall et al. 2007). The approach originated in the social sciences in the 1920s as a means of understanding the social lives of a society's members through *first-hand experience*. It is an 'immersive' approach, which involves a researcher actually visiting social settings and looking at whatever it is that people do within them. Going and looking or doing 'fieldwork' also, and importantly, relies on the adoption and use of an analytic perspective. Ethnography is fieldwork *plus* analytic perspective and the social sciences offer a multitude of different ones. The one that came to the fore in systems design derives from a branch of sociology called 'ethnomethodology'. Thus, the 'turn to the social' in design became in significant part a turn to ethnomethodology for help in addressing the challenge of understanding the real world, real time character of work and its organisation.

Ethnomethodology represents a distinctive approach to sociology. Uniquely, it takes the view that the ordinary members of society are practical sociologists. That sociology is not something that only occurs in the academy but is part and parcel of our own daily lives. That sociology is done by you and me and the other people around us. That the conduct of our activities relies upon our practical mastery of sociology: of knowing how to *conduct* ourselves in the company of others and how to *orchestrate* our actions with theirs so that we can get our business done, no matter how ordinary and mundane that business may be. It might otherwise be said that as they are practical sociologists members know how to *organise* their ordinary affairs. Ethnomethodology wants to know how members do that. It wants to know as an empirical matter so it exploits fieldwork to study practical sociology and the ways in which a setting's members organise the business of their everyday lives.

In place of the business of everyday life we might instead speak of the ordinary 'work' of a setting and in saying that one might recognise that it takes 'work' to do the ordinary things that we do, whether we are paid for them or not (Sacks 1992b). From ethnomethodology's perspective, everything we do takes 'work' – i.e., takes practical effort, skill and competence to accomplish, even if it seems unremarkable to us. When doing ethnography the first thing we want to know is *what* does the work of a setting consist of? What are the activities that the members of a setting *do*? More specifically, what is involved in the doing or making or putting together or *assembly* of ordinary activities? Developing detailed empirical descriptions of the work involved in assembling ordinary activities is the first prerogative of ethnography (Sacks 1984). The second, and primary prerogative, is to explicate *how* the work involved in assembling ordinary activities is made 'naturally accountable', as this is where practical sociology and the real world, real time organisation of work is to be found.

The natural accountability of ordinary activities stands in sharp contrast to their 'classical' accountability – i.e., what ordinary activities come to look like in social science papers and textbooks (Garfinkel 2002b). The natural accountability of ordinary activities speaks of their *recognisability to a setting's members*, rather than their recognisability to professional social analysts. The concept of natural accountability reflects our ability as members of the settings we operate in to see what is going on around us, to understand what it is that we and those around us are engaged in here and now, and to offer an account of what is happening that other members can recognise and make use of too. Natural accountability is a ubiquitous property of human action that in an enormous variety of ways makes it *visible* for any and every competent member of a setting just what is being done here and now. In doing this it enables members to concert their actions accordingly. Our goal in doing ethnography is to unpack how, in the course of assembling their ordinary activities, members provide for the natural accountability of the work they are engaged in: to identify how members *make* their activities naturally accountable so that others can see what is going on and can coordinate their actions with them.

The natural accountability of ordinary activities is ethnography's prize. It is the 'animal in the foliage' that our studies of work seek to reveal – i.e., the real world, real time ways in which a setting's members do their work and organise it as a social enterprise. The natural accountability of ordinary activities is not an abstract thing, not a formula or set of rules or some other formal prescription but a concrete phenomena witnessed and witnessable in the very doing of ordinary activities (Garfinkel 1991). You can see it being done, you can observe it and report it, though you may need to develop competence in a setting's work before it becomes available to you. You will, in other words, need to develop your mastery of practical sociology and the particular, naturally accountable ways in which it is manifest, drawn upon and used in the particular settings you study. You will, in ethnomethodological terminology, need to develop 'vulgar competence' in the work of a setting so that you can see what members see in the course of doing it and in turn can describe the naturally accountable ways in which members do and organise their work. Developing vulgar competence in the work of a setting is the ethnographer's principal challenge and task. It requires that he or she develop a particular sensitivity to studying work in the wild.

10.2 Studying Work in the Wild

So what is involved in studying 'work' in the wild – i.e., in studying through fieldwork the day-to-day business of a setting and the ordinary activities that articulate it? In place of a theory with which to account for and understand everyday life ethnomethodology provides us with a basic set of 'sensitising' concepts (Blumer 1969b) that elaborate a distinctive analytic orientation to the empirical study of ordinary activities. The purpose of these concepts is not to explain ordinary activities but to focus attention on ubiquitous features of the work involved in doing them.

The aim is to orient oneself to them *in situ*. To see what they look like 'on the ground'. To explicate or elaborate them through careful investigation and detailed empirical description so that the ethnographer comes to see how the work of a setting is accountably organised by its members as a real world, real time social enterprise.

The first of these concepts suggests that the work of a setting consists of *practical action and practical reasoning* (Garfinkel and Sacks 1970). Whether the work of a setting is concerned with the production of knowledge, provision of goods and services, is artistic or creative in nature, or about entertainment or leisure, whatever the work is, in short, it is done through the practical action and practical reasoning of the parties to it. Practical action and practical reasoning provide us with a starting point and segue into practical sociology and the naturally accountable organisation of a setting's work. It begs basic questions: what do members do, what kind of reasoning is involved in doing it? Answers start to drive our enquires and propel fieldwork forwards. They provide empirical topics which we can 'bracket' off – i.e., hold up to scrutiny and subject to further elaboration. If we were to ask someone how they get their music or videos they might well say "by searching the internet and downloading stuff", for example, and 'searching the internet' and 'downloading stuff' become empirical topics that warrant continued investigation. We might then look at the practical action and practical reasoning involved in doing 'searching the internet' and 'downloading stuff' and in turn elaborate the work that provides for the accomplishment of these most ordinary of everyday activities.

When we look at the practical action and practical reasoning involved in doing ordinary activities – when we actually see it being done – we see that it is done through *interactional work* (Garfinkel 1986). This concept sensitises us to the fact that practical action and practical reasoning implicates other people, either through direct interaction (e.g., through conversation) or indirect interaction (e.g., by browsing web content written by someone else), and it implicates equipment (computers, software apps, tools, documents, etc.) as well. Furthermore, we can see if we look that members do practical action and practical reasoning through concrete courses of interactional work – 'searching the internet', for example, by launching a web browser, loading bookmarked pages, formulating search terms, browsing retrieved lists of items, inspecting items on a list, etc. There is a sequential order to interactional work and elaborating it is key to our studies. The ordering of sequences of interactional work starts to reveal the naturally accountable character of work whether or not one is working alone or working together with someone else.

Specifically, the sequential order of interactional work reveals members' *work practices* (Button and Harper 1996). This concept draws our attention to the 'methodical' or procedural ways in which members both accomplish and order concrete sequences of interactional work. Work practices do not consist of the kind of things you find in textbooks, manuals or job descriptions – what might generally be called 'formal' methods. Work practices are, by way of contrast, *members'* methods for conducting and ordering interactional work. Take a formal method for 'searching the internet', by way of example. Your browser's manual might tell you to do something like the following: "Type a word or phrase in the space next to the magnifying glass. As you type, a list of suggestions based on what you've typed so far appears. Press return or click on one of the suggestions." But what words do you type to find something that will give you want you want? How do you go about stringing a phrase together that will return sought after items or information? What the formal method does not specify is the methodical ways in which members formulate and can formulate search terms: e.g., by exploiting topical knowledge to specify words and phrases that are relevant to the search, by exploring alternate combinations when that fails, by browsing results and reformulating search terms as a way of doing that, even by asking others when nothing else works. The interactional work of 'searching the internet' is conducted and ordered by members in real time through practical methods of search term formulation.

Members' methods or work practices are 'seen but unnoticed' – i.e., we know and recognise them when they are pointed out to us but we pay no heed to them in the ordinary course of doing our work. People who write formal methods ignore them too. That means we cannot read formal methods of any kind to find out how people actually do their work and, with that, to find out how they actually organise it as a real world, real time social enterprise. In that case we need to attend carefully to the interactional work of a setting and explicate the work practices members observably and reportably use to conduct and order their work. In turn, this will bring an incarnate or embodied *machinery of interaction* into view (Sacks 1984). This concept draws our attention to the social character of members' methods. Methods of search term formulation, for example, while often but not exclusively enacted by individuals working alone, are known, used and recognised by other members to conduct and order 'searching the internet' too: the methods constitute a shared machinery of interaction that we all use to do the job of 'searching the internet'. It is a naturally occurring and naturally accountable machinery that enables us to asynchronously coordinate our actions with a host of anonymous members who post content on the internet, and its use consists in members' mastery of practical sociological methods for organising the accomplishment of the most commonplace of ordinary, everyday activities.[1]

---

[1] It may seem strange to speak of 'searching the internet' in terms of the coordination of ordinary activities. We are not, however, simply interacting with machines when we 'search the internet'. We are interacting with other people, albeit indirectly. Furthermore, the production, distribution and use of digital media may be done by a host of anonymous members working alone but it is social through and through. Practical sociological methods of search term formulation stitch members' anonymous actions together. They enable you to find something that someone else has made and to subsequently make use of it yourself. So you need to understand more than the technical infrastructure and computing methods at work to understand how 'searching the internet' is organised and accomplished in the real world.

10.3   Finding the Animal in the Foliage

Studying work in the wild requires of the fieldworker that they unpack a setting's work by orienting to and focusing on practical action and practical reasoning to identify empirical topics; that they elaborate those topics by attending to the interactional work through which they are observably and reportably achieved; and that they examine concrete sequences of interactional work to identify the work practices members use to accomplish and order them. This, in turn, elaborates the machinery of interaction that members' use to conduct and organise their work. The machinery of interaction is naturally accountable. It consists of practical sociological methods for doing and orchestrating ordinary activities. Practical sociological methods – members' methods, *their* procedures or work practices – are not like the professional sociological methods one might learn in school. They are incarnate or embodied methods, features of a living and lively society and the myriad ordinary activities that compose it, devised and used by members to do their work without recourse to the methodological canons of professional social science.

Practical sociological methods represent a distinctive domain of study. They are alternate to professional social science methods: alternate to the methods of anthropology, sociology, social psychology, etc. They are not available to professional social science methods. They are *members'* methods for doing and organising social life, and they are ignored by members and professional social analysts alike. They are ignored because they are seen but unnoticed – taken for granted, used not reflected upon or studied as topics in their own right, yet they are *practically indispensable*: without them we could not get around a world inhabited by others or get our activities done. The purpose of ethnography as we know and understand it is to uncover and explicate this ignored and indispensable domain of social life to find the 'animal in the foliage' (Garfinkel et al. 1981), the seen but unnoticed methods and distinctive machineries of interaction they constitute that the actual conduct and organisation of a setting's work relies upon. If we are to find the animal it is important that we attend to concrete sequences of interactional work. We cannot find practical sociological methods by interviewing members or asking questions of them. We have to see the work being done. We have to describe actual sequences of practical action and practical reasoning being interactionally achieved to find them. There is no substitute for looking.

How can we find what is right in front of our eyes but usually ignored: seen but unnoticed, like the cat hiding in the bush? Despite the seemingly infinite character and variety of ways in which members might sequence their activities and conduct their work, there is a stable feature of interaction that we might 'grab onto' and make use of to find the animal in the foliage. Whether synchronous or asynchronous in nature, and whether done 'here and now' or distributed over longer time scales, concrete sequences of interactional work are *built up* or assembled and they are assembled by members as social phenomena through the *pairing* of adjacent actions (Sacks 1992c). The formulation of search terms is paired with browsing lists of retrieved items, for example, and the viewing of particular items on the list may be paired with the formulation of further search terms or one of a range of other possible actions. Whatever the action, the ways in which one is paired with another makes the methodical ways in which members do their work (e.g., searching the internet) visible. The pairing of adjacent actions inhabits concrete sequences of interactional work. They are built up out of them, especially where two or more members are working together. The thing to look out for is how the particular actions that elaborate any sequence of interactional work complement and complete one another. Look to see how particular actions are treated by members as being part of a pair of *mutually constitutive* actions that belong together; how they are, in the actual course of interaction, seen by members who do the work to be *accountably related*. If you can see that you can find the methods that members use to conduct and organise the work, as those methods provide for and elaborate the accountable relationship of the actions that make up the sequence.

It is no doubt tempting to understand what we are saying here as being to do with some kind of 'task' analysis. You should only do so in an ordinary sense of the word, however. That is, in the sense that we are analysing peoples work. In a technical sense, task analysis is a formal method in HCI (Diaper and Stanton 2004). It provides a cognitive perspective on work that seeks to decompose it into the particular steps that individuals must take to accomplish the tasks it consists of. Task analysis provides an abstract view on work, which removes individuals from the social context of that work (Grudin 1990). Instead we aim to *see the social* in an individual's performance of their work tasks. The sociality of work becomes visible in the pairing of adjacent actions which elaborate work tasks and which reveal the methodical ways in which members make their actions into naturally accountable features of social life. Thus, and for example, in seeing members formulate search terms, browse retrieved lists, select and view items on the list or reformulate the search, we see what it is that someone is doing: 'searching the internet'. That's a social phenomenon, you do it, I do it, others do it too. It is a naturally accountable phenomenon, with the ways in which it is accomplished *making it accountable* to us all. Those 'ways' are the animal in the foliage. They are the stuff of practical sociology. They are seen but unnoticed in the ordinary course of our affairs. We may come to notice them by attending carefully to the particular pairings of adjacent actions that concrete sequences of interactional work are observably and reportably assembled through. To do that you will need to move beyond our gloss of 'searching the internet' and go and find for yourself the methods that members use to make their work accountable, thereby enabling others to recognise what they are doing and to gear their own actions in with that when and where they have need to do so.

10.4   Dispensing with Method

You don't need any special methods to uncover the naturally accountable character of a setting's work. Indeed, you need to dispense with special methods, with 'formal' methods – i.e., with research methods, the methods that you are taught in HCI classes or by social science researchers, etc. Formal methods are not required because they lose the phenomenon: they lose the methodical ways in which *members* make their work accountable to one another and other parties too, including nosy ethnographers. Members' methods are not available to formal methods of any kind, which is to say that you cannot find them using formal methods. If you use formal methods you will lose sight of the naturally accountable work of a setting. You have a choice to make then, a foundational one, between using formal methods (such as task analysis) to study work or to abandon formal methods and instead explicate the methods that members use to do their work. You have a choice between understanding what work looks like through your use of formal methods to account for what the members of a setting do or what it looks like from a members' point of view in the details of the methods that they use to make their work accountable. The two are not the same and they cannot be reconciled: you see what a setting's work looks like through your use of professional methods or you see what it looks like through members' methods for doing the 'job' (Garfinkel 1996).

If you wish to see what members' methods look like and uncover what they consist of you will need to address the unique adequacy requirement of methods (Garfinkel and Wieder 1992). The unique adequacy requirement replaces a concern with formal methods with a concern to find and explicate the *particular* methodical procedures that members use to make *particular* activities accountable. It replaces the generic methods that professional analysts use to account for work with the situationally relevant and situationally specific methods that members use to do their work. It replaces generic methods designed and used by professional analysts to study a broad range of human activities with specific methods designed and used by members to do specific 'jobs'. In place of generic methods it demands of the fieldworker that she or he understand the specific methods that a setting's work is uniquely possessed of, methods which make the work the very particular thing that it accountably is for the members who do it. It requires of the fieldworker that he or she throw professional research methods in the bin, turn around, walk away and go and develop competence in a setting's work instead.

In place of research methods our approach to ethnography would have you develop 'vulgar competence' in a setting's work (ibid.). Vulgar competence does not mean 'rude', 'offensive', 'unrefined'. It means ordinary, commonly used. It refers to the ordinary competences that are in common use in the setting and it is a requirement that the fieldworker become thoroughly acquainted with them so that he or she understands the day-to-day work of that setting. It requires that you go down onto the shopfloor or wherever it is that work is happening, that you watch it being done, that you talk to those who do it so that you can see the sense of the particular things they are doing, and develop your understanding of the work by being thoroughly immersed in it. The aim is to see and understand work as members see and understand it; to recognise how it is done in the same ways that members recognise it; to be 'in a concerted competence of methods' with members (ibid.). Developing vulgar competence in a setting's work is key to the ethnographic endeavour as we know and understand it. It is what doing fieldwork is all about. Without it you cannot provide an account of the work of a setting or the uniquely adequate ways in which it is done and made accountable. Without it you cannot find the real world, real time social organisation of a setting and its work. Without it you cannot uncover the animal in foliage.

10.5 Assembling the Ethnographic Record

There are no formal methods for developing vulgar competence. You have to go to the setting, get down on the shop floor, immerse yourself in the work and learn through first-hand experience what doing it consists of. In place of a formal methodological account you will need to assemble an 'ethnographic record' – i.e., a corpus of data that elaborates the work of a setting and the methods that members use to conduct and organise it. There are a great many tools and resources that you can use to develop the ethnographic record: audio-visual recordings, photographs, transcripts, diagrams of the workplace, fieldnotes describing activities of work and what is involved in doing them, documents describing the work (job descriptions, accounts of processes and work procedures, etc.), and materials used in the doing of the work itself (notes, emails, memos, etc.). What tools and resources you use will depend on the work being studied – on the modality of the work, the ways in which it is organisationally accounted for, the materials used, and how the parties to it do their work and concert it with others. Whatever tools and resources you do decide to use it is important to remember what it is that you are trying to do when assembling the ethnographic record: to document concrete sequences of interactional work in the details of the unique interactionally achieved courses of practical action and practical reasoning that elaborate them. This, in turn, will enable you to identify the work practices and distinctive machineries of interaction that members use to do particular activities of work and make them into an accountable feature of the setting.

While there are no formal methods for doing fieldwork and assembling the ethnographic record – no recipe, no formula, no prescription – we have found a useful approach that cuts across settings consists of mapping work through 'horizontal and vertical slicing'. This approach recognises that a setting's work is composed of various activities and that these activities hang together in sequential order: at it's most simple, work has a beginning, a middle, an end. We have found it useful to elaborate the sequential order of work in details of the sequencing of activities that compose it, which is to say first identify the activities that compose a sequence of work and the order in which they occur (the horizontal slice). Then drill down into the particular activities that compose a sequence of work, mapping out the concrete sequences of interactional work that each consists of and is accomplished through (the vertical slice). Horizontal and vertical slicing is a simple and flexible approach to doing fieldwork. It can be used to study complex organisations and their work (e.g., large companies) and smaller units within them (e.g., the work of the sales, delivery, or accounts department). The slices hang together to create a detailed empirical portrait of a coherent whole and allow designers to drill down at various levels: from departments and their role in the overall sequential order of a setting's work, to individual departments, the sequential order of their work and the sequencing of activities that compose it, to the particular sequences of interactional work that elaborate each component activity. Horizontal and vertical slicing can be used to map the work of other kinds of setting too. Indeed, wherever we look we find the work of a setting consists of distinct sequences of activities and that these may be mapped out accordingly.

It may seem in advocating this approach to fieldwork that we are saying that everything is reducible to processes insofar as sequences may be understood as such, and in a sense we are, but with some important caveats. Process mapping techniques are common currency in systems design, having a long tradition as a means of understanding and representing work (e.g., Gilbreth and Gilbreth 1924). It is important to appreciate that in mapping work through horizontal and vertical slicing we are not elaborating formal processes (business processes, information processes, workflow models, etc.) or 'the best way' to do work. We are representing human processes, social processes, actual interactional processes (Blumer 1969a), and we are doing so in lively details of the methodical procedures that a setting's members employ to construct them. These do not correspond to formal processes. They are not the same as them and the mapping exercise will not provide design with the same kinds of resource. What it will do is sensitise designers to what formal processes of work look like 'on the ground' as an accountable feature of work. In turn, this may enable the construction of computing systems that resonate with and support how it is that a setting's members construct and accomplish processes of work in fine, methodical, detail.

10.6   Thick Descriptions and Praxeological Accounts

If ethnography is to sensitise design to the real world, real time organisation of work we need to dispense with formal methods and instead elaborate the unique adequacy requirement of methods. This happens through immersion in the work of a setting and the assembly of an ethnographic record that elaborates the sequential order and interactionally accomplished sequencing of setting specific activities of work. This, in turn, will enable the production of 'thick' descriptions and praxeological accounts of work. The notion of thick description was popularised by anthropologist Clifford Geertz (1973), who suggested that "ethnography is thick description". Geertz "borrowed" the notion of thick description from Gilbert Ryle (1968) and put it to work in the service of ethnography. For Geertz, the ethnographer is an interpreter of a social reality that is both "enigmatical" and "strange", someone who is obliged to "contrive somehow to first grasp and then render ... interworked systems of construable signs" which "can be intelligibly – that is, thickly – described". Thick description is a solution to the problems of anthropology for Geertz, for doing the job of 'interpreting interworked systems of construable signs' (whatever that might mean), but that is not what Gilbert Ryle had in mind when he originally coined the phrase.

Gilbert Ryle was a philosopher who was deeply concerned to understand what is involved in "doing something" (1968). His solution to that problem is 'thick' description, which is to say that if you want to provide a *recognisable* account of what a person or persons are doing you need to provide a very detailed and specific description of their actions and interactions. Thick description contrasts with thin description. Take, for example, someone 'searching the internet'. To say that *that* is done by typing in words is to offer a thin description, one that ignores the formulation of search terms. However, even if we include the formulation of search terms in our account it still requires 'thickening up' if we are to see what someone is doing when they are searching the internet. We need also to describe the kinds of search terms they are formulating and we need to describe how they are paired with other accountable actions if we are to see what is being done. Thus, and for example, we might see someone formulating a search for a camera. We might see that this is paired with browsing the retrieved list. That some items on the list are selected and viewed and that another search for a particular make and model of camera is issued. That the manufacturer's website is selected, the model specification reviewed, then associated equipment (SD cards, long life batteries, lenses, etc.) is searched for, and costs written down on paper. That customer reviews are searched for and read too, and that consumer electronics websites are reviewed for costs and they are written down as well. 'Searching the internet' is a gloss on a host of *particular actions and interactions* that make it visible what a person is doing: in this case, finding and pricing up a new camera.

The notion of thick description is an instruction for us to describe the particular actions and interactions that are involved in the accomplishment of particular activities of work. This is not so much an invitation to an enigmatic and strange social reality as it is an injunction to explicate in fine detail the particular actions and interactions that make whatever activities it is that members do in a setting into the very particular activities that they accountably are for them. Ryle's original notion of thick description contrasts sharply with Geertz's, who used the notion to substitute the careful description of practical action and practical reasoning with an intellectual apparatus – an anthropological apparatus – for describing culture and interpreting social life:

> ... descriptions of culture ... must be cast in terms of the constructions we imagine [members] to place upon what they live through ... this does not mean that such descriptions are ... part of the reality they are ostensibly describing; they are anthropological ... they are anthropological because it is, in fact, anthropologists who profess them ... In short, anthropological writings are themselves interpretations, and second and third order ones to boot. They are, thus, fictions ... anthropology exists in the book, the article, the lecture, the museum display, or the film ... its source is not social reality but scholarly artifice (Geertz 1973).

This is not a criticism of ethnography. On the contrary such artifice is seen as a virtue and the hallmark of contemporary ethnographic studies in the social sciences and, increasingly, in a design context too (e.g., Dourish 2006;

Salvador et al. 2010; Irani et al. 2010; Rode 2011; Dourish and Bell 2011, etc.).
We recommend that the ethnographer dispense with it and return to Ryle's original
concern with thick description to elaborate *what is done in the doing* of practical
action and practical reasoning.

Thick description may be used to move us beyond abstractions – beyond
interworked systems of construable signs or, more tangibly, process or sequence
maps – to elaborate what is actually involved in doing particular activities of work.
Given that design is essentially concerned with abstraction, with reducing the
complexity of work so that computational models may be developed, you might
wonder why we need to move beyond abstraction in the first place: surely the
specification of processes and the sequential order of activities that elaborate them
will suffice? The problem is this: we need to appreciate how a setting's work *is done*
if our abstractions are to be 'practically adequate' – i.e., if they are to enable
the modelling of solutions that support work as it is done and can be done in real
time (Crabtree et al. 2001). Just specifying the activities that work is composed of
and the sequential order in which they hang together is not sufficient. We need to
drill down into the actual doing of work so that we can see the naturally accountable
ways in which it is interactionally achieved and ordered. The fieldworker can do
this through horizontal and vertical slicing *and* thick description of the activities
that compose the sequential order to provide 'praxeological' accounts of work.

As with the notion of thick description, you will find different meanings and uses
of 'praxeology' in the social sciences, particularly in economics (Rothbard 1973).
In an ethnomethodological context, however, it means that thick descriptions of
work can be 'praxeologised' (Garfinkel 2002a) – i.e., they can be read to find the
real world, real time orderliness of ordinary activities in accountable details of the
concrete sequences of interactional work that elaborate them. Thick descriptions
of concrete sequences of interactional work are not cultural interpretations. Their
description makes 'instructably observable' the work of a setting in the details, as
Garfinkel (1996) puts it,

> ... of ordinary, unremarkable worksite specific practices ... chained bodily and
> chiasmically to places, spaces, architectures, equipment, instruments, and timing.

We take it that what Garfinkel means in saying this is that thick descriptions of what
people do, and especially of what is done in the doing, should convey the *situated*
character of work (Suchman 1987) such that they enable the reader to see the work
in the details of the interactionally achieved and naturally accountable particulars of
specific jobs, done by specific people, in specific places, being accomplished in
specific ways, through the use of specific equipment, and having a specific temporal
order (see, for prime example, Button and Sharrock 1997). If the situated character
of a setting's work cannot be seen in its description then the work has been glossed
over, either as a result of your descriptions being too 'thin' or your engagement in
scholarly artifice. There *is* a world beyond the anthropologist's text however
(Sharrock 1995) and we recommend that you develop, through thick description,
praxeological accounts to make its work visible and available to design reasoning.

10.7 Informing Design

How can we use sequence maps and praxeological accounts of the sequentially ordered activities that make up a setting's work to 'inform' or shape the design of computing systems? Over the last 20 years a range of practices have emerged and been appropriated to leverage ethnographic findings into the design life-cycle and development process. At its most basic level you might derive 'implications for design' from ethnographic studies of work – i.e., you might reflect upon the significance that ethnographic findings have for design to elaborate what is important about the work of a setting, particularly what aspects of it *cannot* be dispensed with and are critical to maintain and factor into design. Such matters may actively be factored into the development of computing systems through a range of design practices, including software requirements specification (Sommerville 2011), use case modelling (Jacobson et al. 1992), scenario-based design (Carroll 1995), and the construction of mock ups and prototypes (Greenbaum and Kyng 1991). Each of these in their way enables the specification of work activities and, to varying degrees, their sequential ordering. These design practices marry well with ethnography's foundational concern to specify work in details of concrete sequences of interactional work and to elaborate, through their use, what future sequences of work might consist of in fine-grained details of *human-computer interaction.*

These design practices are also complemented by ethnographic approaches to evaluation, including assumptions testing and the study of prototypes deployed in the wild or of systems that are already in use. Assumptions testing is concerned to unravel and make explicit the assumptions that design concepts trade on about the social world and the contexts in which new technologies are envisioned to operate in. It elaborates what is taken for granted about how the social world works and is organised by novel design concepts and seeks to assess their viability in relation to what we know and understand about how the world works and is organised from an ethnographic point of view. Assumptions testing is particularly useful in research contexts and often draws upon pre-existing studies. It may be complemented by 'sensitising studies' if there is need to elaborate design concepts – i.e., by conducting short, focused studies of real world activities that are deemed to be of relevance to the design challenge. Sensitising studies provide detailed snapshots of a setting's work and salient activities that may drawn upon to 'pump prime' design reasoning. They may be built upon through scenario construction, prototyping, and the evaluation of prototypes deployed in the wild to assess their 'workability' – i.e., their resonance with the activities of work they are intended to support (Twidale ét al. 1994).

Assumptions testing and sensitising studies are two ways in which ethnography may be configured to meet the needs of design. In contrast to ethnography in social science research, ethnography in design is part of a fast-paced process having short lead times. Design happens over relatively short periods of time and this has a direct impact upon the use of ethnography for the practical purposes of systems development. The rapidity of design life-cycles makes it necessary to *configure ethnography* for design purposes. In addition to assumptions testing and sensitising studies, configurations of the approach for design also include quick and dirty studies (which are used to get an overview of the work of a setting), concurrent studies (which go hand in hand with systems development and drill down into aspects of a setting's work that are salient to the task to hand), and evaluation studies (which provide sanity checks on development and assess the 'workability' of solutions). These configurations of ethnography for design give lie to the myth that ethnography takes a long time and ensure that diminishing returns for design do not set in (Hughes et al. 1994).

The various configurations of the approach situate ethnography in distinct positions in the design life-cycle: up front in the initial stages of design as part of the effort to work out what should be built and at the backend as a part of the effort to formatively assess developed solutions. Its use is wrapped in an iterative process, where ethnography is used to shape initial development and then assess developing solutions with the results being fed back into ongoing development cycles. It is not something that stands alone but is woven into and relies upon a host of interdisciplinary competences. In short, using ethnography in design, for design, relies upon *collaboration*. There is no focus to ethnographic work without it, no concepts to assess, no virtue in going and looking at work in and of itself, and no possibility of producing design artefacts. The use of ethnography in design is shot through with design concerns. These direct our studies, give purchase to our critical assessments, and warrant our investigations. Furthermore, unless designers are to develop competence in ethnography themselves, collaboration is essential to the translation of detailed accounts of work into design artefacts. SRSs, use cases, scenarios, mock ups, etc., are necessarily co-productions, relying on the interleaving of social and technical competences to formulate practically adequate design solutions (Diggins and Tolmie 2003).

Over the last 20 years ethnographers and designers have worked together to figure out ways of leveraging the approach into the design process. They have moved from mutual interest in practical sociology – from a concern to understand how a setting's members organise their work together and to develop solutions that support accountable organisations of work – to specific configurations of an ethnographic approach and the use of distinctive design practices to leverage members' mastery of practical sociology into the actual development of computing systems. The collaborative achievements of ethnographers and design practitioners involved in the enterprise are significant and have made a real impact on design efforts to factor the social into systems development. It should not be forgotten, however, that ethnography is 'no silver bullet' to the very practical problems encountered in building computing systems (Brooks 1987). It is, as Ian Sommerville (2011) reminds us, "not a complete approach to requirements elicitation on its own and should be used to complement other approaches." If ethnography is to have any lasting impact on systems design it is not only imperative that it be configured to meet design needs but also that it is done as an interdisciplinary activity. Collaborative design practice is key.

10.8 Myths and Mistakes

A great many myths have accompanied ethnography on its journey into design practice. That it takes a long time to do is an often cited one, one that derives from anthropological readings of the approach, and if one is doing anthropology it probably does. Going and looking at what people do need not take years, however. Indeed, it can be done over very short periods of time: hours, days, occasionally weeks. That the myth still persists is something of a curiosity, given that one of the early contributions of the approach in a design context was to make it clear that ethnography need not necessarily take a great deal of time and that the various configurations outlined above may be exploited to ensure fieldwork delivers to design's demands (Hughes et al. 1994). Accompanying this is the myth that fieldwork and ethnography are the same: that going and looking at what people do *is* ethnography. This is a common view in the computer science literature, particularly in HCI where ethnography is frequently characterised as an observational method. Let's be frank – anyone, absolutely anyone, can go and look at work, assuming they have permission to do so. There is absolutely *nothing special* about going and looking at what people do, *nothing at all*. Members do it all the time. Going and looking is an ordinary competence that we all possess. Seeing what's happening and seeing it in a particular way such that, for example, you see the social in what individuals are doing? Now that takes skill and competence. It's a matter of adopting a particular *analytic perspective* on human action.

That's what ethnography is: a particular analytic perspective on human action. So just going and looking at what people do is not enough to qualify your work as ethnographic, you also need to adopt and *apply* a particular analytic perspective on human action, and ethnography has a great many to choose from. There is no single analytic perspective. There are lots of analytic perspectives and they are all different: all of them focus on different features of human action and offer different characterisations of it. Ours focuses on the interactional work involved in the accomplishment of ordinary activities and how, in doing that work, members make whatever it is they are doing accountable such that other members can see what is being done and can concert or orchestrate their actions accordingly. The naturally accountable character of action is its real world, real time social character, and the ways in which it is made accountable are the ways in which it is intersubjectively or socially organised. The social sciences offer a plethora of perspectives accounting for social organisation. In their place we seek to elaborate through fieldwork how that organisation is accountably produced or assembled by members in the actual *in vivo* course of doing their work. In short, our perspective on human action reverses the substitution of practical sociology for professional sociology, anthropology, social psychology, and the rest. We dispense with professional social science accounts of social organisation and seek to uncover members' mastery of practical sociology instead.

There is no recipe for doing that, no series of steps you should take, and this belies the idea that ethnography is an observational method. It is not. To reiterate, anybody can go and look at everyday life and the ordinary activities it consists of, no special skills are required. In place of method stands *epistemological discipline* or analytic rigor. The rigor of the matter is to both find and explicate the naturally accountable character of ordinary activities whatever the setting. How you do that will very much depend on the work of the setting, on the modality of the work, the tools and resources used, the nature of collaboration, and so forth. You will have to dispense with professional methods and instead develop vulgar competence in the work so that you can find the methods that members use to make their work accountable. Ethnography as we know and understand it is as simple and as exacting as that, and in place of professional methods we offer sensitising concepts to attune you to the accountable character of ordinary activities and practical strategies for explicating it through fieldwork.

Our rejection of professional methodological concerns leads to a range of myths and mistaken understandings about the approach: ethnography is a users champion, it tells us what anyone knows, its findings are subjective. We are not interested in users, however, but have a distinctive disciplinary interest in the *accountable* character of their work and thus with the ways in which a setting's members conduct their work as a social enterprise in real time. Nor are we in the business of telling designers what anyone knows – 'common sense' is not what we trade in but rather, the explication of accountable conduct which enables members to trade in common sense accounts of their work. The accountable character of work is not subjective – it is not a personal interpretation of work and its organisation. It is a social and thus *intersubjectively recognisable* phenomenon. Were it not, members could not and would not see what was going on around them and be able to respond accordingly or offer common sense accounts of what is being done in a setting. Forget users, forget common sense, forget subjectivity then: our approach to ethnography replaces each with a concern to explicate the recognisably social character of a setting's work in details of the distinctive machineries of interaction that members use to make their work accountable. If you succeed in developing competence in the work of a setting that social machinery will be recognisable to you as well (Sacks 1984, 1992a).

The perceived subjectivity of ethnographic studies leads to the charge that findings cannot be reproduced, as they are merely the product of the individual researcher's personal interpretation. Many in the social sciences have been happy to except the charge and to champion it, especially in light of the work of Geertz and other leading anthropological luminaries. The view has even been attributed to ethnomethodology and Garfinkel's 'early' work (e.g., Atkinson 1988), which emphasised the "necessarily interpretive" character of everyday conduct and the intersubjective achievement of common understandings (Garfinkel 1967). Those who would chain us to the necessity of interpretation ignore what more Garfinkel had to say about the achievement of common understandings even as long ago as the 1960s, particularly that any course of interpretive work "necessarily has an operational structure." That operational structure consists of and is equivalent or identical to "methods of concerted actions and methods of common understanding; not *a* method of understanding but immensely varied methods". In other words, interpretive work is done through the use of distinctive social machineries, machineries of interaction that members use to make a setting's activities "detectable, reportable, analysable – in short, *accountable*" (ibid.). We need not be chained to the fallacy of interpretation then. We might instead explicate the operational structure of everyday activities and (thus) the methods members use to make the work of the setting's they inhabit accountable. That is not an outcome of our interpretive work but of members', and as a constitutive feature of a setting's everyday work those methods are both reproduced and reproducible.

Ethnographic findings need not be mere subjective interpretations, then. They may explicate and make visible the social machinery that *members use* to produce and reproduce ordinary activities. Nonetheless, our critics are still unlikely to be satisfied and will argue that our findings lack validity. What this means is that our findings have no explanatory power: they do not explain why people do the things that they do in the ways that they do them. It is not necessary to buy into the objection. Instead you might ask why we need to explain ordinary activities at all? The very idea that we do arises from natural science, where it is necessary to develop theories to account for natural phenomena. However, unlike the objects of natural scientific inquiry our objects – ordinary activities – are already possessed of their own means of accountability. *They explain themselves.* Unlike natural science you don't need a theory to explain what members are doing as it is, for members, already and accountably plain to see. As Wittgenstein (1992) put it, "since everything lies open to view there is nothing to explain." Consequently, explanation and the need for it comes to an end (Malcolm 1993). There is nothing to be had in explaining ordinary activities, other than the professionalisation of practical sociology and with that we are guaranteed to lose sight of members' mastery of it. What our studies require is not that we explain ordinary activities, but that we explicate in observable and reportable or empirical detail what members do and how they do it as a social enterprise.

Our rejection of professional practice – of theory and method – ultimately leads to the view that we are advocating epistemological anarchy: to use Paul Feyerabend's infamous phrase, anything goes! Reality as usual is far less exciting than fiction. Feyerabend wasn't arguing that and neither are we. We are not rejecting professional conduct in dispensing with both theory and method or, more to the point, we are not rejecting rigorous study. We are respecifying what that demands of us if we are to adequately address and not lose sight of our phenomenon: *practical sociology*, that is, sociology *in* everyday life, sociology *in* the mundane things you do, sociology *in* the things that I do, sociology *in* the things that we do, sociology *in* the things that make up our daily lives, sociology as a living, breathing thing that *inhabits* our ordinary activities and the particular actions and interactions that observably and reportably animate them. Practical sociology is a ubiquitous feature of ordinary activities, of practical action and practical reasoning everywhere. It is inescapable but it eludes professional sociology and social science more generally. Practical sociology is 'asymmetrically alternate' to professional social science, at odds with it, irreconcilably so (Garfinkel and Wieder 1992). Unlike professional social science, practical sociology is indispensable to us as incarnate members of society, as people who *exist* in space-time, as people who are *flesh*, as people who are *unavoidably connected in our embodied movements around the world,* and as people who are always *accountable to one another in doing so*, whether we like it or not. Without practical sociology we simply could not do the things we do. It shapes our ordinary activities. It is the operational structure that shapes, and that we use to shape, our actions and interactions, all of them, no matter how personal we think they may be, without exception, with no time out, and with absolutely no possibility of evasion. Were we not masters of practical sociology our conduct would grind to a halt. We would all exist in private worlds. Nothing would connect. Nothing would work. Not even computers, which are inexorably situated within practical sociology and inevitably accountable to it (Suchman 1987).

10.9   Doing Design Ethnography

Computers are accountable objects. You might not think they are, you might not care, but that does not change the unalterable fact that computers *are* accountable objects. Lucy Suchman's seminal achievement was to demonstrate that, to show it, and to make visible in doing so the mismatch between computers and practical sociology: that is, the mismatch between systems functionality and the methods that members use to organise their interactions and do their work. Suchman's work was foundational to the turn to the social and specifically to the turn towards factoring practical sociology into design so that computers support the operational structure of a setting's work – i.e., so that computers support *how* it is that members actually *do* their work. The turn to the social was a turn towards understanding that operational structure and avoiding, as Tom Rodden puts it in chapter two, "mass embarrassing systems failures", of avoiding systems "not being workable" and "not fitting to organisations." The organisation of a setting's work is not separate from the operational structure of that work. It is the same as, *identical to*, that operational structure. It consists of the methods that members use to assemble and conduct a setting's work and in doing so members make what they are doing accountable to one another – i.e., intelligible to one another and thus available as something that others can see, recognise, take heed of and gear their own activities into where and when they have need to. In short, the accountable character of a setting's work provides for cooperation and collaboration. It enables members to weave their actions and interactions together. It *is* the real world, real time organisation of ordinary activities.

The need to make computers accountable to the operational structure of work – to make them fit with work as it is done, to make them workable – occasioned the use of ethnography in systems design. There are lots of different versions of ethnography but the ethnomethodologically-informed approach we practice has had the most impact on design to date. It was first on the scene, first to try and leverage the social into design, first to demonstrate that you can make computers accountable to the real world, real time character of human activities (Szymanski and Whalen 2011). Curiously, then, it is an approach that is often and mistakenly taken by designers to be inimical to change, to privilege the status quo over technological intervention and transformation. Nothing could be further from the truth (Anderson 1997). That ethnographers don't leap up and down at the latest grand vision for the future does not mean that we have no interest in technologically-driven change. It means that we would have designers hold such visions up to account. That you see what you are proposing not only in technological terms but recognise that technology is inexorably bound up with the social as well. That technology is and will continue to be enmeshed in the operational structure of ordinary activities and that it must, therefore, be *made* accountable to it. Our studies – that is, the studies of a large cohort of ethnographers working in the ethnomethodological tradition – have sought to sensitise designers to the operational structure of ordinary activities in order to avoid the mismatch between systems and the ways in which people actually do and organise their activities. It is not a conservative approach then but one that actively seeks to incorporate practical sociology *in* design so as to avoid mass embarrassing system failures and more modest ones too.

Our commitment to actively shaping systems development, to actually helping or at least trying to help designers build better systems, in turn opens us up to criticism from our colleagues in the social sciences. We have become slaves to capital culture, cultural dopes who advocate an outmoded version of ethnographic practice. We are not ignorant of developments in anthropology and the social sciences more generally, however. We simply do not buy into the idea that ethnographic texts (field reports, research papers, books, etc.) have no necessary connection to social reality, that it is all a matter of interpretation and scholarly artifice. There is a real world beyond the text and if it is described thickly enough, in praxeological detail, our texts will be indexical to it. They will provide 'corrigible sketches' of the operational structure of ordinary activities (Garfinkel 1996), sketches of work and its organisation that can be verified by members and can be drawn upon to help devise new socio-technical systems that are accountable to work and its organisation. In place of contemporary concerns with the artifice of interpretation, no matter how elaborate and appealing those interpretations may be, it is possible to develop a real world, real time understanding of a setting's work and the practical sociology that orchestrates it. It's not easy and it won't commend your work to the social sciences but it may well help you develop computing systems that meet the demands of real people, doing real activities, in real settings.

The message then is do not conflate ethnomethodologically-informed ethnography with ethnography in the professional social sciences. They are not the same. They don't give you the same kinds of insight. We focus on practical sociology. They focus on scholarly interpretations of social life. We show what ordinary activities look like in the 'raw', as they are observably and reportably done on the shopfloor, on the street, at home, etc. They show what ordinary activities look like once they have been interpreted in terms of the latest social and cultural theories. It would be best that you think of ethnography as we understand and advocate it not so much as a variant of ethnography in the social sciences but as a branch of *natural philosophy*, as an empirical discipline that sees and reasons about sociology as a feature of the natural world. We are not suggesting that our kind of sociology is a primitive natural science (Lynch and Bogen 1994), something that will develop over time through the development of theories and methods, but rather that it is an *epistemological discipline* that investigates sociology as a feature of our natural history: as a feature of the myriad activities that members do and which make up society at large as we know and encounter it in the course of our daily lives.

Our kind of sociology, and our ethnographic approach towards investigating it, dispenses with scholarly artifice and puts in its place the ordinary things that people do and how they do them as a social enterprise. Our kind of sociology would have you attend to the particular ways in which people assemble their activities, no matter where they are, no matter what they are doing, and would have you explicate how, in the course of putting their activities together, members make whatever it is that they are doing naturally accountable. You don't need any special methods to do that. Instead you need to immerse yourself in the work of a setting, see it being done, and develop competence in it by mapping out the sequential order of activities and the concrete sequences of interactional work that elaborate each activity in turn. This will enable you to inspect the work to see how it is put together through the adjacent pairing of the particular actions that animate particular activities. The pairings elaborate the procedures, methods, or work practices that members use to make the work accountable, to make it mutually intelligible and, thereby, to orchestrate the actions and interactions of the parties to it. These procedures, methods or work practices constitute distinctive machineries of inter-action that members use to do their activities. The machineries are social. They are what practical sociology consists of and looks like as a naturally occurring feature of the natural world. They are the operational structure that shapes, and we use to shape, our natural history.

Our kind of sociology – ethnographic 'studies of work' to give it its proper title – may be used to ground design in the operational structure of everyday life. These studies are not confined, as the name might misleading suggest, to everyday activities in the workplace but to the interactional work involved in *any and all* of the activities that human beings do. Ethnographic studies of work do not confine you to the workplace, then, and may be used to shape the design of computing systems as they move ever deeper into our everyday lives. Ethnography is not a panacea to the practical challenges involved in building computing systems but if it is done with due diligence, with particular respect to its epistemological principles, it will sensitise you to the real world, real time organisation of a setting's work, which you can then factor into design through a variety of tried and tested design methods, notably use cases, scenarios, and mock ups of new socio-technical systems of work, and you may also make use of the approach to help you evaluate the solutions you develop too. This book provides a little advice as to how you might actually go about doing that. It elaborates the foundations of the approach, key issues involved in doing fieldwork, what is involved in analysing the social character of a setting's work, and techniques you might use to factor practical sociology into design. Ultimately, it requires that you dispense with the text: that you get out of the office and go and look for the animal in the foliage yourself. It isn't hidden. It's in plain view. Noticing it is just a matter of adopting the right perspective.

> The infirmities of the Senses arises from a double cause, either from the *different proportion of the Object to the Organ*, whereby an infinite number of things can never enter into them, or else from *error in the Perception*, that many things, which come within their reach, are not received in a right manner.

> Robert Hooke

References

Anderson, R. (1997). Work, ethnography and systems design. In A. Kent & J. G. Williams (Eds.), *Encyclopaedia of microcomputers* (Vol. 20, pp. 159–183). New York: Marcel Dekker.

Atkinson, P. (1988). Ethnomethodology: A critical review. *Annual Review of Sociology, 14*, 441–465.

Blumer, H. (1969a). The methodological position of symbolic interactionism. In *Symbolic interactionism: Perspective and method* (pp. 1–60). Berkeley: University of California Press.

Blumer, H. (1969b). Science without concepts. In *Symbolic interactionism: Perspective and method* (pp. 153–170). Berkeley: University of California Press.

Brooks, F. (1987). No silver bullet: Essence and accidents of software engineering. *Computer, 20*(4), 10–19.

Button, G., & Harper, R. (1996). The relevance of 'work-practice' for design. *Computer Supported Cooperative Work: The Journal of Collaborative Computing, 4*(4), 263–280.

Button, G., & Sharrock, W. (1997). The production of order and the order of production. *Proceedings of the 5th European Conference on Computer Supported Cooperative Work* (pp. 1–16). Lancaster: Kluwer.

Carroll, J. (Ed.). (1995). *Scenario-based design: Envisioning work and technology in system development*. New York: Wiley.

Crabtree, A. (2003). *Designing collaborative systems: A practical guide to ethnography*. London: Springer.

Crabtree, A., Rouncefield, M., & Tolmie, P. (2001). There's something else missing here: BPR and requirements process. *Knowledge and Process Management: The Journal of Corporate Transformation, 8*(3), 164–174.

Diaper, D., & Stanton, N. (2004). *The handbook of task analysis for human-computer interaction*. New Jersey: Lawrence Erlbaum Associates.

Diggins, T., & Tolmie, P. (2003). The 'adequate' design of ethnographic outputs for practice: Some explorations of the characteristics of design resources. *Personal and Ubiquitous Computing, 7*, 147–158.

Dourish, P. (2006). Implications for design. *Proceedings of the 2006 CHI Conference on Human Factors in Computing Systems* (pp. 541–550). Montreal: ACM.

Dourish, P., & Bell, G. (2011). *Divining a digital future: Mess and mythology in ubiquitous computing*. Cambridge: MIT Press.

Garfinkel, H. (1967). What is ethnomethodology? In *Studies in ethnomethodology* (pp. 1–34). Englewood Cliffs: Prentice-Hall.

Garfinkel, H. (Ed.). (1986). Introduction. In *Ethnomethodological studies of work* (pp. vii–viii). London: Routledge.

Garfinkel, H. (1991). Respecification. In *Ethnomethodology and the human sciences* (pp. 10–19). Cambridge: Cambridge University Press.

Garfinkel, H. (1996). Ethnomethodology's program. *Social Psychology Quarterly, 59*(1), 5–21.

Garfinkel, H. (2002a). Two propaedeutic cases. In *Ethnomethodology's program: Working out Durkheim's aphorism* (pp. 149–162). Lanham: Rowman & Littlefield.

Garfinkel, H. (2002b). Classical versus natural accountability. In *Ethnomethodology's program: Working out Durkheim's aphorism* (pp. 173–175). Lanham: Rowman & Littlefield.

Garfinkel, H. (2002c). Instructions and instructed actions. In *Ethnomethodology's program: Working out Durkheim's aphorism* (pp. 176–181). Lanham: Rowman & Littlefield.

Garfinkel, H., & Sacks, H. (1970). On formal structures of practical action. In J. C. McKinney & E. Tiryakian (Eds.), *Theoretical sociology: Perspectives and developments* (pp. 160–193). New York: Apple-Century-Crofts.

Garfinkel, H., & Wieder, D. L. (1992). Two incommensurable, asymmetrically alternate technologies of social analysis. In G. Watson & S. M. Seiler (Eds.), *Text in context: Contributions to ethnomethodology* (pp. 175–206). Newbury Park: Sage.

Garfinkel, H., Lynch, M., & Livingston, E. (1981). The work of a discovering science construed with materials from the optically discovered pulsar. *Philosophy of the Social Sciences, 11*, 131–158.

Geertz, C. (1973). Thick description: Toward an interpretive theory of culture. In *The interpretation of cultures: Selected essays* (pp. 3–30). New York: Basic Books.

Gilbreth, F., & Gilbreth, L. (1924). *The quest of the one best way.* Easton: Hive Publishing.

Greenbaum, J., & Kyng, M. (1991). *Design at work: Cooperative design of computer systems.* Hillsdale: Lawrence Erlbaum Associates.

Grudin, J. (1990). Interface. *Proceedings of the 1990 ACM Conference on Computer Supported Cooperative Work* (pp. 269–278). Los Angeles: ACM.

Hughes, J., King, V., Rodden, T., & Andersen, H. (1994). Moving out of the control room: Ethnography in systems design. *Proceedings of the 1994 ACM Conference on Computer Supported Cooperative Work* (pp. 429–438). Chapel Hill: ACM.

Irani, L., Vertesi, J., Dourish, P., Philip, K., & Grinter, R. (2010). Postcolonial computing: A lens on design and development. *Proceedings of the CHI Conference on Human Factors in Computing Systems* (pp. 1311–1320). Atlanta: ACM.

Jacobson, I., Christerson, M., Jonsson, P., & Overgaard, G. (1992). *Object-oriented software engineering: A use case driven approach.* New York: Addison-Wesley.

Lynch, M., & Bogen, D. (1994). Harvey Sacks' primitive natural science. *Theory, Culture and Society, 11*, 65–104.

Malcolm, N. (1993). The limit of explanation. In P. Winch (Ed.), *Wittgenstein* (pp. 74–83). Ithaca: Cornell University Press.

Randall, D., Harper, R., & Rouncefield, M. (2007). *Fieldwork for design: Theory and practice.* London: Springer.

Rode, J. (2011). Reflexivity in digital anthropology. *Proceedings of the 2011 CHI Conference on Human Factors in computing Systems* (pp. 123–132). Vancouver: ACM.

Rothbard, M. (1973). Praxeology as the method of the social sciences. In M. Natanson (Ed.), *Phenomenology and the social sciences* (pp. 31–61). Evanston: Northwestern University Press.

Ryle, G. (1968). *The thinking of thoughts: What is 'Le Penseur' doing?* (University Lectures No. 18). Saskatoon: University of Saskatchewan.

Sacks, H. (1984). Notes on methodology. In J. M. Maxwell & J. Heritage (Eds.), *Structures of social action: Studies in conversation analysis* (pp. 21–27). Cambridge: Cambridge University Press.

Sacks, H. (1992a). On sampling and subjectivity. In G. Jefferson (Ed.), *Lectures on conversation* (Vol. I, Part III, Spring 1966, Lecture 33, pp. 483–488). Oxford: Blackwell.

Sacks, H. (1992b). Doing 'being ordinary'. In G. Jefferson (Ed.), *Lectures on conversation* (Vol. II, Part IV, Spring 1970, Lecture 1, pp. 215–221). Oxford: Blackwell.

Sacks, H. (1992c). Adjacency pairs: Scope of operation. In G. Jefferson (Ed.), *Lectures on conversation* (Vol. II, Part VIII, Spring 1972, Lecture 1, pp. 521–532). Oxford: Blackwell.

Salvador, T., Bell, G., & Anderson, K. (2010). Design ethnography. *Design Management Journal, 10*(4), 35–41.

Sharrock, W. (1995). Different kinds of ethnography: Ethnomethodology and constructionism, COMIC Deliverable 2.4 *CSCW Requirements Development* (pp. 159–177). http://www.comp.lancs.ac.uk/computing/research/cseg/comic/ deliverables/D2.4.ps

Sommerville, I. (2011). Requirements engineering. In *Software engineering 9* (pp. 82–117). New York: Pearson.

Suchman, L. (1987). *Plans and situated actions: The problem of human-machine communication.* Cambridge: Cambridge University Press.

Szymanski, M., & Whalen, J. (Eds.). (2011). *Making work visible: Ethnographically grounded case studies of work practice.* Cambridge: Cambridge University Press.

Twidale, M., Randall, D., & Bentley, R. (1994). Situated evaluation of cooperative systems. *Proceedings of the 1994 ACM Conference on Computer Supported Cooperative Work* (pp. 441–452). Chapel Hill: ACM.

Wittgenstein, L. (1992). *Philosophical investigations.* Oxford: Blackwell.